The
United States
and Lithuania

THE UNITED STATES AND LITHUANIA

The Stimson Doctrine of Nonrecognition

Robert A. Vitas

New York
Westport, Connecticut
London

Library of Congress Cataloging-in-Publication Data

Vitas, Robert A.
    The United States and Lithuania : the Stimson doctrine of
nonrecognition / Robert A. Vitas.
        p.   cm.
    Bibliography: p.
    Includes index.
    ISBN 0-275-93412-8 (alk. paper)
    1. United States—Foreign relations—Lithuania. 2. Lithuania—
Foreign relations—United States. 3. World War, 1939-1945—
Diplomatic history. 4. Lithuania—History—Russian occupation,
1940-1941. 5. United States—Foreign relations—1933-1945.
6. Recognition (International law)—History—20th century.
I. Title.
E183.8.L8V57   1990
327.730475—dc20   89-16063

Library of Congress Catalog Card Number: 89-16063
ISBN: 0-275-93412-8

First published in 1990

Praeger Publishers, One Madison Avenue, New York, NY 10010
An imprint of Greenwood Publishing Group, Inc.

Printed in the United States of America

The paper used in this book complies with the
Permanent Paper Standard issued by the National
Information Standards Organization (Z39.48-1984).

10 9 8 7 6 5 4 3 2 1

Contents

Acknowledgments

The author acknowledges Dr. Sam C. Sarkesian, Dr. Vasyl Markus, Dr. Barbara A. Bardes, and Dr. John Allen Williams of Loyola University of Chicago, and Dr. Roger Hamburg of Indiana University for their advice and encouragement.

The Arthur J. Schmitt Foundation provided funding during 1987-1988, which enabled me to complete the necessary research and begin the task of writing. Dr. John A. Rackauskas, president of the Lithuanian Research and Studies Center, and Mr. Ceslovas V. Grincevicius, director of archives, allowed me free use of the library and archival facilities. The late Dr. Constantine R. Jurgela and Dr. Alan R. Gitelson, chair of political science at Loyola, helped provide the impetus for the work.

Mr. John L. Rackauskas at the Lithuanian Research and Studies Center, and Mr. Dan Eades, Ms. Michelle Scott, Mr. Ken Morris, Mr. Karl Nyberg, and Ms. Nicole Balant at Praeger oversaw the production of the book. Mr. Audrius Kirvelaitis of the University of Illinois prepared the index.

Other individuals who provided moral support include Mrs. Jan R. Brynda, Mr. John J. Brynda, Ms. Kathy L. Marrero, Mr. Thomas R. Miglinas, Dr. Thomas Remeikis, Mr. Steve Sanders, Ms. Maria Smilga, and Ms. Birute Tamulynas.

Finally, this study is dedicated to three people: my parents and the late Mr. Loy Wesley Henderson, who served his country at the U.S. State Department for 39 years. Without him, there might never have been a nonrecognition policy and, hence, there would not have been this book.

1

Introduction

THE UNFINISHED WAR

As World War II was a continuation of the unfinished business of World War I, so too the contemporary geopolitical situation is very much a reflection of the global conflict of the 1940s. To the many refugees who had to flee to distant shores, World War II is still very much a daily experience; exile is a reminder of the battles that raged around them. To this day, the conflict has an impact on people of all backgrounds and in all places, be it in an ethnic neighborhood in the urban United States or on maneuvers with the U.S. Army's Berlin Brigade.

One daily reminder of World War II in the United States is the anomalous presence of the Lithuanian Diplomatic Service. The members of the service, ministers and consuls, defend the interests of the Lithuanian nation whenever and wherever possible, and are living symbols of that nation's aspirations for freedom and the resumption of sovereignty. One reason that the service exists may be found in a postwar memorandum issued by the Supreme Committee for the Liberation of Lithuania, which states:

> Determined to fight on uncompromisingly until the exercise of the sovereignty of the Lithuanian State is restored, the Lithuanian people will consider null and void and not binding any and all decisions made without the participation of their lawful representatives, and which might prejudice or deny the basic rights of Lithuania and her vital interests.[1]

Be that as it may, practically it is not within the power of the Lithuanian people to decide their own governmental or national fate. Thus, it is not according to the discretion of that people that the Lithuanian Diplomatic Service continues to function. The necessary discretion lies elsewhere. As legal scholars and diplomats are aware, international law, both statutory and customary, is not carved in stone. Law among nations is interpreted by those nations themselves, in each respective capital. In the U.S., it is Washington D.C. that determines the existence of the Lithuanian Diplomatic Service and the juridical existence of the Lithuanian state.[2]

In order to understand the paradox of a practically nonexistent state possessing diplomatic representation in the U.S., it is necessary to understand the circumstances of World War II, and Washington's application of international law thereto.

At the outset of World War II, following the dissolution of Poland by Germany and the Soviet Union, the Kremlin issued an ultimatum to Lithuania demanding the formation of a new government and the entry of an unlimited number of Soviet troops into the country. This was in line with the plan adopted in a secret protocol to the Molotov Ribbentrop Non-aggression Pact of 23 August 1939. The Lithuanian government, having decided that opposition would be futile, reluctantly decided to accept the ultimatum. In procedures that violated Lithuanian constitutional law, a new Soviet regime was installed in the provisional capital of Kaunas in June 1940. The Seimas parliament was dissolved the following month, and was succeeded by a so-called People's Seimas, which petitioned the Kremlin for entry into the USSR. The Supreme Soviet obliged on 3 August 1940.[3]   T h e implications for Lithuanian municipal law were enormous. The prime minister, Antanas Merkys, who was acting as president in the wake of the departed president Antanas Smetona, was forced both to appoint a new government and transfer the presidency to a Soviet sympathizer. The dissolution of the Seimas, rump elections to a new parliament, the promulgation of various decrees, and the method of incorporation into the Soviet Union were all in violation of Lithuanian law. Due to these violations, the nonrecognition policy announced by the United States on 23 July 1940 was valid and legitimate, for it was the USSR, and not the U.S., that was interfering in the internal affairs of another country.

U.S. APPLICATION OF INTERNATIONAL LAW

The struggle for national self-determination has been a major component of twentieth century history. While geophysically unequal, states great and small have claimed moral and intrinsic equality, as well as the right to rule themselves under international law. The process of creating states and governments has necessarily touched on the question of recognition extended to these new entities. Traditionally, effective administrative control over a territory and population and the capacity and willingness to discharge international obligations have sufficed to receive recognition, although there is never any obligation to extend recognition. Usually, in the case of a new government which comes to power through extra-constitutional means, political factors outweigh legal ones in the decision to recognize. Recognition has not usually been utilized as a moral tool. Furthermore, recognition does not necessarily translate into approval of the new regime.

The Japanese conquest of Manchuria and the creation of the puppet state of Manchukuo in 1931-1932 added a new factor to recognition. U.S. Secretary of State Henry Stimson announced that the United States would not recognize the new regime and situation in Manchuria, as it had come to power in violation of the Kellogg-Briand Pact and accepted principles of international law. The League of Nations agreed with him and, subsequently, Latin American governments took the lead in formally making nonrecognition a principle of international law.

Nonrecognition is mainly a moral sanction possessing relatively little concrete impact. However, the declaration of nonrecognition is a positive reaffirmation of the international legal order, namely, that illegal actions cannot be the source of legal title to territory and power. The displaced regime possesses juridical continuity in the eyes of those countries not recognizing the new rulers.

Nonrecognition as applied to Lithuania means that the independent prewar government of that country possesses a vestige of international legal personality. There is no legal foundation to the country's incorporation into the USSR; it is null and void. Lithuania is considered to be under a military occupation, with the occupant possessing limited rights and obligations under the Geneva Conventions. The events that occured there in the summer of 1940 are deemed to be manifestations of a misrepresentation of sovereignty by the Soviet installed Lithuanian government. Furthermore, the sovereignty of the prewar regime has been suspended, and can be exercised following the occupant's evacuation.

When Lithuania and the other Baltic States of Latvia and Estonia were occupied by the Soviet Union in 1940, the act was met by the protests of Lithuanian-Americans and the Lithuanian minister to the United States, Povilas Zadeikis. On 15 July 1940, Loy Wesley Henderson, assistant chief of the U.S. State Department's European Affairs Office, authored a memorandum in which he asked if the United States would fight Hitler while ignoring Stalin's aggression. The day the document was written, President Franklin Roosevelt stated that Lithuania's sovereignty had been temporarily suspended and issued Executive Order 8484, which froze all Baltic assets in this country, making them inaccessible to Soviet authorities. On 23 July, U.S. Undersecretary of State Sumner Welles, in an announcement condemning the occupation, implied the application of the Stimson Doctrine of Nonrecognition to the Baltic situation.

Despite Soviet protests, Washington proceeded to implement nonrecognition with regard to the Baltic States. Although Antanas Smetona, the Lithuanian president, was allowed to live in the U.S. only in a private capacity without the possibility of heading a government in exile, Lithuanian diplomats and consuls retained their formal status. U.S.-Lithuanian treaties were considered to be in force but suspended. The activities of official personnel were supported from the frozen assets. Furthermore, consuls were given standing in the U.S. courts to defend their country's economic interests from the Soviets.

It was in this area that nonrecognition had the greatest impact. U.S. courts, taking the executive's nonrecognition policy into account, held that an unrecognized government possesses no standing in court. Hence, the nationalization decrees promulgated in the Baltic in 1940 were considered to be without legal effect in the U.S., and the Kremlin could not claim Baltic assets and property. Thanks to nonrecognition, actual physical resources were kept out of reach of the occupier. The Stimson Doctrine thus became both a moral and a practical tool in the condemnation of illegal aggression.

WARTIME EXPEDIENCY WEAKENS THE POLICY

One year following the incorporation of the Baltic States, Germany broke the Molotov Ribbentrop Pact and attacked the Red Army. The U.S., U.K., and USSR now had a mutual enemy in Adolph Hitler. As the *Wehrmacht* advanced eastward, the Soviet Union was able to attract sympathy and support in the West, with the unintended result that the Soviet aggression of 1939-1940 was deemphasized.

The Atlantic Charter was signed by President Roosevelt and British Prime Minister Winston Churchill on 14 August 1941. It applied the principle of self-determination to European territorial changes and forms of government. Joseph Stalin initially announced his acceptance of the charter's principles, but, as the tide of the war shifted in his favor, he indicated that he would not be bound by them. The Western allies, seeing that they could practically do little on behalf of Eastern Europe, declared that the charter was not a formal treaty and that there would be no predetermination of the postwar situation in Europe. In other words, all settlements would be negotiated following the successful conclusion of hostilities.

The negotiations over the Anglo-Soviet treaty of alliance of 1941-1942 witnessed a fight between East and West over the nonrecognition policy. Stalin pressed Churchill for recognition of the Soviet regimes in the Baltic. In turn, the prime minister asked the Roosevelt administration to moderate its stance, which Washington refused to do. This caused U.S.-U.K. tensions at a time when the war itself was at stake. Stalin, however, agreed to drop the matter of nonrecognition and a simple treaty of alliance was signed on 26 May 1942. The policy condemning Soviet aggression had survived this assault when political expediency would have dictated its retreat.

The wartime conferences at Moscow, Teheran, and Yalta did not alter the nonrecognition policy, but they also did not alter the fact that the Soviets controlled Eastern Europe. Indeed, Roosevelt stressed the importance of friendly contacts and concessions as strategies in placating Stalin and mitigating his rule over the Continent. In employing this approach, the president even jokingly informed Stalin that he was sure the Baltic people would vote to remain in the USSR provided that there would be a vote. Stalin, of course, refused to discuss the matter. With the Baltic used as a bargaining chip, nonrecognition failed to win liberation for the area.

The postwar Potsdam Declaration of 3 August 1945 did not repudiate nonrecognition, but it did not support it either. Konigsberg and the adjacent area was turned over to Moscow for its administration. It is difficult to see how "adjacent area" could not have included Lithuania. As the war had approached its conclusion, the West did not press Stalin for concessions in Eastern Europe. Some commentators believe that even broken agreements would have strengthened the status of the Baltic States. As it turned out, the Cold War was merely an afterthought.

INCOMPLETE IMPLEMENTATION OF THE POLICY

Since World War II, numerous statements, resolutions, and certifications have reaffirmed the policy of nonrecognition in the United States, even to the point of the maintenance of a Baltic desk at the State Department, the noting of the policy on official maps, and the forming of an Ad Hoc Congressional Committee on the Baltic States and Ukraine in the House of Representatives. Of course, the existence of the policy has had some effect on U.S.-USSR relations. Protests during 1940-1941 from the Kremlin went unheeded by Washington. The war crimes trials at Nuremberg also saw a reservation attached to the indictment, which contested the use of the phrase "Soviet Socialist Republic" in conjunction with Lithuania, Latvia, and Estonia. The U.S. and Soviet Union have clashed over the Baltic at numerous conferences and negotiations.

Practically, however, the routine of international intercourse has not been interrupted by the policy. Nonrecognition has not hindered U.S.-USSR dealings regarding specific issues and individuals. The diplomacy of the early 1940s and the detente of the 1970s proceeded in spite of nonrecognition. In short, it is unavoidable to deal with the Soviet regimes in the Baltic, due to the necessary requirements of diplomacy, political expediency, and the lack of tools for concrete action.

Several case studies have indicated why nonrecognition cannot be perfectly implemented. The cases described in this study are postwar repatriation, the Simas Kudirka incident, the Helsinki Accords, and the activity of the U.S. Office of Special Investigations. Among U.S. officials who are supposed to be apprised of the policy, it has sometimes either been ignored or unknown. Nonrecognition has also often been submerged under the issues of asylum, political persecution, diplomacy, and the prosecution of war criminals. Indeed, during the Helsinki negotiations, the policy itself was called into question by several senior officials. Finally, Baltic diplomats have unavoidably been able to play a limited role in defending the interests of their nations and their independent governments.

Be that as it may, the policy has not been forgotten. This conclusion can be reached when noting its various reaffirmations and the controversy surrounding even perceived attempts to undermine it. Unfortunately, it is too often invoked only in a pro forma declaration only after it has been violated and then only after the matter has come to the public's attention. Although the policy has been designed to protect people, it has not always proved successful at this task.

Initially, only diplomatic officers commissioned as of 15 June 1940 could succeed Baltic ministers who died. The advent of the 1980s witnessed a rebirth of the policy, the means of supporting it, and the people who embody it. The year 1980 saw the pooling of the frozen assets of Lithuania, Latvia, and Estonia into a single fund. This money continues to support diplomatic and consular facilities. Furthermore, U.S. President Jimmy Carter waived the rule that only officers active in 1940 could succeed as ministers. When Stasys Lozoraitis, Jr., who was not a commissioned officer in 1940, succeeded Dr. Stasys Backis as minister in Washington in 1987, the Carter policy was successfully implemented for the first time. Prior to this policy switch, consular officers had been appointed with little difficulty, for they filled honorary posts with no authority to defend their nationals in court.

Does a state exist because of recognition, or because of fulfilling certain requirements of statehood? For the Lithuanian nation, statehood, although occasionally interrupted, has existed since the thirteenth century, both in the national consciousness and in the formal trappings of government. Its manifestations have occured even under occupation. Despite practical limitations, international law recognizes all states as morally and juridically equal. The United States recognizes Lithuania, Latvia, and Estonia as legitimate members of the international community, despite the fact that their sovereignty has been suspended.

Obviously, the Soviet presence in the Baltic cannot be ignored indefinitely. Nonetheless, under the law, the presence of Soviet authority could only be legitimated in three ways: precription, that is, the lack of opposition; validation by the residents; or formal validation by the international community. None of these methods have been employed. Hence, Washington is not being unreasonable in maintaining a policy of not recognizing the legitimacy of the Soviet government in the Baltic.

The nonrecognition policy finds its roots in traditional U.S. foreign policy, which eschews a Machiavellian approach.[4] Values are ultimately at the heart of nonrecognition. Of course, morality, in order to be effective, may need power to back it up. This lack of power is where nonrecognition has fallen short for nearly five centuries. However, nonrecognition has been limited in scope from its very inception. Nonrecognition has proceeded as far as originally intended. In other words, it was always meant to be primarily a moral statement supporting Baltic sovereignty. Actual sovereignty must be reconstituted by the Balts themselves.

In another sense, nonrecognition is active intervention, for it asserts the rule of law, regardless of how imperfectly enforced. The Stimson Doctrine is not gathering dust on diplomatic shelves. Nonrecognition is, and always has been, a long-term policy. It has yet to reach its logical conclusion in the restoration of the Baltic States. Thus, in terms of its original purpose, it has been successful. However, in terms of its goal, it is incomplete.

NOTES

1. Supreme Lithuanian Committee of Liberation, *Memorandum on the Restoration of Lithuania's Independence* (n.p.: Lithuanian Executive Council, 1950), p. 15.

2. For accounts in U.S.-Lithuanian diplomatic history, see David Martin Crowe, Jr., *The Foreign Relations of Estonia, Latvia, and Lithuania, 1938-1939*, Ph.D. dissertation, University of Georgia, 1974; William Morris David, Jr., The Development of United States Policy toward the Baltic States, 1917-1922, Ph.D. dissertation, Columbia University, 1962; Constantine R. Jurgela, Lithuania and the United States: The Establishment of State Relations (Chicago: Lithuanian Research and Studies Center, 1985).

3. George F. Kennan writes: "It is ironic to reflect that these little countries, the first to establish normal relations with Moscow, should also have been, together with Poland, the first to be swallowed up again by Moscow." See his *Russia and the West under Lenin and Stalin* (Boston: Little, Brown, 1961), p. 172.

4. Others view foreign policy, in general, differently:

Most writers in the modern tradition of political theory, and many contemporary students of international politics, have conceived of international relations on the analogy of the state of nature. States are pictured as purposive and autonomous agents coexisting in an anarchic environment without significant social, political, or economic activity and devoid of stable expectations regarding the agents' behavior with respect to one another. According to the most extreme views, like Hobbes', moral judgements are inappropriate in such an environment.

See Charles R. Beitz, *Political Theory and International Relations* (Princeton, NJ: Princeton University Press, 1979), p. 179.

2

The Twilight of
Independence, 1939-1940

PRELUDE TO OCCUPATION

In order to fully understand the circumstances that led to the U.S. nonrecognition policy, it is first necessary to acquire a familiarity with the events that led to the extinction of Lithuania's independence. Lithuania's major diplomatic difficulty during the interwar period was the Vilnius dispute. Vilnius had been the ancient capital of Lithuania during the time of the Kingdom and Grand Duchy. Wars with Muscovy in the sixteenth century forced Lithuania to seek aid from her old ally Poland. Poland, however, agreed to give aid only in return for a political union with Lithuania. After a series of high-level maneuvers, the Union of Lublin was signed in 1569, creating the unified Kingdom of Poland and Lithuania. Gradually, Vilnius became more Polish in nature and more cosmopolitan. Poles came to outnumber Lithuanians, while the latter continued to predominate in the countryside. The partitions of Poland and Lithuania in 1772, 1793, and 1795 by Prussia, Russia, and Austria placed Lithuania under czarist rule.

At the conclusion of World War I, new states began carving niches for themselves on the European continent. Two such countries were the formerly united Poland and Lithuania. Immediately upon reconstitution, both sides clashed over Vilnius and its surrounding territories. Lithuania declared her independence on 16 February 1918. This was followed by two years of turbulence. The vanquished Germans retreated and the Bolsheviks entered the Vilnius territory in late 1918. Polish and Lithuanian volunteers drove the Red Army out of Lithuania, with Poland entering Vilnius first on 19 April 1919. During the summer of 1920, the Bolsheviks reoccupied the territory. Subsequently, Russia concluded an armistice with Lithuania, turning over to her the capital and surrounding areas. The peace treaty caused renewed fighting to break out between Poland and Lithuania. Finally, after much maneuvering, including the intervention of the League of Nations, the Treaty of Suvalkai was signed on 7 October 1920; the Vilnius territory was to remain in Lithuanian hands.

The situation was to change with lightning speed. Just two days after the signing of the treaty, Polish general Lucjan Zeligowski, with Polish strongman Marshal Jozef Pilsudski's blessing, staged a rebellion and led Polish forces back into the eastern third of Lithuania, occupying Vilnius. The Lithuanian counterattack was halted by an order of the League of Nations; diplomatic efforts failed to bring Vilnius back to Lithuania, which set up a provisional capital in Kaunas. The Conference of Ambassadors recognized the existing situation in 1923.

The interwar years were to see continuing tensions between the two countries over the Vilnius question. Lithuania would not officially renounce the capital; Poland would not relinquish the predominantly Polish city. A stalemate ensued for 18 years, despite secret and sometimes high level contacts between the belligerents. Nothing appeared able to break the deadlock, which included the lack of diplomatic relations and a technical state of war. An administration line was created between the two antagonists. Diplomats on the Continent saw the unresolved situation as a tinderbox ready to ignite; they hoped for a resolution to the conflict. Their wish came true in March 1938. A border incident in which a Polish soldier was killed was followed by Warsaw's ultimatum demanding the restoration of diplomatic ties. Seeing the massing of Polish troops along the administration line, the Lithuanian government acquiesced. This was, in many respects, the actual start of World War II for the country.

Adolph Hitler decided to add the Klaipeda (Memel) Territory to his empire in March 1939. An ultimatum was issued to the Lithuanian government demanding its cession to Germany. The Lithuanian government, feeling powerless against the military might of the Third Reich, grudgingly accepted Hitler's ultimatum. On 22 March 1939, a treaty was signed by both governments which transferred Klaipeda to Germany. The Germans moved into the area very quickly, indicating premeditation, and Lithuanian private citizens, government agencies, and military components suffered many losses in the sudden move to Lithuania-Major.[1]

The nation was forced to adjust to the economic dislocation that emerged following the ultimatum. In addition, approximately 12,000 refugees from the Klaipeda Territory had to be absorbed. Lithuania was simultaneously maneuvering through the troubled continental political situation brewing before the outbreak of outright hostilities. Despite external pressure, Prime Minister Jonas Cernius was charged by President Antanas Smetona with executing a policy of strict neutrality.[2]

Another problem was constructed by Berlin and Moscow:

When German Foreign Minister [Joachim von] Ribbentrop signed the famous Russo-German Non-Aggression Pact on August 23, 1939, the public announcement of the pact made no mention of a secret protocol signed between the two parties the same day. By terms of this secret protocol the Baltic area, including Finland, Estonia, Latvia, Lithuania, and the entire territory of the Polish Republic, was partitioned between the U.S.S.R. and Nazi Germany. The northern boundary of Lithuania provided the dividing line between the two spheres of interest. The Vilnius area was recognized as part of Lithuania. Finland, Estonia, Latvia, and the Polish territories east of the line of the rivers Narev, Vistula, and San were declared the spheres of influence of the U.S.S.R., whereas Lithuania and the Polish territories west of these rivers would constitute the German sphere of influence. The ultimate fate of Poland was also sealed in this secret protocol, which provided that "whether the interests of both parties make the maintenance of an independent Polish state desirable can be determined only in the course of further political developments."...Later Germany traded [Lithuania] away...to...the U.S.S.R.[3]

This opened the way for the dissolution of Poland. On 1 September 1939, the German blitzkrieg began swallowing the country. The Red Army moved into the Polish-occupied Vilnius territory on the 17th of that month. Ten days later, the two powers carried out the "fourth partition" of Poland according to the terms of the secret protocol. Lithuania was immediately mobilized, albeit temporarily, and began absorbing and interning Polish refugees and military personnel. In October, the Kremlin placed pressure on Kaunas to sign a mutual assistance pact, allowing the establishment of four Soviet bases in Lithuania. For the tiny country, this was a two-edged sword. On the one hand, Lithuania, under the provisions of the pact, received most of the Vilnius territory, the territory for which it had been fighting for 19 years. On the other hand, the Soviet bases were Trojan horses in the subsequent occupation of the country.[4]

Technically, the Treaty on the Transfer of Vilnius and Soviet-Lithuanian Mutual Assistance, signed at Moscow on 10 October 1939, was intended solely to guarantee Lithuania's borders with the help of 50,000 Soviet troops. Article VII stated that the treaty had no effect on sovereign rights or internal affairs. The following article stated that the treaty would come up for review in 15 years. On 14 November, the first of 20,000 Red Army soldiers entered Lithuania.

Soldiers also entered the other Baltic States, under the terms of mutual assistance pacts concluded at the same time. Ostensibly, the Soviet troops were there to guarantee the independence of the three countries. However, as Kazys Pakstas writes, this was not to be:

In November, 1939, the mechanized units of the Russian army (about 70,000) were already established in...the three Baltic countries. Juridically the Baltic states were in the position of Cuba or Egypt, but the "protecting" partner was not the law-abiding Anglo-Saxon or Yankee.[5]

THE SOVIET UNION INTERVENES

The final cabinet meeting of independent Lithuania took place during the night of 14 June 1940. The president himself was presiding, for the government was considering an ultimatum from Moscow. The ultimatum included a demand for the arrest of Interior Minister Brigadier General Kazys Skucas for allegedly ordering the kidnapping of Red Army soldiers stationed in Lithuania, although it was apparent that they had actually deserted. Another point of the ultimatum was permission to allow an unlimited number of Soviet troops into Lithuania for the purpose of "guaranteeing" the Soviet-Lithuanian mutual assistance pact. Finally, the Kremlin called for the formation of a government acceptable to it. Divisional General Stasys Rastikis, former commander in chief of the army, was invited to the meeting and appointed prime minister. He began forming a government, but word soon arrived from Moscow that Rastikis was unacceptable. Following further discussion, the cabinet decided that President Smetona should leave the country and turn presidential power over to Prime Minister Antanas Merkys, who had been appointed to succeed Prime Minister Cernius on 22 November 1939.

The Red Army began occupying Lithuania and the other Baltic States, which had been induced by similar ultimatums on 15 June 1940. This was managed on the scene by functionaries from the Soviet Commisariat for Foreign Affairs. In Lithuania it was Vladimir Dekanazov, assisted by the Soviet minister to Kaunas, Pozdniakov. In Latvia it was Andrei Vishinsky, while Andrei Zhdanov managed the takeover in Estonia. Prime Minister Merkys was forced two days later to name communist sympathizer and journalist Justas Paleckis as new prime minister and de facto president, although, as will be seen below, Merkys's action did not conform with the requirements of Lithuanian constitutional law.

As far as public Soviet justifications were concerned, the occupation was necessary because the Baltic States were engaged in a secret military collaboration in violation of the Baltic-Soviet mutual assistance pacts. Indeed, it was asserted by the Soviet Union that the occupation was benign and designed to preserve the Baltic States:

> The U.S.S.R. never, either in words or in deeds, threatened the independence of the Baltic countries. On the contrary, she was herself interested in their independence. There was therefore no reason whatever for the formation in the Baltic States of various blocs and coalitions directed ostensibly against "threats on the part of the U.S.S.R." In any case, none of these blocs and coalitions could have defended the Baltic States had the U.S.S.R. really desired to violate their independence.[6]

It soon became, obvious, however, that it was indeed the Soviet Union's intent to liquidate Lithuania's independence and incorporate the country.[7]

LITHUANIA'S INCORPORATION INTO THE USSR

The new Lithuanian government created under the direction of Dekanazov was a mixture of patriots and communist sympathizers. However, there was no question that it would perform at the will of the Kremlin. On 19 June, a number of communists jailed by Smetona for their agitation were released from imprisonment and communist-sponsored public rallies were held. That same day the Lithuanian Nationalist Association, President Smetona's political faction which had ruled Lithuania since the coup of 17 December 1926, was outlawed. On 25 June, Interior Minister Mecislovas Gedvilas announced that the Communist Party would be the only legal political party and entered it in the register of societies and associations. Three days later came the legalization of the Young Communist League. The Seimas was dissolved on 1 July. The following day the Lithuanian army was renamed the People's Army, and would later become the 29th Territorial Corps of the Red Army; political commisars joined the ranks. Nationalization and collectivization of property were also begun.[8]

On 5 July, the government announced that elections to a People's Seimas would be held on the 14th of that month. Acting President Paleckis published the new electoral law the following day. Only candidates of the Communist Party were allowed to run, and there would be only as many candidates as there were seats in the Seimas.[9] Because only 15 to 20 percent of those eligible actually voted on election day, the voting was extended to 10:00 P.M. the following day. The official tally stated that 1,386,469 individuals (95.51% of the population) voted to elect 79 Seimas deputies.[10]

The People's Seimas convened in the Kaunas State Theater on 21 July 1940. Red Army soldiers, secret police agents, members of the Soviet legation, and representatives from Moscow sat among the deputies, some of whom had been elected against their will. Their names commanded respect among the citizenry, and it was thought by the Soviets that their presence would give the proceedings at least superficial legitimacy. The convocation was marked by almost continuous shouting and turmoil. During the voting, non-deputies raised their hands and resolutions were recorded as having passed unanimously. Only two were passed. The first declared that the Soviet system would be introduced into Lithuania; the second requested admission into the Soviet Union.[11]

The following month, the second resolution was presented by a Lithuanian delegation to the Supreme Soviet of the USSR, which admitted the Lithuanian Soviet Socialist Republic into the nation on 3 August. On the 24 August, a new constitution was promulgated for Lithuania, and Justas Paleckis was named chairman of the Presidium of Lithuania's Supreme Soviet.[12]

It was no surprise that Germany, the Soviet Union's ally in dividing Eastern Europe, did not hinder Soviet actions in the Baltic States. On 22 July, the Lithuanian minister to Berlin, Kazys Skirpa, handed a letter of protest regarding Soviet activities to Ernst Woermann, director of the political department of the

German foreign ministry. Woermann transmitted the letter to Foreign Minister Ribbentrop with a request for instructions. The Latvian minister presented a similar letter that day. Two days later, Woermann returned these letters and refused to accept one from the Estonian minister. By the middle of the following month, German legations in the Baltic States were converted to consulates.[13]

August Rei, former president of Estonia, wrote of the incorporation:

> Every observer who followed with any attention the so-called "incorporation" of the Baltic States into the Soviet Union in the summer of 1940, was aware from the very first that this was an act of violence brutally disregarding both international law and the agreements then in force, even though terrorist methods were applied in such a manner as to suggest that the nations concerned had themselves freely renounced their political independence, declared themselves Soviet Republics and applied for admission to the Soviet Union as federal States.[14]

It was thus at bayonet point that Lithuania became the 14th Soviet Republic.

NOTES

1. Juozas Audenas, *Paskutinis posedis: Atsiminimai* (Final meeting: Reminiscences) (New York: Romuva, 1966), p. 127; Julius P. Slavenas, "Klaipeda Territory," Encyclopedia Lituanica, 1973, vol. 3, p. 137.

2. U.S. House of Representatives, *Third Interim Report of the Select Committee on Communist Aggression*, 83rd Congress, 2d Sess. (Washington, D.C.: U.S. Government Printing Office, 1954), pp. 154-155.

3. Bronis J. Kaslas, "The Lithuanian Strip in Soviet-German Diplomacy, 1939-1941," *Journal of Baltic Studies*, 4, 3 (Fall 1973), 211.

4. For accounts of these events, see Audenas, *Paskutinis posedis*, p. 150; Adolfs Klive, "Pacts of Mutual Assistance between the Baltic States and the USSR," Baltic Review, 18 (November 1959), 31-40; Stasys Rastikis, Ivykiai ir zmones: Is mano uzrasu (Events and personalities: From my notes), ed. Bronius Kviklys (Chicago: Academic Press, 1972), p. 44; Stasys Rastikis, Lietuvos likimo keliais: Is mano uzrasu (On the roads of Lithuania's destiny: From my notes), ed. Jonas Dainauskas (Chicago: Academic Press, 1982), p. 225; Adolfas Sapoka, Vilnius in the Life of Lithuania (Toronto: Lithuanian Association of the Vilnius Region, 1962), pp. 153-161. Many military officers and citizens did not understand why Lithuania did not invade and take back the Vilnius territory when Poland was attacked and Berlin was urging Kaunas to move. This, however, would have violated Smetona's policy of strict neutrality. See Vaclovas Sliogeris, Antanas Smetona: Zmogus ir valstybininkas. Atsiminimai (Antanas Smetona: Person and statesman. Reminiscences) (Sodus, MI: Juozas J. Bachunas, 1966), pp. 135-136.

5. Kazys Pakstas, "The Baltic Victims of the Present War," *World Affairs Interpreter*, 12, 1 (April 1941), 36-37. See also Bronis J. Kaslas, ed., The USSR-German Aggression against Lithuania (New York: Robert Speller and Sons, 1973), pp. 149-151; Benedict V. Maciuika, ed., Lithuania in the Last 30 Years. Subcontractor's monograph prepared in the Division of the Social Sciences at the University of Chicago. HRAF Subcontract HRAF-1 Chi-1 (New Haven, CT: Human Relations Area Files, 1955), pp. 70-72. For an overview of the prewar military situation in the Baltic, see Edgar Anderson, "Die militarische Situation der Baltischen Staaten" (The Military Situation in the Baltic States), Acta Baltica, 8 (1968), 106-155; Edgar Anderson, "Military Policies and Plans of the Baltic States on the Eve of World War II," Lituanus, 20, 2 (Summer 1974), 15-34.

6. Soviet Information Bureau, *The Soviet Union, Finland and the Baltic States* (n.p.: Soviet War News, 1941), p. 6.

7. Soviet military maps printed in 1939 already indicated Lithuania and the other Baltic States as components of the USSR.

8. Algirdas J. Kasulaitis, *Lithuanian Christian Democracy* (Chicago: Leo XIII Fund, 1976), p. 153.

9. Officially called the Union of Working People of Lithuania.

10. Maciuika, *Lithuania in the Last 30 Years*, pp. 73-74; U.S. House of Representatives, Communist Takeover and Occupation of Lithuania. Special Report No. 14 of the Select Committee on Communist Aggression (Washington, D.C.: U.S. Government Printing Office, 1955), pp. 12-13. The reporting of the election results sometimes went to rather interesting extremes. For example, on 16 July, one newspaper reported that some areas had a 138% voter turnout. The following day, Vilniaus balsas (Voice of Vilnius) reported that some Vilnius precincts saw a turnout of 133%. See Albertas Gerutis, "Occupied Lithuania," in Lithuania 700 Years, 2d rev. ed., ed. Albertas Gerutis (New York: Manyland, 1969), p. 273.

11. Liudas Dovydenas, *Mes valdysim pasauli: Atsiminimai II* (We will rule the world: Reminiscences II) (New York: Romuva, 1970), p. 284; Gerutis, "Occupied Lithuania," p. 276; Kaslas, USSR-German Aggression, pp. 237-243. Similar events were occuring in Latvia and Estonia at the same time. Indeed, the wording of the resolutions was almost identical. See August Rei, Nazi-Soviet Conspiracy and the Baltic States: Diplomatic Documents and Other Evidence (London: Boreas, 1948), p. 5.

12. On 30 August 1942, in Kaunas, after the Germans had invaded and occupied Lithuania, 10 members of the People's Seimas issued a public declaration repudiating the elections and the incorporation process. They cited threats against them and their families. See Conference of Free Byelorussians, Estonian World Council, Lithuanian World Community, World Congress of Free Ukrainians, World Federation of Free Latvians, *To the United Nations General Assembly: A Resolution with Appended Documents Concerning the Decolonization of the Union of Soviet Socialist Republics* (Toronto/New York: Joint Committee/Ucrainica Research Institute, 1978), pp. 109-111.

13. U.S. Department of State, *Documents on German Foreign Policy 1918-1945*, Series D (1937-1945), Vol. X: The War Years June 23-August 31, 1940 (Washington, D.C.: U.S. Government Printing Office, 1957, pp. 264, 267, 286, 483.

14. Rei, *Nazi-Soviet Conspiracy*, p. 5.

3

International Law and
the Lithuanian Situation

SELF-DETERMINATION

The emergence of the European nation-states in the nineteenth century and the decolonization of Africa and Asia that began in the middle of this century point up the importance of the concept of self-determination as the basis for the existence of states as well as the relations among them. Obviously, in geophysical terms not all states are equal, for "the survival of small states depends to-day, as in the past, on the policy the dominant great powers adopt."[1] However, intrinsically, as far as the law of nations is concerned:

> The principle of equality is not affected by differences of power, and it precedes the idea of self-determination. It is a basic principle of international law, and goes back to the time when a state was personified in the person of its ruler or sovereign body.[2]

When examining the development of international law since World War II, it is apparent that self-determination has been an explicit consideration in interstate relations. To demonstrate this, the following passage is quoted *in extenso*:

> The Second Inter-American Conference of Foreign Ministers, held in July, 1940, in Havana, Cuba, confirmed the right of self-determination in Latin-American countries. The Third International Conference of Jurists held in August, 1943, in Mexico City, reaffirmed it. The Charter of the United Nations (Articles 1(2) and 55) consider the right of peoples to self-determination as a basic pre-requisite for the maintenance of friendly and peaceful relations among nations. The British-Egyptian agreement of February 12, 1953, granted the right of self-determination to the Sudanese people, and Sudan became an independent state. The resolution adopted by the Asian Socialist Conference held in Rangoon in January, 1952, emphasized the right of self-determination for Asian peoples. The Inter-American

Conference held in Caracas in March, 1954, also stressed this right as essential for the maintenance of international peace and order. The Pacific Charter of September 8, 1954, reaffirmed the right of self-determination to all nations of the world, and the Afro-Asian Conference held in April, 1955, in Bandung, demanded the right of self-determination for all Afro-Asian peoples.[3]

The United Nations has on numerous occasions declared the importance of self-determination for the successful maintenance of the global community.[4]

RECOGNITION

Recognition in interstate relations deals with the existence of a new state or government, and the decision whether to enter into relations with it. Recognition, in and of itself, is not a legal matter, but rather "a political act with legal consequences."[5] Legal effects stem from this political act, as when national courts depend on executive policy for determining judgments in cases involving foreign governments, property, or nationals. There is never any duty to recognize another state or government and, when dealing with the idea of implied or tacit recognition, "there must be a very clear *indication of intent to recognize*."[6]

When the recognition of a completely new state is at issue, the important factors to examine are the possession of a distinct territory and population, and the presence of a government that has effective control over both, is not itself controlled by outside forces, and has the capacity to responsibly enter into foreign relations. These, once again, are matters of fact, not law.[7]

Recognition of governments differs from that of states. Unless there are political objections to recognition, there are three objective tests that must be successfully met. First, the government must possess de facto administrative control. Second, there must be an absence of meaningful resistance to it. Third, it must have the backing of a substantial segment of public opinion. Beginning with the second half of the nineteenth century, a fourth, subjective, test was applied, namely, the capacity and willingness to discharge international obligations. Thus, the United States and Cuba, for example, have obligations toward each other as states under customary international law, treaties, and international agreements, regardless of the differences between their governments.[8]

It must be noted that recognition has two degrees. "Recognition is either definite and complete (*de jure*) or provisional and limited to a certain juridical relation (*de facto*)."[9] De jure recognition is retroactive from the date of the actual independence of a state. De facto recognition is either expressed or implied, such as in an agreement with a limited or provisional purpose.[10]

Recognition is a matter not only in regard to new states and governments, but also to changes within governments.

Normally a state does not concern itself legally with a change of government in another state. When a change of government occurs in a foreign state that is in accord with the domestic law of that state, the legal relationship between the two governments remains unaffected. For example, Great Britain does not recognize a new government in the United States whenever a new President is elected.

However, under established principles of international law, the legal relationship between two states is affected if a government assumes power in a manner that violates domestic law. When such a change of government occurs, the question of recognition of the new government is said to arise.

The line between a lawful and an unlawful change of government is not always clear, and problems may arise in determining whether a particular change of government raises the question of recognition.[11]

When an extra-constitutional change occurs, political factors often overshadow legal factors, depending on the interests of the recognizing government. In practice, both law and politics are blended in a decision. The three major approaches to recognition reflect the interplay between politics and law. They are the traditional approach, the Estrada Doctrine, and the Tobar or Betancourt Doctrine.[12]

The traditional approach deals with the standard objective and subjective tests, namely control of territory and government, public acquiescence, and indication of willingness to discharge international obligations. This approach is flexible and depends mainly on political interests. Recognition may either be deemphasized, or it may be used as a bargaining chip in seeking elections, economic advantage, or greater civil liberties. Recognition may even be withheld until certain conditions are met. An example is the U.S. refusal to recognize the Albanian government after World War II, which is still in effect.

The second approach to recognition was announced by Mexican foreign minister Don Genaro Estrada in 1930. Under this approach, extra-constitutional acquisition of power is not subject to consideration. New states are recognized, but governmental changes of any kind do not affect interstate relations.

The Estrada Doctrine embraces the principle of unfettered national sovereignty and rejects interference with the domestic affairs of one state by another through the granting or withholding of recognition. States that have adopted the Estrada Doctrine often say they recognize states, not governments; however, as a practical matter, many states depart from the doctrine whenever they perceive a major political advantage in using the recognition instrument.[13]

Developed by a foreign minister of Ecuador, the Tobar Doctrine takes exactly the opposite approach. It refuses to recognize any government that comes to power through extra-constitutional means. Free elections must be held, for coups and revolutions are unacceptable even if the citizenry constitutionally approves the change. Though operative for a time in South America and applied by the United States as the Wilson Doctrine from 1913 to 1929, the Tobar Doctrine has met with little acceptance.[14]

For the most part, recognition has not been utilized as a moral tool to sanction unconstitutional behavior. Indeed, as far as the U.S. Department of State and most international law texts are concerned, recognition does not necessarily translate into approval of a regime.[15]

> No rule of law has ever ascribed anything like a sacred character to the constitution of any country. No rule of the law can be held to deprive a people of its right to change its form of government, whether by ballot or by bullet, nor does any existing rule maintain that such a change must be the handiwork of a majority in any nation.[16]

Most scholars assert, thus, that recognition is a matter of fact and politics, not of law or morality. In fact, relations and trade can exist between two governments that do not recognize each other. On the other hand, two governments that recognize each other may lack formal relations and even engage in trade interdiction and economic warfare.[17]

> Recognition of foreign governments, for all its long history and frequent use, has little substantive content....One might logically inquire why states attach importance to [recognition]. The answer appears to be that the importance attached to recognition derives in part from the weight of tradition and in part from the sense of legitimacy recognition confers.[18]

This cursory look at the concept of recognition has paved the way for an examination of a matter more directly affecting relations between the United States and Lithuania since the summer of 1940, namely the explicit nonrecognition of the Soviet occupation of Lithuania. The use of nonrecognition by the U.S. did not begin with the Lithuanian occupation, but actually commenced about a decade earlier in conjunction with events in Asia. It is this, in the context of the Stimson Doctrine, to which we now turn.

THE STIMSON DOCTRINE

In the early 1930s, Japan and China were at war. Japan had been the aggressor, attacking the Chinese province of Manchuria. The beginning of 1932 saw a culmination of the fighting. As Japan established effective control in Manchurian areas, it replaced Chinese authorities with puppet agencies acting as autonomous local administrative bodies. On 17 February, the Supreme Administrative Council was established at Mukden, which issued a declaration of independence the following day and established the new state of Manchukuo. Huan-tung, a former emperor of China who had been dethroned as a boy in 1912, was asked to become the leader of the new state. He accepted. 9 March 1932 saw an Organic Law promulgated as the constitution.[19]

U.S. Secretary of State Henry L. Stimson began responding to the Manchurian situation in January, prior to the official formation of Manchukuo. On 7 January he dispatched a note to China and Japan, that stated that the United States:

> cannot admit the legality of any situation de facto nor does it intend to recognize any treaty or agreement entered into between those Governments [of China and Japan], which may impair the treaty rights of the United States or its citizens in China, including those which relate to the sovereignty, the independence, or the territorial or administrative integrity of the Republic of China...and that it does not intend to recognize any situation, treaty, or agreement which may be brought about by means contrary to the covenants and obligations of the [Kellogg-Briand] Pact of Paris of August 27, 1928.[20]

16 January saw the Japanese reply, which asserted that treaties relative to China must occasionally be applied with an eye toward the changing situation. Tokyo added that the confusing state of affairs in China could not have been foreseen by diplomats signing international agreements.[21]

The following month saw the Assembly of the League of Nations responding to events in Manchuria. On 24 February the assembly adopted the Lytton Report on Manchuria, which contained a statement of recommendations based on the idea that China possessed sovereignty over Manchuria. In addition, the recommendations dealt with behavior toward the new regime in Manchuria:

> The recommendations made do not provide for a mere return to the status quo existing before September, 1931. They likewise exclude the maintenance and recognition of the existing regime in Manchuria, such maintenance and recognition being incompatible with the fundamental principles of existing international obligations....The Members of the League...will continue not to recognize this regime either de jure or de facto.[22]

League actions were based on Article Ten of the organization's covenant which read, in part, that "the Members...undertake to respect and preserve as against external aggression the territorial integrity and the existing political independence of all Members."[23] With Japan abstaining, on 11 March 1932 the League unanimously resolved "that it is incumbent upon the Members...not to recognize any situation, treaty or agreement which may be brought about by means contrary to the Covenant...or to the Pact of Paris."[24] On the following day, Secretary Stimson stated that "this action will go far towards developing into terms of international law the principles of order and justice."[25]

As far as the development of nonrecognition is concerned, the Latin American nations have taken the lead in incorporating "the principles of order and justice" into international law. This is most probably rooted in Latin America's general approach to its own regional law. Former Chilean member of the World Court Alejandro Alvarez

> mentions some five principal characteristics of American international law. These are: 1. a sentiment of continental solidarity; 2. an American juridical conscience; 3. an American moral conscience; 4. pacifism, idealism, and optimism; and 5. respect for law and international morality, condemning all violation of their precepts.[26]

Indeed, the years immediately following the Stimson Doctrine saw Latin American diplomats embracing it in actual regional conflicts.[27] During the 1933 Chaco War between Bolivia and Paraguay, the representatives of the other 19 American states issued the following statement:

> The American nations...declare that they will not recognize any territorial arrangement of this controversy which has not been obtained by peaceful means nor the validity of territorial acquisitions which may be obtained through occupation or conquest by force of arms.[28]

The Chaco Declaration inspired Argentina's foreign minister, Dr. Saavedra Lamas, who suggested that a formal treaty be constructed. On 10 October 1933 at Rio de Janeiro, the Anti-War Treaty of Non-Aggression and Conciliation was signed by Argentina, Brazil, Chile, Mexico, Paraguay, and Uruguay. The first two articles of what is usually referred to as the Saavedra Lamas Anti-War Treaty spell out the nonrecognition of territorial and juridical arrangements carried out through the use of force.[29] Two months later, the Seventh Inter-American Conference met at Montevideo and signed the Convention on the Rights and Duties of States. Article Eleven broadened the meaning of the use of force:

> whether this consists in the employment of arms, in threatening diplomatic representations, or in any other effective coercive measure. The territory of a State is inviolable and may not be the object of

military occupation nor of other measures of force imposed by other States directly or indirectly or for any motive whatever even temporarily.[30]

The Eighth Inter-American Conference in 1938 at Lima reaffirmed the principle of nonrecognition. However, this time the Latin American diplomats went one step further, not merely stating that nonrecognition is a duty, but also declaring on 22 December that it is "a fundamental principle of the Public Law of America."[31]   "It can therefore be maintained that the Stimson doctrine of nonrecognition represents a basic principle of regional inter-American law."[32]

NONRECOGNITION

Nonrecognition has usually been employed as an expression of moral disapproval. It is rarely concretely disruptive to the recipient or indicative of the actual strength of the nonrecognizing government. However, the act possesses definite legal and political consequences.[33] "While non-recognition assumes in specific instances a negative form, it is in fact a positive affirmation of the validity of the existing legal order, as contrasted with acts of violence destructive of that order."[34]

Under nonrecognition, acts contrary to international law are null and void, and cannot be a source of justification for the aggressor. Illegality cannot be a source of legality (*ex iniuria non oritur*). Such a policy "is an attempt to carry over into the domain of international law viewpoints and judgements of a moral or ethical character which have become deeply rooted in municipal and constitutional law."[35]   In the global arena, nonrecognition "prevents any law-creating effect of prescription."[36]   In other words, the occupation of territory, for example, does not necessarily lead to title of ownership.

Nonrecognition is applied in several ways.[37]   First, it may be applied to subjects of international law, either new states or new regimes in old states, when their existence is brought about by illegal means. For the latter, both international law and the municipal law of the country in question must be examined in order to determine if succession has been properly executed.[38]   Second, nonrecognition may also be directed against treaties or agreements if it is determined that they violate international norms. This is especially true if one of the parties to an agreement is itself unrecognized.

Third, it may also be applied to situations. An objective legal criterion must be examined in this case. For example, violations of treaty provisions would bring about a situation wherein norms have been broken. Accepted principles of international law, in the absence of specific treaty obligations, could also be utilized to examine a situation to determine if it is illegal and, hence, subject to nonrecognition.[39]   As a corollary, nonrecognition has been expanded to cover treaties, persons, consular exequaturs, currency, passports, postage stamps, membership in international public unions, court decisions, and assets.   It should be noted that nonrecognition of a lawful act does not impair its validity or render it legally ineffective.   It is significant only in regard to unlawful acts, "to prevent the validation of what is a legal nullity."[40]   Also, while "logically and practically...it is not possible to recognize more that one government at a time in one state,"[41] it is often unavoidable to continue personal and business relations, as well as some official contact, with the unrecognized regime.[42] Furthermore, an unrecognized power still possesses obligations in the occupied territory.   Robert Langer draws an analogy between hostile territorial transfer and belligerent occupation. The occupant possesses no sovereignty over the area in question and cannot annex it during wartime.   However, it is incumbent on him to continue competent administration and normal existence.[43]

There is no obligation of nonrecognition in general international law. Concomitantly, silence in the face of an annexation, for example, does not necessarily imply recognition of the new situation.   "International law does not recognize the formula of *qui tacet, consentire videtur* (he who is silent seems to agree)."[44]

As long as...recognition has not been withdrawn [from the old regime], it is still effective. The withdrawal of recognition must not necessarily be explicit; however, because of its far-reaching consequences, it may be inferred only from acts which are unequivocally, and not by mere implication, expressive of the intention of the state in question. Of course, *de jure* recognition, but not *de facto* recognition, of the new authority replacing the state from which recognition is withdrawn, has also the effect of a withdrawal of recognition.[45]

There are several effects that flow from a policy of nonrecognition. The legal status of the government of the still-recognized regime, its treaties with the non recognizing government, and diplomatic and consular representation are preserved. Legal acts are accorded full legitimacy and, conversely, the legal acts of the unrecognized regime are not. The recognized power is thus guaranteed legal continuity. Nationals of the recognized regime are accorded separate status and the protection of their governmental and diplomatic authorities. Property is also protected from claims by the unrecognized regime.[46]

In the *North Sea Continental Shelf* case, the International Court of Justice formulated the conditions necessary to create a positive rule of customary international law:[47]

First, it must be ascertained whether there has been a constant and uniform usage. Such usage must include consistent repetition, a sufficient degree of generality and a certain lapse of time. Second, those states acting in accordance with the claimed precription must do so because they regard their adherence to it as being a legal duty incumbent upon them as members of the international community, that is, in conformity with the ancient Roman maxim *"opinio iuris sive necessitatis."*[48]

Nonrecognition of territorial acquisition through conquest has seen consistent repetition by states. This is visible, for example, in the postwar reconstitution of Albania, Austria, Czechoslovakia, Ethiopia, and Poland. The United Nations has also reacted negatively to postwar territorial occupations by Israel in 1967, by Morocco and Mauritania in the Western Sahara in 1975, by Indonesia in East Timor in 1976, by Vietnam in Cambodia in 1979, and by the USSR in Afghanistan that same year. Furthermore, nonrecognition as a principle has been adopted by the Inter-American Conference on Problems of War and Peace in its Declaration on Reciprocal Assistance and American Solidarity in 1945, by the Organization of American States and the Organization of African Unity in their charters, and by the U.N. General Assembly in 1970, acting on a recommendation by the U.N. Special Committee on Principles of International Law Concerning Friendly Relations and Cooperation.[49]

To see if nonrecognition meets the requirement for a sufficient degree of generality, one can examine the practice of states and discover that the principle is universally applied. It is not limited to a specific group of states. The lapse of time can be seen in view of the fact that no major nation has yet recognized the legitimacy of the Soviet occupation of Lithuania since 1940. In addition, there are now approximately six other areas of controversy where the legality to territorial title has been denied for a decade or more.[50]

The World Court's second major point is that a rule must be considered legally incumbent, not merely politically expedient. Nonrecognition had, indeed, been mainly a political instrument through the Ethiopian and Manchurian controversies of this century. However, in view of the above discussion, especially when the policy has been applied for more than 10 years, it is difficult to see it as politically expedient. In most cases, including that of the Baltic States, it would be politically more convenient to recognize the new status quo.[51]

Thus, recent state practice, measured by the standards of the International Court of Justice, backed by the generally conforming practice of international organizations, expressed in conventional law such as the U.N. Charter, and supported by a considerable volume of national court decisions, would form a strong case for asserting the existence of a new customary rule in international law proscribing the forcible seizure of territory and requiring the nonrecognition of any claim to title based uniquely on such a *tour de force*.[52]

NONRECOGNITION AND LITHUANIA

If indeed the events described in Chapter 2 happened as they did, then the incorporation of Lithuania into the Soviet Union occured *via facti*, that is without any legal foundation whatsoever. Thus the incorporation is null and void (*nul et non avenue*). International law does not allow one state to eliminate the constitution and laws of another; the former cannot occupy the latter without freely given consent.

It is of no consequence that the Soviets claim "historical importance" to the previous union of Lithuania to Russia. Furthermore, the true national will and sovereign aspirations of the citizenry have been expressed in the emergency diplomatic powers conferred on Stasys Lozoraitis, the Lithuanian minister in Rome, shortly before the occupation; the president's exit from the country; the 1941 revolt; the eight year postwar partisan movement; and Lithuanian diplomatic protests and activities to the present day. Boris Meissner writes that the Soviet argument that Russia was too weak in 1920 not to recognize Lithuanian independence is fiction. Many times the Soviet Union *expressis verbis* (with clear words) stated its recognition. Even on 13 July 1940, before the formal incorporation, Soviet President Michail Kalinin greeted Lithuanian President Justas Paleckis. The illegal aggression cannot easily be hidden.

By way of nonrecognition, Lithuania has not disappeared in the juridical sense, and it has retained some vestige of international personality, subject to international rights and obligations. No international act, no formal treaty or agreement, and no peace or armistice has legally changed the status of independent Lithuania. This has come about not merely because of the Lithuanian actions cited above, but because of the attitude of the members of the world community:

> By its refusal to recognize the Soviet rule in Lithuania as legal, the family of Western nations has assumed quasi-judicial rights "as bearers of international functions" not only in the interest of Lithuania and their own political expediency but also in the interest of the international community as a whole and the law which regulates the intercourse among nations. The Western nations are thereby applying "a rule protecting the continual existence of states against illegal acts," thus "upholding the principle of the legal continuity of an illegally suppressed state even as a mere ideal notion" -- a practice which "acquires a wider meaning of action not only in defense of an individual state, but, indeed, of international law itself."[53]

However, in the final analysis, the arbitrary act of nonrecognition on the part of the international community is not sufficient to guarantee legal continuity. The legal principle that prevents the fruits of illegal acts to be legalized is really the foundation of nonrecognition and the continued existence of Lithuania.[54]

Finally, a number of commentators have pointed out that Lithuania, notwithstanding the formal annexation, is legally still under occupation by the Soviet Union's armed forces. The occupation, whether one considers it of the military or the belligerent (enemy) variety, must be recognized as fact. The annexation, however, is null and void. No occupational authority possesses the legal competence to transfer sovereignty over the area in question. International law does not permit annexation, even where domination is effective, for effectiveness is a necessary but not sufficient precondition for absorption; it requires finality:

> Of the three stages of the process of final conquest which are distinguished by international law -- namely, invasion, occupation, and transfer of sovereignty over occupied territory by a treaty of cession concluded with the legitimate sovereign or by subjugation of an enemy state in war without such a treaty of cession -- Lithuania's present status still is in the stage of war occupation, no transfer of sovereignty having taken place by any legally valid means.[55]

In creating a quisling government, the Soviets were responsible for a misrepresentation of sovereignty. The rights and obligations of that government do not extend beyond those enumerated for an occupant in the Hague Convention. The rights of an occupant certainly do not extend to a new oath of allegiance, the holding of elections, introduction of new criminal and civil law, expropriation of property, conscription, and deportation. Thus, the 3 August 1940 decision by the USSR Supreme Soviet transforming the occupation into an act of internal Soviet public law was an exercise in illegal annexation.[56] Furthermore, as Krystyna Marek points out, "for the continuity of a State, as for its birth, its reason of validity must be directly rooted in international law; it cannot be situated within the legal order of another State. Its basic norm cannot be the concretisation on a lower level of a basic norm of that other State."[57]

In sum, then, the military occupation of Lithuania did not confer any title of territory to the Soviet Union and did not legally extinguish the independent government of the nation, despite the proclamation of annexation, which itself overstepped the authority of the occupant. Sovereignty persists as long as it is evident that the occupation is challenged by those living under it. In turn, sovereignty can be effectively exercised as soon as the occupying forces are withdrawn from the country.

NOTES

1. Alfred Cobban, *The Nation State and National Self-Determination* (New York: Crowell, 1970), p. 290.

2. Cobban, *The Nation State,* p. 303.

3. Antanas Trimakas, "The Soviet Disregard of the Right of Peoples to Self-Determination," *Baltic Review,* 16 (April 1959), 38.

4. Trimakas, "The Soviet Disregard," p. 41. It is ironic that the first bilateral treaty embodying the principle of self-determination was the Estonian-Russian peace treaty of 2 February 1920. Article II stated,

> On the basis of the right of all peoples freely to decide their own destinies and even to separate themselves completely from the State of which they form a part, a right proclaimed by the Socialist Republic of Soviet Russia, Russia unreservedly recognizes the independence and autonomy of the State of Estonia, and renounces voluntarily and forever all rights of sovereignty formerly held by Russia over the Estonian people and territory.

See E. Krepp, *Security and Non-Aggression: Baltic States and U.S.S.R. Treaties of Non-Aggression* (Stockholm: Estonian Information Centre/Latvian National Foundation, 1973), p. 7. See also G. Mennen Williams, "Global Self-Determination and the Baltic States," Baltic Review, 31 (April 1966), 3-6.

5. Gerhard von Glahn, *Law among Nations: An Introduction to Public International Law,* 4th ed. (New York: Macmillan, 1981), p. 90.

6. Von Glahn, *Law among Nations,* p. 91.

7. L. Thomas Galloway, *Recognizing Foreign Governments: The Practice of the United States* (Washington, D.C.: American Enterprise Institute for Public Policy Research, 1978), p. 3; von Glahn, Law among Nations, p. 92.

8. Gerard J. Mangone, *The Elements of International Law,* rev. ed. (Homewood, IL: Dorsey Press, 1967), p. 52; von Glahn, Law among Nations, pp. 98-100.

9. Institut de Droit International (Institute of International Law), "Resolution," *American Journal of International Law,* 30 (1936), p. 185.

10. Institut de Droit International, "Resolution," p. 185. As the U.S. did with Israel, it is possible to recognize a new state de jure while granting de facto recognition to a provisional government. See von Glahn, *Law among Nations,* p. 96.

11. Galloway, *Recognizing Foreign Governments,* pp. 3-4. Galloway also writes that following the recognition of a state, it retains its identity regardless of any internal organizational or governmental alterations, even if extreme. In another technical point, he adds that recognition does not necessarily lead to diplomatic relations, although that is the normal procedure. The United States has recently

moved to merge the two actions in an effort to deemphasize recognition. See Galloway, p. 3.

12. Ibid., p. 5. The following passage is distilled from his pp. 5-10.

13. Ibid., p. 9.

14. Ibid., p. 10; von Glahn, *Law among Nations*, p. 99.

15. Galloway, *Recognizing Foreign Governments*, p. 2.

16. Von Glahn, *Law among Nations*, p. 99.

17. Galloway, *Recognizing Foreign Governments*, pp. 11-12; von Glahn, Law among Nations, p. 101.

18. Galloway, *Recognizing Foreign Governments*, pp. 11-12.

19. Robert Langer, *Seizure of Territory: The Stimson Doctrine and Related Principles in Legal Theory and Diplomatic Practice* (Princeton: Princeton University Press, 1947), p. 57. His pp. 50-56 recount the troubled history of Manchuria in the late nineteenth and early twentieth centuries, which involved competition among, and interference from, Russia, China, and Japan.

20. Ibid., p. 58. See also Bronis J. Kaslas, *The Baltic Nations-The Quest for Regional Integration and Political Liberty* (Pittston, PA: Euramerica, 1976), p. 276; E. Krepp, Security and Non-Aggression: Baltic States and U.S.S.R. Treaties of Non-Agrression (Stockholm: Estonian Information Centre/Latvian National Foundation, 1973), p. 30.

21. Langer, *Seizure of Territory*, p. 60.

22. Ibid., p. 69.

23. Vaino J. Rusmandel, "The Continued Legal Existence of the Baltic States," *Baltic Review*, 12 (7 November 1957), 66.

24. Kaslas, *The Baltic Nations*, p. 276.

25. Ibid., pp. 276-277.

26. H. B. Jacobini, *A Study of the Philosophy of International Law as Seen in the Works of Latin American Writers* (the Hague: Martinus Nijhoff, 1954), p. 128.

27. However, it was actually the League of Nations that first intervened in a Latin American dispute by invoking the Stimson Doctrine. In a dispute between Peru and Colombia over the Leticia district, the League Council on 18 March 1933 adopted a report that recommended that Peru evacuate the district and urged league members not to recognize "any situation, treaty or agreement" contrary to the covenant or the Kellogg-Briand Pact. See Langer, *Seizure of Territory*, pp. 69-70.

28. Ibid., p. 68.

29. Ibid., pp. 75-76.

30. Ibid., p. 77. See also Kaslas, *The Baltic Nations*, p. 277.

31. Langer, *Seizure of Territory*, p. 79.

32. Von Glahn, *Law among Nations*, p. 325.

33. William L. Tung, *International Law in an Organizing World* (New York: Crowell, 1968), p. 54; von Glahn, Law among Nations, pp. 107-108.

34. Malbone W. Graham, Jr., "What Does Non-Recognition Mean?" *Baltic Review*, 1, 4-5 (July-August 1946), 171.

35. Graham, "Non-Recognition," p. 171. See also H. Lauterpacht, *Recognition in International Law* (Cambridge: Cambridge University Press, 1947), p. 420.

36. Rusmandel, "Continued Legal Existence," p. 49.

37. The following passage is derived from Graham, "Non-Recognition," pp. 171-174.

38. Von Glahn writes that nonrecognition of a state itself is ineffective and disadvantageous, in that a government's interests and citizens cannot be adequately protected in the nonrecognized state. See his *Law among Nations*, p. 92.

39. As will be seen in the next chapter, the U.S. invoked the principle that she is opposed to the threat or use of force. The Welles statement of 23 July 1940 did not cite any specific treaties.

40. Lauterpacht, *Recognition*, p. 413.

41. Thomas M. Franck and Michael J. Glennon, *Foreign Relations and National Security Law: Cases, Materials and Simulations* (St. Paul, MN: West, 1987), p. 431.

42. This even for the sake of possessing an observation point or for staging underground action against the occupant. See Langer, *Seizure of Territory*, p. 287.

43. Ibid., p. 106.

44. Boris Meissner, *Die Sowjetunion, die Baltischen Staaten und das Voelkerrecht* (The Soviet Union, the Baltic States, and international law) (Cologne, West Germany: Verlag Politik und Wirtscahft, 1956), reviewed by Jonas Maziulis, Baltic Review, 7 (16 June 1956), 78.

45. Rusmandel, "Continued Legal Existence," pp. 49-50. Also Lauterpacht, *Recognition*, pp. 406, 416-421.

46. Graham, "Non-Recognition," p. 174.

47. *North Sea Continental Shelf* (W.Ger. v. Den.; W.Ger. v. Neth.), 1969 I.C.J. 3 (judgment of February 20).

48. William J.H. Hough, III, "The Annexation of the Baltic States and Its Effect on the Development of Law Prohibiting Forcible Seizure of Territory," *New York Law School Journal of International and Comparative Law*, 6, 2 (Winter 1985), 449.

49. Ibid., pp. 449-450, 460, 465.

50. Ibid., pp. 466-467.

51. Ibid., p. 467.

52. Ibid., p. 468. See also Baltic Committee in Scandinavia (BCS), *Memorandum Regarding the European Security and Cooperation Conference and the Baltic States* (Stockholm: BCS, 1972), p. 4.

53. Martin Brakas, "Lithuania's International Status: Some Legal Aspects 2," *Baltic Review*, 38 (August 1971), 12.   See also Hough, "Annexation," p. 481. Graham, "Non-Recognition," p. 173, writes:

> A special situation arises when third parties, which have conformed their foreign policy to the relations established between two countries by treaty, are faced by a unilateral violation of such treaty by one of the contracting parties. The mere fact of such unilateral violation does not require the party to conform its policy to the accomplished fact. Such is believed to be the situation confronting the United States in the light of the violation of the fundamental treaties of peace between the [USSR] and the three Baltic States.

54. Krystyna Marek, *Identity and Continuity of States in Public International Law* (Geneva: Librairie E. Droz, 1968), p. 414.

55. Brakas, "Lithuania's International Status," p. 14.

56. Meissner, *Die Sowjetunion*, in Maziulis, review, pp. 76-77; Konstantinas Rackauskas, "Power Politics vs. International Law," Baltic Review, 14 (1 August 1958), 72-73.

57. Marek, *Identity and Continuity*, p. 396.

4

Genesis of the U.S. Nonrecognition Policy

LITHUANIAN-AMERICAN ACTIONS

From the inception of an independent state of Lithuania, Lithuanian-Americans came to the country's aid. The years 1918-1922 were crucial in Lithuania's development. Having declared her independence from the Russian empire, she was still forced to fight the Germans, Poles, and Bolsheviks in order to assure that the declaration of independence of 16 February 1918 would not be hollow. Lithuania naturally sought support from Britain, France, and the United States. Over one million signatures requesting de jure recognition of Lithuania by the U.S. were presented to President Warren G. Harding during a campaign by Lithuanians aimed at the U.S. government. Their goal would become a reality in 1922.

During the period of independence, Lithuanian-Americans remained active. Lithuanian lawyers, bankers, and organizers were politically prominent in both major political parties. Furthermore, Lithuanian journalists were adept at using the non-Lithuanian media to publicize their causes. As David Truman writes:

> A primary concern of all organized political interest groups in the United States is the character of the opinions existing in the community. Group leaders, whatever else they may neglect, cannot afford to be ignorant of widely held attitudes bearing upon the standing and objectives of their organizations. Estimating the direction and incidence of public opinions, moreover, goes hand in hand with more or less continuing efforts to guide and control them. In fact, almost invariably one of the first results of the formal organization of an interest group is its embarking upon a program of propaganda, though rarely so labeled, designed to affect opinions concerning the interests and claims of the new group.[1]

If this sort of work had been important during the interwar period, it became critical beginning with the events of 1940.[2]

A Lithuanian-American delegation met with Minister Povilas Zadeikis at the Lithuanian Legation in Washington, D.C. on 29 June. At first, it appeared that Zadeikis was hesitant to speak out against the government of Justas Paleckis, not yet being certain exactly what was transpiring in Lithuania. The delegation stated that it would vigorously oppose the occupation, and would protest against Lithuanian diplomatic and consular personnel who would not break ties with the new government. It was noted that the legation had assisted the Paleckis regime in relaying information to the Lithuanian-American media. The consultation ended with a consensus that the Soviet regime in Lithuania would be opposed. Minister Zadeikis gave his blessing to the formation of a unitary Lithuanian American Council.

A general meeting of Lithuanian-American groups met at Pittsburgh on 9-10 August. The provisional bylaws of the Lithuanian American Council and the Lithuanian Rescue Board (*Lietuvos Gelbejimo Taryba*) were approved.

An idea to send a delegation to President Franklin D. Roosevelt germinated. A telegram was dispatched to U.S. Representative A. Sabath, a Roosevelt supporter, raising the idea. A letter to that effect was also sent to Minister Zadeikis. Both responded that the president was too occupied to receive a delegation. Assistance was then rendered by Viktoras Solis (or Sholis), a journalist and assistant to Secretary of Commerce Harry Hopkins. Solis made the necessary arrangements, and President Roosevelt received the delegation on 15 October 1940. It presented the following memorandum:

> The delegation before you, Mr. President, represents most of the Lithuanian people of the United States; it is here to encourage you in the task of bringing reason and law to reign again in a distracted world. With the world aflame, with ruthless might attempting to conquer the earth, the Lithuanian people were moved to great depths of sorrow when their native land and land of their forebears lost her freedom. When Lithuania fell, it seemed that the nations of the earth, particularly those who had recognized her as independent, were disinterested, none condemned the act of extirpation which to the Lithuanians of America seemed so needful of condemnation. Then, on the twenty-third day of July, 1940, your State Department, Mr. President, announced the [Welles declaration[3]]....
>
> That was a clear, understandable, and unequivocal statement of policy. It was an act of condemnation of a wrong committed by a great power against a weak nation. At last the clamor of destruction was overcome by the call to reason and justice, and our people were glad that voice came from the greatest liberty-loving nation on the earth -- the United States of America. We are proud that [the United States] stands firmly behind a policy that knows no compromise with aggression. Your courageous stand, Mr. President,

on the side of justice, law and reason enkindled the flame of hope -
- a hope that Lithuania may again take her place amongst the nations
of the [E]arth.[4]

Roosevelt responded that Lithuania had not lost her independence, but that it had
merely been suspended:

> The address mentioned that Lithuania had lost its independence.
> That is a mistake. The independence of Lithuania is not lost but only
> put temporarily aside. The time will come when Lithuania will be
> free again. This may happen sooner than you may expect.[5] It was
> a mistake on behalf of one of the speakers to say that Lithuania is a
> small country. In Latin America there are states even smaller than
> Lithuania, but they live a free and happy life.
>   Even the smallest nation has the same right to enjoy independence
> as the largest one.[6]

Though Roosevelt was speaking in October, the policy of the U.S. toward the Soviet
occupation had been decided in July. A central figure in this episode was Loy
Wesley Henderson, the career diplomat who prodded the U.S. government into
taking a firm stand with regard to the Lithuanian situation.

THE HENDERSON MEMORANDUM

Actions outside U.S. control were certainly the driving force behind
Lithuania's new situation in the summer of 1940. However, the application of the
Stimson Doctrine to the Lithuanian occupation was brought about by internal
bureaucratic forces, as well as by the actions of Lithuanian-Americans. Within the
U.S. government, a combination of practical and moral considerations guided policy
toward Lithuania. A leading player behind the scenes at the State Department was
Henderson, at that time the assistant chief of European Affairs.

On 15 July 1940, exactly one month following the occupation, Henderson
addressed an internal memorandum to the assistant secratary of state, Adolph A.
Berle, Jr., and to the adviser on political relations, James Clement Dunn. The
document described and evaluated recent events, raising the dilemma the U.S.
faced not only in terms of policy, but also in terms of principle:

> Is the Government of the United States to apply certain standards of
> judgement and conduct to aggression by Germany and Japan which
> it will not apply to aggression by the Soviet Union[?] In other words,
> is the Government...to follow one policy with respect to, say,
> Czechoslovakia, Denmark, and German-occupied Poland, and another

policy with respect to Latvia, Estonia, Lithuania, and Finland...[?] Is the United States to continue to refuse to recognize the fruits of aggression regardless of who the aggressor may be, or for reasons of expediency to close its eyes to the fact that certain nations are committing aggression upon their neighbors[?][7]

Not being one to ignore practical consequences, Henderson added:

It seems likely that the assets of all three countries in the United States will not amount to much more than 12 or 13 million dollars. In this connection it will be observed that if the three countries in question are absorbed into the Soviet Union, the United States will probably not receive one cent of the several million dollars which the governments of these three countries owe us. Furthermore, American interests in those three countries will probably be a total loss.[8]

Henderson concluded the memorandum by urging the U.S. to move swiftly in this regard, before the Soviets gained possession of the Baltic funds. He added that the U.S. Maritime Commission should look into the matter of Baltic vessels in the same manner.[9]

Although it is uncertain whether any of Henderson's actions prior to writing the memorandum had any influence on the matter, the U.S. Treasury Department decided that the measures outlined by Henderson should be implemented. On the same day that Henderson dispatched his memorandum, President Roosevelt issued Executive Order 8484:

By virtue of the authority vested in me by section 5 (b) of the Act of October 6, 1917 (40 Stat. 411), as amended, and by virtue of all other authority vested in me, I, FRANKLIN D. ROOSEVELT, PRESIDENT of the UNITED STATES OF AMERICA, do hereby amend Executive Order No. 8389 of April 10, 1940, as amended,[[10]] so as to extend all the provisions thereof to, and with respect to, property in which Latvia, Estonia or Lithuania or any national thereof has at any time on or since July 10, 1940, had any interest of any nature whatsoever, direct or indirect.[11]

The actions of 15 July 1940 (that is, the Henderson memorandum and the Roosevelt order) were the first official responses to the occupation. In order for the nonrecognition policy to be fully framed, however, it was necessary for the United States to formally act on the diplomatic front. This task fell to Acting Secretary of State Sumner Welles who, in applying the Stimson Doctrine of nonrecognition to the European continent in general, and to the Baltic States in particular, forged a new trail in the U.S. interpretation of international law.

THE WELLES DECLARATION AND ITS AFTERMATH

One week following Henderson's and Roosevelt's measures, on 23 July 1940, the U.S. State Department announced to the global community the U.S. policy regarding the occupation, which is reproduced in its entirety:

> During these past few days the devious processes whereunder the political independence and territorial integrity of the three Baltic Republics -- Estonia, Latvia, and Lithuania -- were to be deliberately annihilated by one of their more powerful neighbors, have been drawing rapidly to their conclusion.[12]   From the day when the peoples of these Republics first gained their independence and democratic form of government, the people of the United States have watched their admirable progress in self-government with deep and sympathetic interest.   The policy of this Government is universally known.   The people of the United States are opposed to predatory activities, no matter whether they are carried on by the use of force or by the threat of force.   They are likewise opposed to any form of intervention on the part of one State, however powerful, in the domestic concerns of any other sovereign State, however weak.   These principles constitute the very foundation upon which the existing relationship between the twenty-one sovereign republics of the New World rest.   The United States will continue to stand by these principles, because of the conviction of the American people that unless the doctrine in which these principles are inherent once again governs the relations between nations, the rule of reason, of justice, and of law -- in other words, the basis of modern civilization itself -- cannot be preserved.[13]

Though seemingly vague and obfuscating, the declaration is pregnant with meaning. Welles did not mention nonrecognition per se, but in the context of the Baltic States, the phrase "doctrine in which these principles are inherent" refers to the Stimson Doctrine.[14] By making this statement, and backed by the actions of the Treasury Department, the United States came out foursquare in favor of a nonrecognition policy aimed at Soviet actions in the Baltic States. The U.S. did not consider the USSR a legitimate successor state in the area and, at least in Washington's eyes, Lithuania, Latvia, and Estonia maintained some vestige of international personality.[15]

Needless to say, the U.S. actions brought a storm of protest from the Soviet Union and from the new Soviet regimes in the Baltic States.[16] On 27 July 1940, Welles met with Soviet ambassador Constantine A. Oumansky:

The Ambassador went on to say that the action taken by the Soviet [*sic*] should have been applauded by the [U.S.] since it had obliterated the growth of "fascism" in the three Baltic republics and had made it possible for the suffering peoples . . . to come under the sheltering protection of the Soviet Government as a result of which they would obtain the blessings of liberal and social government.[17]

Welles responded that he could not discuss the matter with the ambassador because the U.S. would stand by its stated policy. The ambassador stated that the U.S. appeared to be viewing Soviet actions as being similar to German invasions in Western European countries. Welles made it clear that the U.S. "saw no difference in principle between the two cases."[18]

In addition to the continuity of Baltic diplomatic and consular functions in the U.S., the Soviets took particular umbrage at the freezing of assets. In a conference with Welles, Henderson, and Acting Chief of European Affairs Ray Atherton, Oumansky remarked that:

So long as the [U.S.] Government addressed communications to the Soviet Government of such a nature as that stick of dynamite on the subject of the frozen Baltic funds which had been given to him..., an improvement in the relations between the two countries would not be easy to achieve....He noticed in one of these communications such offensive expressions as "duress", "force", etc.[19]

The U.S. chief of mission in Moscow, Walter C. Thurston, in a 20 July conversation with Assistant Commisar for Foreign Affairs A. Lozovski received a strong protest against Executive Order 8484. In defending Roosevelt's action, Thurston said that it was not illegal, as Lozovski had said.[20] The formal U.S. reply to the Soviet protest included mention of U.S. losses in Soviet-controlled territories due to nationalization and confiscation.[21]

In addition to these protests, U.S. diplomats in the Baltic also received expressions of disapproval from the new governments there. The evening before the Lithuanian People's Seimas met, U.S. Minister Owen J. C. Norem was called to the foreign ministry in Kaunas to receive a protest that stated that responsibility for losses due to Executive Order 8484 would fall to the U.S. government. However, the representative of the ministry quietly added: "Please disregard all of our protests. We do not act independently anymore. We appreciate what Washington is doing more than we dare tell. People are listening and I cannot say any more."[22]

As the events of World War II and thereafter would demonstrate, it was not always practically possible or desirable to maintain an ironclad interpretation of the nonrecognition policy. Indeed, before the year was out, there was already some questioning of the policy by senior officials in the context of Western war aims; one of them was U.S. Secretary of State Cordell Hull. In a conversation with the British ambassador and his counselor of embassy, Hull said

> that if Russia should show a real disposition to move in our common direction with respect to the axis countries, then I would be disposed to deal with the Baltic assets and ships on a sort of *quid pro quo* basis rather than to adhere inflexibly to our non-recognition policy in this case.[23]

In other words, it was clear from its inception-at least privately in government circles-that the nonrecognition policy would never be allowed to harm U.S. interests.

NOTES

1. David B. Truman, *The Governmental Process: Political Interests and Public Opinion*, 2d ed. (New York: Knopf, 1971), p. 213.

2. For a short summary of Lithuanian-American action at that time, see Kucas, pp. 276-277.

3. See below for details of the Welles statement.

4. Leonardas Simutis, *Amerikos Lietuviu Taryba: 30 metu Lietuvos laisves kovoje 1940-1970* (Lithuanian American Council: 30-year struggle for the liberation of Lithuania 1940-1970) (Chicago: LAC, 1971), p. 458. See also p. 24.

5. History would prove Roosevelt wrong.

6. Ibid., p. 458. See also Algirdas M. Budreckis, ed., *The Lithuanians in America 1651-1975: A Chronology and Fact Book* (Dobbs Ferry, NY: Oceana, 1976), pp. 109-110; E. J. Harrison, Lithuania's Fight for Freedom, 3d ed. (New York: Lithuanian American Information Center, 1948), p. 28; Simutis, Amerikos Lietuviu Taryba, p. 25.

7. U.S. Department of State, *Foreign Relations of the United States*, Diplomatic Papers, 1940, vol. I, General (Washington, D.C.: U.S. Government Printing Office, 1959), p. 390.

8. U.S. Department of State, *Foreign Relations*, 1940, I, General, pp. 390-391. A note by Dunn at the beginning of the document states: "I feel funds of all 3 of these countries should be blocked on same basis as those of countries occupied by Germany." See p. 389.

9. U.S. Department of State, *Foreign Relations*, 1940, I, General, p. 391.

10. This order froze Norwegian and Danish assets following the German occupation of those countries. See U.S. Office of the Federal Register, *Code of Federal Regulations*, Title 3-The President, 1938-1943 Compilation (Washington, D.C.: U.S. Government Printing Office, 1968), pp. 645-647.

11. U.S. Office of the Federal Register, *Code*, 1938-1943, p. 687. In 1950, acting on the advice of the State Department, the Treasury Department modified its regulations implementing Executive Order 8484 so as to allow the Baltic funds to be invested in certain securities.

12. Two days prior to the Welles declaration, the Lithuanian People's Seimas had voted to enter the USSR.

13. U.S. Department of State, *Department of State Bulletin*, 3, 57 (27 July 1940), 48.

14. Robert Langer, *Seizure of Territory: The Stimson Doctrine and Related Principles in Legal Theory and Diplomatic Practice* (Princeton: Princeton University Press, 1947), pp. 263-264.

15. Gerhard von Glahn, *Law among Nations: An Introduction to Public International Law*, 4th ed. (New York: Macmillan, 1981), p. 118, cf. pp. 119-123. Shortly before Germany attacked the Soviet Union in June 1941, President Roosevelt had a conversation with General Wladyslaw Sikorski, the premier of the Polish government-in-exile. One year after the fact, Roosevelt still maintained his stance toward the Baltic: "As far as the United States is concerned, we stand by [the Welles declaration]....It is one of our basic policies not to recognize unilateral changes brought about by force or threat of force." See Jan Ciechanowski, Defeat in Victory (Garden City, NY: Doubleday, 1947), p. 20.

16. Cf. Budreckis, *The Lithuanians in America*, pp. 384-385.

17. U.S. Department of State, *Foreign Relations of the United States*, Diplomatic Papers 1940, vol. III (Washington, D.C.: U.S. Government Printing Office, 1958), p. 329.

18. Ibid., p. 330.

19. Ibid., p. 379.

20. U.S. Department of State, *Foreign Relations*, 1940, I, General, p. 395. According to Edgar Anderson, Soviet Deputy Commissar for Foreign Affairs Andrei Vishinsky admitted on 14 September 1940 that the Soviet government possessed no legal claims to Baltic gold. See his "British Policy toward the Baltic States, 1940-41," Journal of Baltic Studies, 11, 4 (Winter 1980), 330.

21. U.S. Department of State, *Foreign Relations*, 1940, I, General, pp. 410-416.

22. Ibid., p. 397.

23. Ibid., pp. 439-440.

5

Political and Legal Effects of Nonrecognition

THE STATUS OF THE LITHUANIAN GOVERNMENT

As spring turned to summer in 1940, the atmosphere on the European continent was tense. Poland had been eliminated from the political map by Germany and the Soviet Union the previous September. Germany was rapidly preparing to strike west toward France and Great Britain. In the East, Finland had been forced to negotiate an unequal peace treaty following the attack by the USSR. Finally, the Baltic States, which now had Soviet troops on their soil thanks to the mutual assistance pacts, sensed that the Kremlin was not satisfied with that arrangement alone.

In order to be prepared for any contingency, Lithuanian Foreign Minister Juozas Urbsys, acting on presidential authority, dispatched telegram number 288 to Lithuanian diplomats abroad on 2 June 1940, just a scant two weeks prior to the occupation. It stated that in case of emergency, the chief of the remaining Lithuanian Diplomatic Service outside Lithuania would be Stasys Lozoraitis, former foreign minister and minister of Lithuania in Rome. His first deputy would be Petras Klimas, minister in Berlin, and the second deputy would be Jurgis Saulys, posted in Bern, Switzerland.

Following the resolution by the People's Seimas to join the Soviet Union, Lozoraitis spoke out as the representative of the Lithuanian diplomats. Ironically, his first protest, on 1 August 1940, was directed against the foreign ministry in Kaunas:

> In view of the resolution of July 21, passed by the so-called Seimas
> and incorporating Lithuania into the Soviet Union I declare:
> *primo*: the so-called Seimas, constituted under military
> occupation, oppression and terror of a foreign country
> which had broken treaties and principles of international law and
> committed an act of aggression, is not a representative body, but
> a tool in the hands of oppressors;

secundo: its resolutions do not express the will of the Lithuanian nation, and bind neither the people of Lithuania nor myself, the legal representative of the independent and sovereign state of Lithuania;

tertio: I protest with horror against the treacherous resolution.[1]

One may ask what became of President Antanas Smetona during this period. When he left Lithuania following the Soviet ultimatum, Smetona entered East Prussia, where he and his party were interned as guests of the German government. His Lithuanian diplomatic passport identified him as president. Constitutionally, Smetona was still president, despite having temporarily relinquished acting powers to Prime Minister Antanas Merkys. Shortly thereafter, the U.S. chief of mission in Berlin issued Smetona a visa to enter the United States, but only on the condition that he not represent himself as acting in an official capacity. Smetona had to declare: "While I am in the U.S. I shall not be considered as the head or member of any government." In return, the U.S. government referred to Smetona as the "distinguished guest, the President of the Republic of Lithuania in exile, residing in the U.S. in private capacity," while State Department correspondence addressed him as His Excellency.[2]

By way of South America, Smetona arrived in New York City on 10 March 1941. On 1 April he paid a visit to Acting Secretary of State Sumner Welles, and on the 18 April he met with President Roosevelt. Roosevelt advised Smetona to work among Lithuanian-Americans for Lithuania's cause, which he did until his untimely death in a fire at his son's home in Cleveland on 9 January 1944.[3]

Smetona's odyssey is related to the question of a Lithuanian government-in-exile. In September 1940, Lithuanian diplomats met in Rome to discuss the future of the nation's independent government. On the 25 September, they endorsed a resolution that created the Lithuanian National Committee. Ernestas Galvanauskas, a former prime minister, was invited to be its president, Lozoraitis was appointed deputy ipso jure. Diplomats Eduardas Turauskas, Kazys Skirpa, and Povilas Zadeikis would also have a hand in the committee's work. The committee's task was "to care for the interests of the Lithuanian State and Lithuanian nation."[4] The Lithuanian National Committee never functioned in a practical manner.

The Supreme Committee for the Liberation of Lithuania has often represented itself as a quasi-government-in-exile, complete with parliamentary organs and political parties:

It is true that certain ministers plenipotentiary and other diplomatic representatives of Lithuania are still recognized and are continuing to fulfill certain functions deriving from the state sovereignty. But they are only executive bodies, and not sovereign political representatives.... Hence the necessity arose for headquarters of some kind, vested with proper authority, to direct and coordinate Lithuanian activities...and provisionally to fulfill the tasks which otherwise would be a matter for the government.[5]

Indeed, in 1947, the Supreme Committee concluded an agreement with the Polish government-in-exile regarding the formulation of a treaty on the common struggle against the Soviet Union. Lithuanian diplomats, however, declined to endorse the draft treaty and the project was ultimately set aside.[6]

In July 1946, at a conference of the Supreme Committee and Lithuanian diplomats in Bern, Switzerland, it was decided to form the nucleus of a Lithuanian delegation to the upcoming peace conference. In a merger of the state and the resistance to the Soviets, an executive council of the committee was formed. Stasys Lozoraitis accepted the invitation to take charge of foreign affairs in the executive council, while the Supreme Committee would remain as a parliamentary and study institution. This arrangement was never ratified, and Lozoraitis later pulled out in order to retain his independence.[7]

The question was never seriously addressed in the United States. On 18 December 1941, following prodding by Smetona, the Lithuanian minister in Washington, Povilas Zadeikis, transmitted a note to Secretary of State Cordell Hull on the matter of a Lithuanian National Council and government in exile. On 12 January 1942, Zadeikis informed Smetona that Hull had stated that consideration of those questions was postponed. It is quite possible that wartime politics, specifically the Soviet Union's participation against the Axis, was instrumental in this. This notwithstanding, even during the Cold War, the U.S. did not wish to commit itself to the idea of recognizing an extraterritorial sovereign body. To this day, the Baltic legations in Washington are not recognized as governments in exile. The role of the Baltic envoys "is to uphold the ideal of a free Estonia, Latvia, and Lithuania."[8]

STATUS OF TREATIES AND DIPLOMATIC PERSONNEL

As far as the United States is concerned, its treaties with the government of independent Lithuania are legally still in force. They deal with matters of customs, extradition, finance, nationality, postal affairs, trade, and other forms of international intercourse. Only abrogation by the executive terminates the validity of a treaty, and no Lithuanian executive recognized by the U.S. government has done so. Of course, the treaties are now suspended, for there is no independent Lithuanian government to implement them. As far as the Soviets are concerned, the treaties are no longer valid, since all meaningful foreign affairs dealing with Lithuania must pass through the Kremlin. In addition, since official contact with the sending state was severed, the Lithuanian minister in Washington could no longer conclude treaties or other agreements with the U.S. government.

Though President Smetona's fate, personally and politically, was not a happy one, Lithuanian diplomatic and consular personnel were more fortunate.

Their status as representatives of the independent Lithuanian government remained unaltered. It was obvious that the U.S. government considered the preservation of the Lithuanian Diplomatic Service a minor and relatively harmless matter. Granting status to a chief executive and government-in-exile, though, would have possessed far-reaching political implications, tying Washington's hands in its relations with Moscow.

Popular lore has it that the Lithuanian legation in Washington refused to carry out the orders of the Lithuanian government as of 15 June 1940. However, as was indicated in the previous chapter, Minister Zadeikis and his staff were confused as to the situation in Lithuania due to Smetona's departure, Merkys's efforts to return him to Kaunas, the reports of Smetona's de facto resignation, and the presence of Foreign Minister Juozas Urbsys in Moscow. Compounding this was the fact that members of the new government themselves, including President Paleckis, were uncertain about the future. Zadeikis was receiving no information or responses to inquiries. The picture became more clear when it was learned that the known communist Mecislovas Gedvilas had been appointed interior minister, and that the first secretary of the Lithuanian Communist Party, Antanas Snieckus, was now the director of the internal security department.

By 13 July 1940, Zadeikis was able to write to Secretary Hull that "from the information available, it appears that the scheduled elections [to the People's Seimas] will be carried out exclusively under the aegis of the Communist party."[9] On 3 August, after the Supreme Soviet admitted Lithuania into the USSR, Zadeikis reaffirmed both his own status and his protest:

> As the duly accredited representative of the Sovereign Republic of Lithuania near the Government of the United States of America I repeat my protest against the unprovoked aggression and illegal incorporation of Lithuania into the Soviet Union and at the same time express the hope of the Lithuanian nation that no State in the world will recognize this international outrage as having any legality or bona fide excuse. I...hope that the American Government will continue to refuse legal recognition of the Soviet's aggressive acts against Lithuania's integrity and independence.[10]

It became abundantly clear to Zadeikis where he stood with the new government in Kaunas when a decision of the Lithuanian Council of Ministers was published on 14 August. Retroactive to 26 July, it stripped Zadeikis of his Lithuanian citizenship, confiscated his property, and forbade him to return to Lithuania. This notwithstanding, there was never any Soviet attempt to assume control of the legation, located at 2622 16th Street NW in Washington, D.C. Zadeikis continued to issue formal protests to the U.S. State Department during the occupations of World War II, and disseminated information regarding the Lithuanian situation. Then, as now, the legation was listed in the State

Department's annual *Diplomatic List.*

The following consular personnel continued to function in the U.S., representing the interests of Lithuanian nationals and their property: Consul General Jonas Budrys, Consul Vytautas Stasinskas, Vice Consul Anicetas Simutis, New York; Consul Petras Dauzvardis, Chicago; Honorary Consul Julius J. Bielskis, Los Angeles; Honorary Consul Anthony O. Shallna, Boston. However, the trade, economic, cultural, and scientific functions of the consulates practically ceased. The consuls were left in the unusual position of defending the interests of their nationals against both the United States and the factual authorities of the sending state, Soviet Lithuania. "[Consular] representation may...be urgently needed in the interest of those whom non-recognition is intended to protect."[11]

Baltic consuls possess standing (*locus standi*) in U.S. courts. A court case confirming the status of the Estonian consul general in New York, but also applicable to Lithuanian consuls, was *Buxhoeveden v. Estonian State Bank*, et al.[12] The plaintiff, Buxhoeveden, contended that he was entitled to certain payments under an Estonian will written in 1837. On 3 December 1941, he obtained a warrant of attachment and caused it to be levied on funds of the Estonian State Bank deposited at the National City Bank of New York.

The Estonian consul general, Jaakson Kaiv, asserted that it was his right under international law, the U.S.-Estonian consular convention, and Estonian municipal law to protect property interests of nationals of the sending state where no power of attorney has been granted to another party. Buxhoeveden maintained that Kaiv did not have the authority to represent the Estonian State Bank as a consular official. The New York Supreme Court stated the problem:

> The basic question of law presented by this application is the extent of the right of a Consul General of a foreign nation, at peace with this country, but completely occupied by an enemy, to protect and guard in our courts the rights and property of one of his own nationals, an Estonian corporation in which the said Republic owns a majority share interest, and which, if indeed it has knowledge of this action, is itself manifestly unable, because of present unprecedented world conditions, to defend the same or to take any steps specifically to authorize such defense.[13]

Kaiv's consular status was affirmed on the basis of both international law and U.S.-Estonian agreements. In other words, he acts in an official capacity, and not as a private agent, when he defends the property interests of his nationals. He also possesses the right to move and take action without authorization from, or communication with, the defendant.[14]

This leads us to a discussion of the notarial acts of unrecognized governments.[15] All governments perform routine notarial acts, such as the issuance of birth, death, and marriage certificates. U.S. courts have been faced with a dilemma when dealing with the acts of unrecognized governments, and have responded in various ways. Courts that have accepted their validity have indicated the nonpolitical nature of such acts, and the fact that citizens have no choice but to accept the acts of a government in actual control of territory. They state that acceptance does not undercut a policy of nonrecognition. Courts that have invalidated such acts stress that executive nonrecognition must lead to judicial nonrecognition, as the unrecognized government is not seen as possessing the legal capacity to act.

Following World War II there occured a series of court decisions that grappled with these issues. Citizens in the Baltic States, who sought their legitimate share of estates in the United States, would sign letters of attorney so that U.S. counsel could represent them. These letters were authenticated by officers of the unrecognized Soviet regimes in the Baltic. A U.S. consul would, in turn, countersign, but would add the note: "This authentication is not to be interpreted as implying recognition of Soviet sovereignty over [Lithuania, Latvia, or Estonia]." The executor of the estate would typically object to these documents once they were introduced in court. Baltic consuls would also object. New York State surrogate courts tended to sustain these objections out of deference to determinations of the executive branch.[16]

In *In re Aleksandravicius*, a New Jersey court followed a different approach and ruled that only political acts are to be unrecognized in U.S. courts.[17] The court added that this did not violate the nonrecognition policy, for the U.S. consul's countersigned statement explicitly stated official U.S. policy. Thus, private notarial acts were separated from political ones. A New York court made a similar ruling in *In re Estate of Bielinis*, and noted practical difficulties facing beneficiaries residing in Lithuania:

> There are no officials of the Republic of Lithuania in Lithuania. To require these legatees to go before a notary of the de jure Republic of Lithuania to prove their signatures is to deny to them the right validly to execute powers of attorney at all. To require them to travel to some part of the USSR where the USSR is recognized by our government as the de jure government in order to execute powers of attorney is to require them to do a useless act and one which, in the light of the small participation they have in the estate, may mean that they would forfeit their interest rather than try to prove it....
>
> It would appear self-evident that almost the last person in the world who would be able to communicate with the principals and to obtain appropriate evidence from the occupied territory of Lithuania would be the Lithuanian consul.[18]

Today, U.S. courts generally distinguish between notarial acts and acts that politically would violate the nonrecognition policy. This was reaffirmed in a relatively recent federal case, *Daniunas v. Simutis*:

> Even though the present government of Lithuania is not recognized
> by this country, since the powers of attorney relate to what has been
> determined to be solely a private, local and domestic matter, the
> inheritance rights of Lithuanian citizens, they will be given effect by
> the courts of this country.[19]

The question of specific consular actions is found in the general context
of U.S.-Baltic consular relations. Evald Roosaare writes:

> [T]he [Vienna] Convention [on Consular Relations[20]] provides only
> that the functions of a member of the consulate come to an end "on
> notification by the sending state to the receiving state" in that respect
> and implies clearly that recalling a consular official by the sending
> state is governed by domestic and not by international law. The only
> question which may arise, and indeed arose, is whether the action was
> taken by the proper authorities and under proper law. Not the
> refusal by Baltic consuls to follow the Soviet order, but the United
> States' refusal to recognize the Soviet Government in the Baltic states
> determined their status within the United States.[21]

Thus, Roosaare concludes, since the U.S. has not changed its recognition of the
independent Baltic governments, the legal status of Baltic consular officials and
their ability to carry out consular functions have not been altered.

While in 1990, as will be seen in the final chapter, the existence of
Lithuanian consulates in the U.S. is mainly a symbolic and informational enterprise,
the war years saw the consuls actively exercising their role in defending the interests
of their nationals. Though challenges to Soviet notarial acts were a part of this, the
most important strides were made in response to Soviet property nationalization
laws and decrees, which Washington did not view as legitimate.

THE STATUS OF ASSETS AND PROPERTY

In the four day period of 22-25 July 1940, the Soviet-run legislatures of
the Baltic States carried out decrees nationalizing banking and credit institutions as
well as industrial enterprises. All orders of the previous owners and directors
became invalid. According to the Act of State Doctrine in international law, one
state respects the validity of another's public acts. As a corollary, courts are not to
pass judgment on the legality or constitutionality of such acts.[22] In other words,
had the executive not intervened in the case of the Baltic States, U.S. courts would
have routinely upheld the Soviet decrees in cases coming before them.

However, the U.S. nonrecognition policy did not permit this. Nonrecognition is a political relationship of which courts must take cognizance and which, under the doctrine of judicial auto-limitation, they must implement in line with stated executive policy. In such a situation, not only are the public acts of the unrecognized government viewed as illegal, but "a nonrecognized [de facto] government does not possess a right of access to the courts of such other states as deny it recognition; that is, an unrecognized government cannot sue in such courts."[23] In *R.S.F. Soviet Republic v. Cibrario*, the court noted that no precedent existed whereby an unrecognized government could seek relief in U.S. courts.[24] The commom practice in such an event is to freeze assets, as indeed the U.S. government did with the funds of the Baltic states, South Vietnam, Cambodia, North Korea, Cuba, and China.

At the time of the Soviet occupation, Gosbank, the official Soviet bank in Moscow, forwarded an order to U.S. banks to transfer Baltic assets to it. This order, thanks to the presidential freeze of 15 July 1940, was not complied with. All subsequent orders requesting the release of assets of nationalized Baltic business enterprises located in the U.S. were ignored. The U.S. departments of State and Treasury began to jointly administer the frozen Baltic assets and gold reserves, which were used to maintain the still-recognized Baltic diplomatic and consular facilities.

While the Soviet orders of the summer of 1940 did not explicitly state that Baltic assets abroad were covered by the nationalization decrees, this was clearly the intent. Soviet juridical literature claims the positive extraterritorial effect of nationalization legislation. However, the U.S. has refused to grant extraterritorial effect in this case.

> American courts have consistently concluded that such decrees had no *extraterritorial* effect, that is, the decrees do not in themselves change the status of property situated in the United States or temporarily outside the borders of the state, or located in a third state at the time of the decree.[25]

The United States has followed one concept in international law, namely that the deprivation of an entity of legal status by a state abroad is not recognized if nationalization injures the vested rights of third parties. The third party here is the U.S.[26] Furthermore, Robert Langer points out that:

> A certain safeguard against the danger of giving effect, on the part of the non-recognizing State, to such measures of spoliation and depredation may consist in the application of the principle . . . that acts of a foreign Power that are irreconcilable with the public policy of the State from which enforcement is sought, are disregarded in the courts of the latter.[27]

One of the more interesting episodes involving Baltic assets dealt with shipping. The "Baltic Ships Cases" were directly related to Soviet nationalization decrees. On this basis, the new governments in the Baltic could issue laws such as the following:

> Any kind of leaving harbours or entering harbours without the permission of the Government of the Republic [of Estonia] is prohibited for Estonian ships in foreign waters....
>
> Masters of ships who transgress the orders of the Government of the Republic regarding the bringing back of Estonian ships to the home country will be treated as persons guilty of high treason, *whereby responsible are also the members of their families and nearer relatives....*
>
> Ships are prohibited to enter the harbours of the United States of America and Britain without the permission of the Government of the Republic (emphasis added).[28]

The Soviet Union asserted that the vessels in question were now the property of the state. As such they were immune from the jurisdiction of foreign courts without the consent of the new sovereign power. This immunity existed whether the vessels were used for public or private purposes, and whether or not they were in the physical possession of the sovereign.[29]

The Soviet Union thus was attempting to gain possession of the vessels. Indeed, following World War II, it occasionally attempted to collect insurance payable for Baltic ships sunk during hostilities.[30] However, claims of ownership or insurance proceeds were rejected because such claims in each case were grounded on some governmental act based on unrecognized Soviet sovereignty.

> [The] Baltic Ship Cases, reinforced by corresponding decisions in a number of other countries, including the United States, helped to establish the doctrine that nonrecognition of an alleged successor state or government resulted in a failure to create immunity claimed for vessels of that state or government.[31]

In *Latvian State Cargo & Passenger S.S. Line v. McGrath*, the U.S. Court of Appeals explicitly took this into account. The court decided that the U.S. did not merely fail to recognize the Soviet nationalization decrees, but deliberately opposed them. "We find ourselves in agreement with other courts which have either implicitly or explicitly recognized the policies of [the executive] in refusing to countenance the confiscation of vessels by the Soviet regime."[32]

In order to gain an idea of how these cases were conceived and how they proceeded, it is worthwhile to quote Langer's synopsis of three of them:

In three cases, namely (1) the *Kotkas*,[33] (2) the *Regent*,[34] (3) the *Signe* (later renamed the *Florida*),[35] libels of persons acting on behalf of the Soviet Government had been filed in order to obtain possession of Baltic ships which their masters refused to surrender. The district courts had first to decide on motions of the libelants for letters rogatory to be issued to a competent court of the Soviet Union for the purpose of procuring testimony of parties residing in the respective Baltic countries. All these motions were denied on the ground that since the United States did not recognize the incorporation..., no court of the latter could issue effective process to residents of those republics. Thereupon the libels were dismissed for failure on the part of the libelants to prove their right of possession.[36]

The case *The Maret* dealt with the question of the validity of acts of an unrecognized occupant.[37] The *Maret* was a vessel of Estonian registry in the territorial waters of the U.S. Virgin Islands at the time of incorporation. The captain was ordered to proceed to Murmansk. He was willing to comply and requested an advance to purchase supplies. The Amtorg Trading Company in New York, which was an agent of the Soviet government, obliged, and provided the funds. However, while the vessel was in port at St. Thomas, the U.S. Maritime Commission requisitioned it. The commission proceeded to deposit $25,000 with the U.S. Treasury "on account of just compensation" for the *Maret*. The Amtorg Company then filed suit seeking a portion of that payment. The Soviet action, in turn, was opposed by Estonian Consul General Jaakson Kaiv, acting for some of the co-owners of the vessel.

Although a federal district court decided in favor of the Soviets, a circuit court reversed the decision, writing that recognition is a political question, not a legal one, and must be decided by the executive branch. The same applies to the validity of decrees of an unrecognized power. When Kaiv produced Acting Secretary of State Sumner Welles's certificate not recognizing the decrees of the regime functioning in Estonia, the circuit court decided that a domestic court cannot examine the decrees of such a sovereign and determine rights in property based on them.[38]

The consequences of these events were certainly not lost on Soviet officials, who complained bitterly that the U.S. government was sanctioning the theft of Soviet property by aiding, as Soviet Ambassador Constantine A. Oumansky stated:

The former Ministers and Consuls of the Baltic States who, in cooperation with the officials of the Department of State, local Customs authorities, and police officials, were continuing to arrest Captains and members of the crews of what are now Soviet vessels only because such persons desired to go home. The Consuls...through fictitious means were changing the registry of these vessels and directing their movements.[39]

People's Commissar for Foreign Affairs Viacheslav Molotov complained to U.S. Ambassador Laurence A. Steinhardt in Moscow that some of the Baltic vessels had been dispatched to South America, where the Soviet Union possessed no diplomatic representation.[40]

The U.S. nonrecognition policy possessed differential political and legal effects. On the one hand, the U.S. would not commit itself to allowing a Lithuanian government in exile function on her soil. On the other hand, treaties and diplomats retained complete status, albeit in a reduced role. The consuls were the most active and potent representatives of the success of the policy. The events surrounding the disposition of Baltic property, as well as the Kremlin's reaction, serve to demonstrate that the effect of the U.S. nonrecognition policy, at least at its inception, was far from merely symbolic. Actual physical resources were involved and removed from the reach of the Soviets.[41]

While the United States remains steadfast in its stated policy toward Lithuania and the other Baltic States, there have been occasions where the policy has been stretched -- or compressed, if you will -- to fit practical exigencies. World War II, along with the question of alliance with Stalin, would be the first major test of the resilience of the nonrecognition policy.

NOTES

1. U.S. House of Representatives, *Third Interim Report of the Select Committee on Communist Aggression*. Report of the Select Committee to Investigate Communist Aggression and the Forced Incorporation of the Baltic States into the U.S.S.R. (Washington, D.C.: U.S. Government Printing Office, 1954), pp. 364-375.

2. Aleksandras Merkelis, *Antanas Smetona: Jo visuomenine, kulturine ir politine veikla* (Antanas Smetona: His social, cultural and political activity) (New York: American Lithuanian National Association, 1964), pp. 644-645, 657.

3. Ibid., p. 652. See also J. J. Bachunas, *Vincas S. Jokubynas* (Sodus, MI: Author, 1954), pp. 10-11.

4. Bronis J. Kaslas, ed., *The USSR-German Aggression Against Lithuania* (New York: Robert Speller and Sons, 1973), p. 314. In an editor's comment on pp. 314-315, Kaslas notes that the committee never aspired to be a government-in-exile, but wished to preserve the Lithuanian Diplomatic Service as well as to organize Lithuanian-Americans.

5. Kazys Sidlauskas, "Supreme Committee for Liberation of Lithuania as Representative of Lithuanian National Interests," In *Twenty Years' Struggle for Freedom of Lithuania*, ed. Juozas Audenas (New York: ELTA, 1963), p. 100. On pp. 102-108 and 115, Sidlauskas, a longtime official of the committee, cites legal

precedents of the recognition of national committees during wartime, and states that the committee should be recognized as representing the Lithuanian people.

6. Juozas Audenas, "The Activities of the Supreme Committee for Liberation of Lithuania," in *Twenty Years' Struggle for Freedom of Lithuania*, ed. Juozas Audenas (New York: ELTA, 1963), pp. 78-79.

7. Vytautas Alseika, *Trys desimtmeciai emigracijoje: Nuo Roitlingeno iki Niujorko* (Three decades in emigration: From Reutlingen to New York) (Vilnius: Mintis, 1977), pp. 120-121; Audenas, "Activities," pp. 76-77.

This conference saw an interesting incident finally make itself public. At the Bern conference, Lozoraitis revealed the existence of the Acts of Kybartai, which were dated 15 June 1940 and supposedly signed by Smetona just before he crossed the border out of Lithuania. The first act removed Antanas Merkys as prime minister and replaced him with Lozoraitis. The second act asked Lozoraitis to act as president. This fact was communicated to the U.S. State Department in 1944 and, indeed, Lozoraitis signed some of his official papers as prime minister and acting president. It later became apparent that the acts were actually signed by Smetona in Switzerland on 23 November 1940 in an attempt to create a legal basis for the formation of governmental organs outside Lithuania. See Albertas Gerutis, "Kybartu aktai" (Acts of Kybartai), Aidai, 4 (April 1976), 164-171.

8. U.S. Department of State, Statement by Robert L. Barry, Assistant Secretary for European Affairs, before the Subcommittee on International Organizations of the House Committee on Foreign Affairs, 26 June 1979, pp. 4-5.

9. U.S. Department of State, *Foreign Relations of the United States*, Diplomatic Papers, 1940, vol. I, General (Washington, D.C.: U.S. Government Printing Office, 1959), p. 387. See also U.S. House of Representatives, Third Interim Report of the Select Committee on Communist Aggression, Report of the Select Committee to Investigate Communist Aggression and the Forced Incorporation of the Baltic States into the U.S.S.R. (Washington, D.C.: U.S. Government Printing Office, 1954), pp. 365-366.

10. Ibid., pp. 366-367.

11. Robert Langer, *Seizure of Territory: The Stimson Doctrine and Related Principles in Legal Theory and Diplomatic Practice* (Princeton: Princeton University Press, 1947), p. 102.

12. *Buxhoeveden v. Estonian State Bank*, The New York Supreme Court, Special Term, Queens County, April 21, 1943; 41 N.Y.S. (2d) 752-757; Ibid., Part I, October 8, 1948; 84 N.Y.S. (2d) 2.

13. *Buxhoeveden v. Estonian State Bank*, 41 N.Y.S. (2d) 753.

14. Ibid., 757. On 26 March 1948, the U.S. State Department sent a letter to all state governors that stated that U.S.-Baltic treaties were still in force, and that Soviet consular officers possessed no right to represent Baltic nationals in U.S. probate proceedings. Only Baltic consular representatives were empowered to do so. See *U.S. Congressional Record*, 1 May 1948, p. 6795.

15. Unless otherwise indicated, the following passage is taken from Thomas M. Franck and Michael J. Glennon, *Foreign Relations and National Security Law: Cases, Materials and Simulations* (St. Paul, MN: West, 1987), pp. 494-497.

16. Franck and Glennon, in ibid., p. 496, note that these rulings were due partly to the prevailing Cold War atmosphere. They also write that:

Some Baltic nationals attempted to evade this result by travelling to Leningrad or Moscow to have their letters of attorney authenticated in the Soviet Union proper. This strategem worked in *Matter of Luberg's Estate*, 19 A.D. 2d 370, 243 N.Y.S. 2d 747 (1963), but failed in In re Mitzkel's Estate, 36 Misc. 2d 671, 233 N.Y.S. 2d 519 (Sur. Ct. Kings 1962). See generally Matter of Adler's Estate, 197 Misc. 104, 93 N.Y.S. 2d 416 (Sur. Ct. Kings), appeal dismissed, 279 App. Div. 745, 109 N.Y.S. 2d 175 (1951), order vacated 110 N.Y.S. 2d 283 (N.Y.A.D. 1952); In re Braunstein's Estate, 202 Misc. 244, 114 N.Y.S. 2d 280 (Sur. N.Y. 1952); In re Kapocius' Estate, 36 Misc. 2d 1087, 234 N.Y.S. 2d 346 (Sur. King's 1962).

See also Evald Roosaare, "Consular Relations between the United States and the Baltic States," Baltic Review, 27 (June 1964), 28-29.

17. 83 N.J. Super. 303, 199 A. 2d 662 (App. Div. 1964), *cert. denied*, 43 N.J. 128, 202 A. 2d 702 (1964).

18. *In re Estate of Bielinis*, 55 Misc. 2d at 197-198, 284 N.Y.S. 2d at 825-826.

19. *Daniunas v. Simutis*, 481 F.Supp. at 134 (S.D.N.Y. 1978). See also In the Matter of the Estate of Julius Yuska, 128 Misc. 2d 98, 488 N.Y.S. 2d 609 (Sur. Kings 1985).

20. United Nations, Doc. A/Conf. 25/12, 23 April 1963.

21. Roosaare, "Consular Relations," p. 32. For an account of how the Estonian consul general in New York City, Jaakson Kaiv, refused to obey Soviet orders, see pp. 23-24.

22. Dietrich A. Loeber, "Baltic Gold in Great Britain," *Baltic Review*, 36 (October 1969), 15-17; Gerhard von Glahn, Law among Nations: An Introduction to Public International Law, 4th ed. (New York: Macmillan, 1981), p. 152.

23. Ibid., p. 108.

24. N.Y.C.A., 1923, 235 N.Y. 255, 139 N.E. 259.

25. Gerard J. Mangone, *The Elements of International Law*, rev. ed. (Homewood, IL: Dorsey Press, 1967), pp. 380-381.

26. Loeber, "Baltic Gold," pp. 17-20. See also p. 26.

27. Langer, *Seizure of Territory*, p. 108.

28. U.S. House of Representatives, Select Committee to Investigate the Incorporation of the Baltic States into the U.S.S.R., *Baltic States* Investigation I (Washington, D.C.: U.S. Government Printing Office, 1953), p. 182. See also U.S. Department of State, Foreign Relations of the United States, 1940, I, p. 408.

29. Von Glahn, *Law among Nations*, p. 149. See also U.S. House of Representatives, Baltic States Investigation I, pp. 20-21, 207-209.

30. Von Glahn, *Law among Nations*, p. 110. Richard A. Schnorf notes that Baltic ships transporting Allied war supplies across the Atlantic were decimated by German submarines. See his "The Baltic States in U.S.-Soviet Relations: The Years of Doubt, 1943-1946," Lituanus, 12, 4 (Winter 1966), 67.

31. Von Glahn, *Law among Nations*, p. 149. In pp. 109-110, he notes that not all legal scholars agree that a nonrecognized state is barred from access to the courts of nonrecognizing states. In turn, not all concur in the disposition of the Baltic ships cases.

32. *Latvian State Cargo & Passenger S.S. Line v. McGrath*, U.S. Court of Appeals, District of Columbia Circuit, 188 F 2d 1000 (1951).

33. 35 *Federal Supplement Reporter* 810, 983 ff., District Court, E.D. New York, November 22, 1940; 37 Federal Supplement Reporter 835 ff., do. March 31, 1941.

34. 35 *Federal Supplement Reporter* 985 ff., District Court, E.D. New York, November 22, 1940.

35. 37 *Federal Supplement Reporter* 810 819 ff., District Court, E.D. Louisiana, New Orleans Division, March 4, 1941; 39 Federal Supplement Reporter 810 ff., do. July 22, 1941; 133 F 2d 719 ff., Circuit Court of Appeals, Fifth Circuit, February 20, 1943.

36. Langer, *Seizure of Territory*, p. 266. Further, the court in the Signe case noted the authority possessed by the Estonian consul general in charge of legation, Jaakson Kaiv, for the "temporarily supplanted government of the Republic of Estonia." Kaiv became involved in approximately 20 cases involving Estonian vessels. See Langer, Seizure of Territory, pp. 266-267; U.S. House of Representatives, Baltic States Investigation I, p. 32.

37. 145 F 2d 431, Circuit Court of Appeals, Third Circuit, October 17, 1944.

38. Langer, *Seizure of Territory*, pp. 267-268; Georg Schwarzenberger, A Manual of International Law, 5th ed. (New York: Praeger, London Institute of World Affairs, 1967), p. 433; William L. Tung, International Law in an Organizing World (New York: Crowell, 1968), pp. 266-268. Franck and Glennon, Foreign Relations, p. 486, note that the court in the Maret did not consider the location of the ship outside Estonia when determining whether to give effect to the decree of the Estonian SSR.

39. U.S. Department of State, *Foreign Relations of the United States*, 1941, Vol. I (Washington, D.C.: U.S. Government Printing Office, 1958), p. 708.

40. U.S. Department of State, *Foreign Relations of the United States*, Diplomatic Papers, 1940, Volume III (Washington, D.C.: U.S. Government Printing Office, 1958), p. 439.

41. Other cases involving Baltic ships and nationals are *Re Adler's Estate*, 122 The New York Law Journal 1777, in the King's County Surrogate Court, New York; Re Braunstein's Estate, 114 N.Y.S. 2d 280 (1952), in the New York County

Surrogate Court; Estonian State Cargo & Passenger S.S. Line et al. v. United States, 116 F.Supp. 447 (Ct. of Cl., 1953); Latvian State Cargo & Passenger S.S. Line et al. v. United States, 116 F.Supp. 717 (Ct. of Cl., 1953); A/S Merilaid & Co. v. Chase National Bank of City of New York, 71 N.Y.S. 2d 377 (1947); The Matter of Mike Shaskus, 131 The New York Law Journal 12 (1954), in the King's County Surrogate Court, New York; United States v. Rumsa, 212 F 2d 927 (7th Cir., 1954), cert. denied, 348 U.S. 838.

6

Nonrecognition and Wartime Politics

THE CHANGING NATURE OF THE WAR

As the year 1940 gave way to 1941, the Soviets were still consolidating their occupation of Lithuania. Obviously, the U.S. nonrecognition policy, while possessing definite political and legal consequences, had not caused their retreat. As the year wore on, however, the situation in the Baltic would change drastically, with great implications for U.S.-Soviet relations.

Historically, the Lithuanian people have always been caught between the Germans and the Russians; World War II was no exception. Hitler's Operation Barbarossa, ending the charade of the Molotov-Ribbentrop Pact, commenced 22 June 1941. Thus began the Third Reich's campaign to become master of the East. The German occupation brought cautious hope to a people who had just lived under a regime which in 12 months had arrested, deported, or killed some 50,000 Lithuanians. The greatest horrors occured about one week prior to the Nazi attack when, during the night of 14 June, 34,260 people were packed off in cattle cars to prisons and hard-labor camps in Siberia and other points deep within the Soviet Union.

A rebellion temporarily reconstituting the Lithuanian government was carried out, but this received no support from the invading Germans. The affairs of the country were, instead, placed firmly under the control of the *Reichskommissar fur das Ostland* (Reich Commissar for the Eastern Territories), based in Riga, Latvia; terror and expropriation continued. For example, on 27 May 1942, four hundred Poles and Lithuanians were executed in retaliation for the murder of two German civilians. On 31 March 1943, in response to anti-German sentiments in Vilnius, a line of about two hundred men was formed-and every fifth one was shot.

CHANGING PERCEPTIONS OF THE SOVIET UNION

Hitler, who was the declared enemy of the West, had now attacked the Soviet Union. As the wartime alliance became cemented, the U.S. was forced to choose the lesser of two evils. In other words, any enemy of Hitler was now considered an ally. The rocky course of this unnatural relationship can be traced in the official propaganda of the time. When Stalin was on the move against Poland, Finland, and the Baltic States, he was branded an international criminal and expelled from the League of Nations. Outcries were heard in the public and the press. However, after the United States entered the war and the Anglo-Soviet Treaty of Alliance was signed on 26 May 1942, attacks on the Kremlin were toned down in an effort to construct harmony and a superficial working relationship during the course of hostilities. The Red Army was perceived as a friend in the battle against the Third Reich -- though, of course, the matter of postwar settlements was in the back of everyone's mind.

In a poll released on 22 December 1939, 70 percent of U.S. citizens questioned believed that communist activities in the U.S. were more serious than Nazi actions. However, less than two months following the commencement of Operation Barbarossa, 38 percent of U.S. citizens favored the inclusion of the Soviet Union in the Lend-Lease program, while 39 percent were opposed.[1]

Of course, there was a small vocal communist movement in the U.S. that fostered such attitudes. Regarding the Soviet occupation of Lithuania, leftist author Anna Louise Strong wrote that "a sovereign state was changing from capitalism to socialism quite constitutionally without destruction of life or property."[2] Gregory Meiksins asserted that Lithuania had never been independent and belonged in the Soviet Union following "liberation" by the Red Army.[3]

Nonetheless, the communists' influence was negligible, for it was members of U.S. mainstream society who were also becoming supportive of the Soviets -- and often overlooking their transgressions. Vice President Henry A. Wallace, Harold Ickes, Senator E. D. Thomas, Walter Lippmann, and news commentator Elmer Davis were among those influential in forming public opinion regarding Soviet intentions during the war. U.S. citizens were inclined to respect the Soviets thanks to their victories in the East, while the Western allies were still waiting to throw all their force against Hitler. Some U.S. writers even supported Russian ethnographic claims to the Baltic States. Though individuals such as Herbert Hoover and Robert Taft cautioned U.S. citizens to be more realistic in their appraisal of the Soviets, the paramount concern of the time appeared to be the maintenance of allied unity.[4]

U.S. officials were acutely aware of their predicament. Once the alliance was on its way to formation, an anticommunist or anti-Soviet message could have been construed as fascist. Officials were hard-pressed to make statements on the Soviet occupation of Lithuania, for they would immediately be branded as harmful to the alliance and the war effort.[5] Other officials, though, urged greater support for the Soviets. In a letter to Breden Bracken, presidential adviser Harry Hopkins wrote:

> We are having some difficulty with our public opinion with regard to Russia. The American people don't take aid to Russia easily....[A] lot of people...sincerely believe that Stalin is a great menace to the world. Still I think it will come out all right in the end.[6]

Another official with similar opinions was Joseph E. Davies, the U.S. ambassador to Moscow, who wrote:

> In my opinion, the Russian people, the Soviet government, and the Soviet leaders are moved, basically, by altruistic concepts. It is their purpose to promote the brotherhood of man and to improve the lot of the common people. They wish to create a society in which men live as equals, governed by ethical ideals. They are devoted to peace.[7]

In an address to 20,000 people in Chicago in February 1942, Davies asserted that "By the testimony of performance and in my opinion, the word of honor of the Soviet Government is as safe as the Bible."[8] Though perhaps Davies' confidence in the Kremlin was greater than that of most U.S. citizens, it at least in part reflected the currents of opinion in the United States during the course of World War II.

THE ATLANTIC CHARTER

The Atlantic Charter, signed by President Roosevelt and British Prime Minister Winston Churchill on 14 August 1941, was a stirring declaration stating that neither the U.S. nor Great Britain would seek increases in territory during and after hostilities. Further, territorial changes and forms of government would be determined in accordance with the wishes of the people of Europe. In addition, the signatories hoped "to see sovereign rights and self-government restored to those who have been forcibly deprived of them." The Atlantic Charter was a moral pronouncement reminiscent of Woodrow Wilson's Fourteen Points. Nevertheless, it was not a formal treaty and did not possess binding force.

By September 1941, Stalin had formally subscribed to the provisions of the Atlantic Charter, telling British Foreign Secretary Anthony Eden that "he thought the Charter was directed against those who were trying to get world domination."[9] Roosevelt was wary of Stalin's true intentions, and Churchill was even more so. Both commented that Stalin's actions were not consistent with the charter.

Specifically, Stalin had agreed to the document on the basis of boundaries existing at the time of Hitler's move east, that is, with the Baltic States within the

Soviet Union.   British officials and some U.S. pragmatists, such as Assistant Secretary of State Adolph Berle, were willing to concede this point, since Roosevelt had put off boundary settlements until after the war.[10]

While, on the one hand, Churchill sincerely declared that the 1941 boundaries were illegally constructed, he could not realistically trade British interests for the Baltic.[11]   Early in 1942, Churchill wrote to Roosevelt:

> The increasing gravity of the war has led me to feel that the principles
> of the Atlantic Charter ought not to be construed as to deny Russia
> the frontiers she occupied when Germany attacked her. This was the
> basis on which Russia acceded to the Charter.[12]

Churchill further was of the opinion that "in the deadly struggle it is not right to assume more burdens than those who are fighting for a great cause [the British] can bear."[13]

Granted, Stalin's public statements expressed adherence to the Atlantic Charter's principles. However, when the scales of war began tipping in his favor, he changed his posture and brought forth a list of territorial claims. As will be seen below, while hardly taken aback by this action, the West was forced to actively reassess its perception of, and position toward, the Soviet Union. The realization that Moscow would be a power to contend with after the war was unsettling, to say the least.   With this grew distrust and ambivalence regarding Soviet behavior following the cessation of conflict. Be that as it may, the Western powers were still concerned with successfully concluding the war, and decided to place the issue on the back burner; boundaries were to be settled at a forthcoming peace conference - - a conference that was never formally completed.

Following the Axis declaration of war on the U.S. on 11 December 1941, the Soviet Union attempted to utilize its new, good relations with the West. In the spring of the following year, the Kremlin requested that the U.S. and Britain recognize Lithuania, Latvia, and Estonia as incorporated components of the USSR, but both powers refused to do so. On the other hand, while the U.S. was willing to symbolically support the Baltic cause, it realized that practical exigencies dictated a cautious approach, knowing full well that the U.S. could not completely influence events in Eastern Europe -- and that U.S. citizens would not support a war with the Soviets following the defeat of the Nazis.

What was the fate of the Atlantic Charter?   Though the protocol of proceedings of the Yalta Conference of February 1945 reaffirmed the Charter's principles, on 19 December 1944 President Roosevelt stated that it had never been formally signed, so that it did not have to be implemented.

> American diplomacy sought and obtained repeated Soviet promises
> that governments and boundaries in liberated areas would be
> determined democratically, but at the price of avoiding further

mention of past unpleasantries such as the Soviet annexation of the
Baltic States and a chunk of Finland.   This was...not a policy of
confrontation, but rather one of accommodation.   The dubious
rationale for this policy was that the Soviets would not feel compelled
to turn their weak neighbors into client states for security reasons if
assured that American friendship and the new international
organization would protect them instead.   American diplomats in
Soviet-liberated countries seemed honestly surprised when in 1944 and
1945 the Soviets set about reordering boundaries and governments
according to their own definition of [democracy].[14]

Bronis Kaslas adds:

Clemenceau said that Wilson talked like Jesus Christ and acted like
Lloyd George; much the same can be said for Roosevelt.   The
dichotomy between lofty principle and mundane action is a traditional
characteristic of American foreign policy, and the Atlantic Charter is
one of the loftier enunciations of principles which American presidents
have produced, but American governments have never implemented.[15]

Perhaps Richard Schnorf sums up the results of the Atlantic Charter best when he
writes that "this famous manifesto is today virtually forgotten except by those whose
hopes of freedom are expressed in its provisions."[16]
        The Atlantic Charter was, of course, the first act in the play of diplomacy
surrounding World War II.   The West had adopted a policy of non-
predetermination, meaning that victory was the immediate priority.   Territorial
questions would be addressed at a postwar peace conference. On 4 February 1942,
U.S. Secretary of State Cordell Hull penned a memorandum to President Roosevelt
where he asserted that permanent political and territorial agreements during the
course of hostilities would be contrary to the Atlantic Charter, and a reversal of
U.S. policy not recognizing forcible annexation.[17]

Hull was an old-fashioned Jeffersonian liberal who remembered the
problems Wilson had in 1919 when confronted with the secret treaties
of the Allies. Hull would adamantly oppose any secret deals while the
war was still in progress. He would strive mightily for an international
organization that could maintain the peace after the war.[18]

Sumner Welles, Adolph Berle, and State Department careerists shared Hull's view
and, further, were suspicious of both British and Soviet imperialism. Old World
diplomacy, with its spheres of influence and balances of power, was to give way to
democratic diplomacy. Roosevelt was a politician who had risen to power through
dealing and trading. He was confident that his charm and negotiating skills would

ultimately carry the day for a democratic Europe.[19] Roosevelt's first wartime test would come during the Anglo-Soviet negotiations of 1941-1942.

THE ANGLO-SOVIET TREATY OF ALLIANCE

As noted above, Stalin pressed for Western recognition of Soviet gains in the Baltic. British Foreign Secretary Anthony Eden spoke with him on this matter in December 1941. Stalin added that this was a condition for an Anglo-Soviet agreement. Eden replied that he could not commit to territorial arrangements. Churchill agreed, yet by early 1942 he did not feel "that this moral position could be physically maintained."[20] Churchill wrote Roosevelt a pleading letter on 7 March 1942:

> The increasing gravity of the war has led me to feel that the principles of the Atlantic Charter ought not to be construed so as to deny Russia the frontier she occupied when Germany attacked her. This was the basis on which Russia acceded to the Charter...I hope, therefore, that you will be able to give us a free hand to sign the treaty which Stalin desires....[T]here is very little we can do to help the only country that is heavily engaged with the German armies.[21]

Hull urged Roosevelt not to endorse such an arrangement. Roosevelt appealed directly to Stalin to omit territorial matters from the treaty. Stalin answered that he was merely taking note of the president's position.[22]

Though Roosevelt's motives appeared noble, George Kennan is of a different opinion:

> One does not get...the impression that Roosevelt had any substantive objections-any real political objections-to seeing these [Baltic and Polish] areas go Russian, or indeed that he cared much about the issue for its own sake. One gets the impression that it seemed to him of little importance whether these areas were Polish or Russian. His anxiety was rather that he had a large body of voting constituents in this country of Polish or Baltic origin, and a further number who sympathized with the Poles, and he simply did not want this issue to become a factor in domestic politics.[23]

In a series of conversations in February-April 1942, Roosevelt, Sumner Welles, and British Ambassador Edward Lord Halifax discussed the negotiations with the Kremlin. Among the options discussed were the right of the Soviets to possess military bases in the Baltic following the war, or their right to control Baltic foreign and defense policy. Roosevelt implied that he favored the latter option.

If this were done, Soviet demands for security could be reconciled with the Atlantic Charter. Halifax noted that the Soviet demands could be greater. Furthermore, the USSR's presence in the Baltic would translate into greater security against possible future German aggression. Welles countered by asking what kind of peace could be created if the U.S. and Britain

> agreed upon selling out millions of people who looked to us as their one hope in the future and if that new world order were based upon the domination of unwilling, resentful, and potent minorities by a State to which they would never give willing allegiance.[24]

Lord Halifax felt that Washington was not being realistic. For him, Baltic self government did not outweigh having a friendly and cooperative Kremlin during and after the war. Soon thereafter, Welles transmitted an idea from Roosevelt. Roosevelt's offer was U.S. approval of British acceptance of Soviet demands if Baltic residents who did not wish to live under a Soviet regime would be allowed to leave with their property.[25]

Assistant Secretary Berle forcefully condemned this idea. He supported a U.S.-style Good Neighbor policy in the Baltic, conceded that the Baltic States could not be springboards for invasion from the west, and felt that the Soviets should have access to the Baltic Sea. However, he urged observance of the Atlantic Charter, saying that implementation of the proposed policy would be a "Baltic Munich." In such a case, the U.S.:

> would have committed [itself] to the seizure of the territory, provided there is added some pious, and in the existing circumstances, meaningless phrase about free immigration of populations to places unknown, on conditions unspecified, and in any case, with the complete sacrifice of their tradition, their property, their habits, and possibly even their language and race.[26]

Evidently the Roosevelt property proposal was a trial balloon. Welles informed Berle that both he and the president were opposed to such a policy. If the current Kremlin demands were met, more would be sure to follow. Emigration would be a last resort to prevent complete enslavement if the Soviets remained in the Baltic.[27] Welles added:

> I have felt more strongly on this issue, namely, the conclusion of this treaty, than on any matter which has [come] before me in recent years. The attitude of the British Government is, in my judgement, not only indefensible from every moral standpoint, but likewise extraordinarily stupid.[28]

Roosevelt was not going to endorse any territorial agreement in the current negotiations, preferring a military alliance creating a second front. Indeed the president may have repudiated a territory-based agreement outright. The Kremlin gave up the territorial clauses, realizing that recognition of its conquests was not forthcoming. In addition, the Germans had halted the Soviet counterattack in the eastern Ukraine, and the Kremlin was increasingly dependent on U.S. aid. Finally, a simple treaty of Anglo-Soviet alliance was signed on 26 May 1942.

THE WARTIME CONFERENCES

Although Roosevelt won this diplomatic battle, he could not ignore practical reality. In a March 1943 conference with British Foreign Secretary Anthony Eden, Roosevelt stated that U.S. public opinion would be opposed to a final postwar absorption of the Baltic States. However, he could not force the Soviets to do anything. The president hoped that Stalin would, at least, go through the motions of a second plebisctite, and was confident that recognition of Soviet control in the Baltic could be utilized as a bargaining chip for Soviet concessions in other areas.[29] In July of that year, Roosevelt told the Polish ambassador: "The problem of the Baltic States, and particularly that of Lithuania will be much more difficult....What can we do if Stalin calmly announces, for instance, that the question of Lithuania must be left out of the discussion?"[30]

As the Moscow foreign ministers' conference of October 1943 approached, the Western Allies were slowly proceeding up the Italian peninsula and Soviet troops were crossing the Dnieper River on a broad front. Secretary Hull did not receive instructions to discuss the Baltic. However, in a 5 October conference, President Roosevelt spelled out his plans for the upcoming Teheran conference:

> As for Poland and the Baltic States, the President said that, when he
> should meet with Stalin, he intended to appeal to him on grounds of
> high morality. He would say to him that neither Britain nor we would
> fight Russia over the Baltic States, but that in Russia's own interest...it
> would be a good thing for her...to hold a second plebiscite in the
> Baltic countries.[31]

Prime Minister Churchill, however, did give Anthony Eden pre-Moscow advice on the Baltic. It turned out, though, to be an oxymoron: "We reaffirm the principles of the Atlantic Charter, noting that Russia's accession thereto is based upon the frontiers of June 22, 1941. We also take note of the historic frontiers of Russia before the two [world] wars.[32]

When Hull returned from Moscow on 15 November, he declared that the Baltic and Balkan States deserved the right of self-determination. Each state, regardless of size, was sovereign and equal, according to Hull. Despite such high-minded -- and vague -- pronouncements, true State Department opinions regarding Moscow were pessimistic. When encountering this, Jan Ciechanowski, Polish ambassador to the U.S., surmised "that, as far as could then be ascertained, America and Britain had had to sacrifice the three Baltic countries and half of Poland to Russia for the sake of understanding with the Soviets."[33]

A number of observers in official circles were not surprised by the outcome of the Moscow conference or the direction that East-West relations appeared to be taking. Indeed, U.S. Admiral William Leahy expressed his pessimism shortly before the conference:

> America's position at this conference might be very difficult because of our reputation for reliability and our previous announcement that the sovereignty of small nations should be reestablished after the war's end. It was inconceivable to me that Stalin would submit to the reestablishment of effective sovereignty in Poland, Latvia, Lithuania, and Estonia.[34]

It is not certain whether Hull ever discussed the Baltic with Stalin at Moscow. What is certain is that the Baltic States failed to emerge in a more favorable position -- a pattern that was repeating itself.[35]

Direct discussion of the Baltic States was not on the agenda of the December 1943 Teheran conference, which was the first time that Roosevelt, Churchill, and Stalin met together. Nonetheless, the issue did arise and Roosevelt immediately sought to appease Stalin. Roosevelt noted the historical place of the Baltic States as a part of Russia, and added that he did not intend to go to war over the territory. He was worried, however, about public opinion in the U.S. toward self-determination and referenda, specifically mentioning Baltic-American voters. He urged Stalin to carry out a plebiscite in the Baltic, for he was certain that Lithuanians, Latvians, and Estonians would vote to join the Soviet Union.

Stalin replied that there had not been any outcry of world opinion when the Czar did not grant autonomy to the Baltic States at the turn of the century. Furthermore, the Baltic people had voted to join the Soviet Union in 1940. He also astonishingly suggested that the Western powers carry out a propaganda campaign in their countries to sway people to accept Soviet power in the Baltic. With that, Stalin closed the door on further discussion of the matter, and Roosevelt left it at that.[36]

Richard Schnorf takes Roosevelt to task for this conversation. He cannot reconcile what the president said with the Atlantic Charter and the Declaration of the United Nations, although he admits that Roosevelt may have attempted to use false flattery to keep the Baltic issue alive.[37] Schnorf also finds a problem with Roosevelt's assertion that the Baltic States have traditionally been a part of Russia, noting that those territories have lived apart from Russia longer than within it.[38] He summarizes the proceedings as follows:

The conversation dulled to a great extent the keen moral edge of the United States policy of July 23, 1940. Although the United States did not renounce that policy, it made no serious attempt to deter the Soviet Union from repeating its rape of the Baltic States. The diplomats from the Baltic countries had been powerless when the massive influence of the Soviet Union came to bear on the United States. Seized with fear of a separate Russo-German peace, the American Government no longer could afford the luxury of condemning devious processes....[T]he Teheran Conference marked the low point in relations between the United States and the Baltic States as represented by its diplomats. The slim thread of non-recognition of the Soviet annexation was not broken, but it was tightly stretched.[39]

Other commentators criticize President Roosevelt's actions at Teheran, noting that he explicitly stated that Stalin's position in the Baltic would not be challenged. The Soviets had made the Baltic a test case -- a test the U.S. failed.[40]

World War II did not stop for conferences. It ground on and the fortunes of the Allies gradually improved. Stalingrad, where the Germans were dealt a crushing defeat, was the beginning of the end of the Third Reich. The Red Army began sweeping the Nazi armies back westward across the Continent. In the West, plans were successfully implemented for the invasion of Europe on D-Day, 6 June 1944, opening a second major front. Coincidentally, the Germans retreated from Lithuania that same month. As the war's end came within sight, political and territorial settlements could no longer be ignored. The Allies would grapple with these matters at the final major wartime conference -- Yalta.[41]

The U.S. and Britain entered the Yalta conference with no illusions as to the fate of the Baltic States in particular and Eastern Europe in general. With the Red Army controlling half the Continent, there was little that the Western powers could do to restrain Stalin.[42] Indeed, during the planning for Yalta, John Hickerson, deputy director of European affairs at the U.S. State Department, wrote a secret memorandum to the secretary of state on 8 January 1945 pointing this out and suggesting a solution:

> We know that the three Baltic States have been re-incorporated into the Soviet Union and that nothing which we can do can alter this. It is not a question of whether we like it...The point is that it has been done and nothing which is within the power of the United States Government to do can undo it....
>
> I would favor using any bargaining power that exists in connection with the foregoing matters to induce the Russians to go along with a satisfactory United Nations organization....*I would favor...our recognition*

of these areas as Soviet territory (emphasis added).[43]

Thus, some U.S. officials were ready to concede everything to Stalin, even the nonrecognition policy, which had been an expression of U.S. morality applied to the international arena.

Yalta was also the place where the Soviets pressed for the admission of Soviet Lithuania, Byelorussia, and the Ukraine to the new United Nations. The Soviet law of 1 February 1944 gave each Union Republic the right to establish direct relations with foreign countries, conclude agreements, and exchange representatives. They were also authorized to establish their own ministries of foreign affairs. Such decisions belong to the Supreme Soviet of each Union Republic. However, concurrently, the USSR ministry of foreign affairs was transferred from the All-Union category of ministry to the Union-Republic class. Whereas the former category means that it possesses no counterpart in the country, the latter class creates corresponding ministries with direction and control emanating from Moscow. Indeed, while the war was still in progress, Lithuania, Byelorussia, and the Ukraine concluded the exchange of population and repatriation agreements with the government reconstituted in Poland, the Lublin Committee. Despite the initial Soviet dream of having all Union Republics represented in the U.N., ultimately only Byelorussia and the Ukraine were admitted.[44]

Although Churchill was more of a realist, Roosevelt and U.S. Secretary of State Edward Stettinius were of the opinion that friendly contacts led to successful diplomacy. However, Churchill achieved the same result in the Baltic, mainly because he saw no other alternative; it was too late.[45] Roosevelt possessed a vision of a postwar world controlled by benevolent powers. He brushed off warnings of Stalin's dubious intentions:

> I just have a hunch that Stalin isnt't that kind of man. Harry [Hopkins] tells me he's not and that he doesn't want anything but security for his country. I think that if I give him everything I possibly can and ask for nothing in return, he won't try to annex anything and will work with me for a world of peace and democracy.[46]

Four years prior to Yalta, Roosevelt had condemned Stalin for the incorporation of Lithuania, Latvia, and Estonia. Now he saw only a benign Stalin, not merely as a diplomatic tactic, but seemingly privately as well.

The Yalta declaration of 11 February 1945 professed adherence to the idealistic principles of the Atlantic Charter, but also confirmed the division of Europe into military zones.[47] By war's end, Roosevelt had abandoned principles of equality and sovereignty in favor of a sometimes arrogant view of smaller nations, whose sovereignties he easily traded. He would not bargain with them, but was prepared to dictate their place in the new world order.[48] This was done not to placate Stalin, but simply because he no longer cared about Lithuania and other secondary powers. As such, the "Yalta decisions necessarily broke the back of opposition to Communist rule, not only in Poland, but in every country that had been or was about to be overrun by Russian armies."[49]

Other observers felt that the West was not completely impotent at Yalta, and that it could have exerted its influence to change the situation in Eastern Europe. Patrick J. Hurley, U.S. ambassador to China during the conference, later testified:

> America was in a position at Yalta to speak the only language the Communists understand, the language of power....One quiet sentence to Marshal Stalin in that language could have indicated that America would require him to keep his solemn agreements....The sentence was not forthcoming. ...[At] the time of Yalta the United States had unquestionable power to make Russia respect her ...agreements, but instead we surrendered them in secret. Russia did not have to break her agreements or commitments.[50]

THE WAR ENDS

According to one scholar, Lithuanians "had the firm belief that Nazi Germany would first crush the Soviet Union and then, in turn, be defeated by the Anglo-American alliance, which would restore Europe on an *ante bellum* status."[51] However, that was not to be, and the victorious powers met at Potsdam in July-August 1945. The Potsdam declaration of 3 August did not mention the Baltic States. However, certain inferences existed in Section VI, "City of Koenigsberg and the Adjacent Area," which grew out of Stalin's claim to the city. He said that this had been agreed to at Teheran by President Roosevelt and Prime Minister Churchill. President Harry Truman did not oppose Stalin's claim, but Churchill contended that the provision would imply recognition. He recommended that the question be deferred until a final peace settlement; Stalin assented to this.[52] As a result, Section VI of the declaration stated that the U.S. and Britain would support at the "forthcoming peace settlement" the Soviet proposal to transfer that area to the USSR. It appears to indicate that ultimately the Western powers intended to agree to the Baltic incorporation, for it is difficult to discern how a transfer of the adjacent area of East Prussia could be accomplished without including Lithuania.

The Paris Peace Conference convened on 29 July 1946. Prior to this, the Soviets had attempted to place the foreign ministers of the Baltic SSRs in the Soviet delegation. This was met with protests by the Baltic diplomats in the U.S. Lithuanian Minister Povilas Zadeikis wrote to U.S. Acting Secretary of State Dean Acheson:

> It actually means that the Soviet Government still persists in selling

to the Western Democratic Powers the false idea that the Lithuanian nation voluntarily discarded their hard-won independence. ...[It] means that the Soviet dictatorship is in fact a foe of democracy, of the Four Freedoms, of the Atlantic Charter, and of the principle of self-determination....The bringing of [Lithuanian SSR Foreign Minister P. F.] Rotomskis to Paris appears to be the latest trick of the Soviet diplomatic game....I consider it my duty to register my protest against any attempts by Mr. Rotomskis to represent the Lithuanian people and against any move to consider him as a legal representative of the Lithuanian Republic.[53]

It was hoped by some that the U.S. atomic weapons monopoly would force the Baltic States onto the conference's agenda. This was not to be. Indeed the Paris conference reinforced the divided Europe that had been created during the wartime consultations, for it never led to any formal peace treaty.

Jazeps Vizulis writes:

Were the Baltic countries the price the Western Allies had to pay the Soviet Union to win the war with Nazi Germany?...The triumph of victory, as Winston Churchill has said, soon turned into the tragedy of the cold war, the cause of Berlin, Korea, and Vietnam. Nor was the cause of international justice served by the subjugation of the Baltic countries by Soviet tyranny....The tragedy now finished, all that was left was for the actors to leave the darkened stage.[54]

Schnorf adds that there was less notoriety surrounding the Baltic absorption of 1944-1945 than the first one in 1940. At the end of the war, "there was no longer a real Baltic issue in the United States."[55]

Many people to this day criticize the West's diplomatic behavior during and after World War II. Leonas Sabaliunas points out that:

The Baltic mentality has never fully understood the Anglo-Saxon conception of diplomacy, which Harold Nicolson has labeled as "mercantile." It rejects the notion that diplomacy is war by other means and, instead, stresses the need for a frank discussion, mutual concessions, conciliation, appeasement, credit, reasonableness. In general, the purpose of such a diplomacy is a peace of accomodation, not victory, and it is certainly more conducive to international stability than a theory which sees negotiation as a military campaign.[56]

Others assert, however, that Stalin took advantage of western war-weariness and utilized an approach to diplomacy far removed from the Anglo-Saxon model:[57]

Stalin was a survivor of the Bolshevik underground and tsarist prisons, the formidable victor in the power struggle and purge, the killer of Trotsky, Bukharin, and literally millions of others. Above all he understood power, how to seize, retain, and wield it. This was a different school than Groton or Harvard, and his political experience involved something more than defeating Republican ward bosses or presidential contenders.[58]

In the final analysis, the West could have pushed Stalin to make concessions at the height of the war when the USSR was at its weakest. A separate Soviet agreement with Hitler was a remote possibility. Hitler would never have retreated from captured territory, and by such an arrangement, Stalin would have had much to lose and little to gain.

However, once Stalin possessed the ability to do so, he would have abrogated any agreement unfavorable to him. The presence of the Red Army in Eastern Europe would have easily enabled him to do so. Be that as it may, such an abrupt Kremlin policy switch as the war progressed would have possessed two positive results. First:

From the standpoint of international law and world opinion, the Soviets would have had to face the consequences of violating their own international pledges and commitments. The Baltic countries could have strengthened their international position by virtue of this legal commitment on the part of the Soviet Union to restore their independence.[59]

Second, had the Soviet Union demurred in its international obligations, "its refusal would have provided the United States with an early indication of Soviet intentions; and American self-interest, as well as international morality, could then better have influenced American conduct at ensuing conferences with the Soviets."[60] Thus, had the West remained firm in its commitment to Lithuania and the other Baltic States, Stalin's actions ultimately would have strengthened their status, as well as serving to warn the U.S. and Britain. That, of course, was never to be. The Truman Doctrine, the Cold War, and the policy of containment emerged not as a result of wartime planning-but more as an unavoidable afterthought.

The policy of nonrecognition had survived World War II, though some U.S. officials had been willing to discard it. However, its ultimate objects of concern, the Baltic States, were now firmly entrenched well beyond the Iron Curtain. Prospects for restored independence as a result of the war did not come to pass. What emerged was a hollow, symbolic independence hanging from the thin political thread of nonrecognition.

NOTES

1. Hardley Cantril, ed., *Public Opinion 1935-1946* (Princeton, NJ: Princeton University Press, 1955), pp. 164, 411.

2. Anna Louise Strong, *The New Lithuania* (New York: Workers Library Publishers, 1941), p. 3.

3. Gregory Meiksins, *The Baltic Soviet Republics* (New York: National Council of American-Soviet Friendship, 1944).

4. Jan Ciechanowski, *Defeat in Victory* (Garden City, NY: Doubleday, 1947), p. 97; Richard A. Schnorf, "The Baltic States in U.S.-Soviet Relations, 1939-1942," *Lituanus*, 12, 1 (Spring 1966), 52-53; Richard A. Schnorf, "The Baltic States in U.S.-Soviet Relations: The Years of Doubt, 1943-1946," *Lituanus*, 12, 4 (Winter 1966), 57-58. Schnorf also writes:

> In one respect it is fortunate that the Soviet Union did not invade the Baltic States later than it did....If the Soviet Union had invaded the Baltic States after it had been invaded by Germany, its argument that the occupation was a defensive move might have been accepted by the Western world. If the Soviet Union had forced anti-German treaties on the Baltic States, with the right of free passage of troops, the situation could have been tolerated in the democratic states in spite of the infringement of Baltic sovereignty.

See his "The Baltic States in U.S.-Soviet Relations: From Truman to Johnson," *Lituanus*, 14, 3 (Fall 1968), 58.

5. Antanas A. Olis, "JAV uzsienio politika sarysy su Lietuvos klausimu" (U.S. foreign policy and the Lithuanian question), in *Amerikos lietuviu tarybos suvaziavimas* (Congress of the Lithuanian American Council), ed. LAC (Chicago: LAC, 1954), p. 40. Although some officials who voiced wartime doubts regarding the Soviets died a professional death, Loy Henderson, an architect of the nonrecognition policy, continued on an illustrious career. See Schnorf, "The Baltic States...1943-1946," p. 75.

6. Quoted in Robert E. Sherwood, *Roosevelt and Hopkins* (New York: Harper and Brothers, 1950), pp. 372-373.

7. Joseph E. Davies, *Mission to Moscow* (New York: Simon and Schuster, 1941), p. 511.

8. Quoted in William C. Bullitt, *The Great Globe Itself* (New York: Scribner's, 1946), p. 22. In the historical section of a handbook issued to U.S. military personnel toward the end of hostilities, there was no mention of the Soviet aggression of 1939-1940. See U.S. Armed Forces, The USSR: Institutions and People. A Brief Handbook for the Use of Officers of the Armed Forces of the United States (Washington, D.C.: U.S. Government Printing Office, 1945).

Even Sumner Welles, who had issued the nonrecognition declaration on 23 July 1940, incorrectly spoke of the "plebiscites of 1939," and added that "perhaps the peoples of the Baltic States desire to form an integral part of the Union of Soviet Socialist Republics." See his Time for Decision (New York: Harper and Brothers, 1944), pp. 330, 333.

9. Herbert Feis, *Churchill-Roosevelt-Stalin: The War They Waged and the Peace They Sought* (Princeton, NJ: Princeton University Press, 1957), p. 27.

10. Earl W. Jennison, Jr., "Review Essay," *Journal of Baltic Studies*, 6, 2-3 (Summer-Fall 1975), 223-224.

11. Winston S. Churchill, *The Grand Alliance* (Boston: Houghton Mifflin, 1953), pp. 584-585.

12. Quoted in Feis, *Churchill-Roosevelt-Stalin*, p. 60.

13. Quoted in ibid.

14. Jennison, "Review Essay," p. 224.

15. Bronis J. Kaslas, ed., *The USSR-German Aggression against Lithuania* (New York: Robert Speller and Sons, 1973), p. 364.

16. Schnorf, "The Baltic States...1939-1942," p. 47.

17. Schnorf, "The Baltic States...1943-1946," p. 57; I. Vizulis, "The Diplomacy of the Allied Powers toward the Baltic States (1942-1945)," *Baltic Review*, 35 (August 1968), 52, 58-59.

18. Edmund R. Padvaiskas, "World War II Russian-American Relations and the Baltic States: A Test Case," *Lituanus*, 28, 2 (Summer 1982), 7.

19. Padvaiskas, "Russian-American Relations," pp. 7-8.

20. Churchill, *The Grand Alliance*, pp. 558-559; Winston S. Churchill, The Second World War (London: Cassel, 1951), IV, 292-294. See also Merkelis, Antanas Smetona, p. 664; Kaarel R. Pusta, "How Has Russia Been 'Rewarded?'" Baltic Review, 1, 4-5 (July-August 1946), 235.

21. Winston S. Churchill, *The Hinge of Fate* (Boston: Houghton Mifflin, 1950), p. 285. W. Phillips Davison attributes an utterance to Churchill, that states that if Hitler invaded Hell, he would speak favorably of the devil in the House of Commons. See Davison's "The Public Opinion Process" in Policy-Making in American Government, ed. Edward V. Schneier (New York: Basic Books, 1969), pp. 17-18.

22. Feis, *Churchill-Roosevelt-Stalin*, p. 59; U.S. Department of State, Foreign Relations of the United States, 1942, III (Washington, D.C.: U.S. Government Printing Office, 1961), pp. 505-512.

23. George F. Kennan, *Russia and the West under Lenin and Stalin* (Boston: Little, Brown, 1961), p. 357. See also Feis, Churchill-Roosevelt-Stalin, p. 60; Vizulis, "Diplomacy of the Allied Powers," p. 53.

24. U.S. Department of State, *Foreign Relations of the United States*, 1942, III, pp. 519-520.

25. Ibid., pp. 512-526, 538.

26. Ibid., pp. 539-540.

27. Ibid., pp. 541-542.

28. Ibid., III, pp. 540-541.

29. Feis, *Churchill-Roosevelt-Stalin*, p. 122; Padvaiskas, "Russian-American Relations," pp. 23-24. Padvaiskas notes that the president informed W. Averill Harriman that he, Roosevelt, would personally negotiate matters involving the Baltic States. He also notes that Sumner Welles resigned in September 1943 over personality clashes with Secretary Hull. Thus was lost a strong defender of the Atlantic Charter.

30. Ciechanowski, *Defeat in Victory*, p. 186.

31. Cordell Hull, *The Memoirs of Cordell Hull*, ed. Walter Johnson (New York: Macmillan, 1948), p. 1266; Arnolds Spekke, Latvia and the Baltic Problem (London: Latvian Information Bureau, 1952), p. 65. See also Schnorf, "The Baltic States...1943-1946," p. 59.

32. Winston S. Churchill, *Closing the Ring* (Boston: Houghton Mifflin, 1952), p. 283.

33. Ciechanowski, *Defeat in Victory*, p. 228.

34. William D. Leahy, *I Was There* (New York: Whittlesey House, 1950), p. 185.

35. Schnorf, "The Baltic States...1943-1946," pp. 62-63.

36. Robert E. Sherwood, *Roosevelt and Hopkins* (New York: Harper and Brothers, 1950), p. 796; US Department of State, Digest of International Law, ed. Marjorie M. Whiteman (Washington, D.C.: U.S. Government Printing Office, 1964), III, pp. 219-222; U.S. Department of State, Foreign Relations of the United States, Diplomatic Papers, The Conferences at Cairo and Teheran, 1943 (Washington, D.C.: U.S. Government Printing Office, 1961), pp. 594-595; Vizulis, "Diplomacy of the Allied Powers," p. 55.

37. Ibid., p. 56, states that Roosevelt's proposal for a second plebiscite was based on genuine disinformation regarding the circumstances surrounding the 1940 plebiscites. Others contend that the president utilized it as a diplomatic tactic.

38. Schnorf, "The Baltic States...1943-1946," pp. 64-65.

39. Ibid., p. 66. By using the phrase "devious processes," Schnorf is making a reference to words used in the Welles Declaration.

40. Padvaiskas, "Russian-American Relations," p. 27; Vizulis, "Diplomacy of the Allied Powers," pp. 55-56. In a letter to a friend dated 2 September 1944, James V. Forrestal angrily wrote:

> I find that whenever any American suggests that we act in accordance with the needs of our own security, he is called a god-damned fascist and imperialist, while if Uncle Joe [Stalin] suggests that he needs the Baltic Provinces, half of Poland, all of Bessarabia, and access to the Mediterranean, all hands agree that he is a fine, frank, candid and generally delightful fellow who is very easy to deal with because he is so explicit in what he wants.

Quoted in Walter Millis, ed., *The Forrestal Diaries* (New York: Viking, 1951), p. 14.40.

41. Vizulis, "Diplomacy of the Allied Powers," p. 54. Sumner Welles, though no longer in government, grappled with those issues at the same time, revealing the ascendancy of pragmatism over idealism:

> To remove all grounds for justifiable criticism and to make doubly sure that the frontiers of the future Russia will incorporate willing, rather than unwilling, Soviet citizens, the Soviet government would be well-advised to permit open plebiscites to be taken in every instance where there is a dispute as to the will of the majority, and *to permit all individuals who do not wish to become Soviet citizens to depart freely with their possessions, and with due compensation for the real property they are obliged to abandon* (Time for Decision, p. 333).

Author's emphasis.   This came from the man who but two years earlier had emphatically rejected similar proposals as "not only indefensible from every moral standpoint, but likewise extraordinarily stupid." See U.S. Department of State, Foreign Relations of the United States, 1942, III, pp. 540-541.

42. Richard F. Fenno, Jr., ed., *The Yalta Conference* (Boston: D.C. Heath, 1955), p. 91.

43. U.S. Department of State, *Foreign Relations of the United States*, Diplomatic Papers, The Conferences at Malta and Yalta, 1945 (Washington, D.C.: U.S. Government Printing Office, 1955), pp. 94-95.   Hickerson also noted the necessity of carrying out a program to prepare public opinion for recognition.

44. Fenno, *The Yalta Conference*, p. 12; Kazimierz Grzybowski, Soviet Public International Law: Doctrines and Diplomatic Practice (Leyden, the Netherlands: A. W. Sijthoff, 1970), pp. 90-92.

45. Fenno, *The Yalta Conference*, pp. 41-49; Schnorf, "The Baltic States...1943-1946," p. 70; Sumner Welles, Seven Decisions That Shaped History (New York: Harper and Brothers, 1951).

46. Quoted in Fenno, *The Yalta Conference*, p. 41.

47. Algirdas Budreckis, "Liberation Attempts from Abroad," in *Lithuania 700 Years*, 2d rev. ed., ed. Albertas Gerutis (New York: Manyland, 1969), p. 379; Fenno, The Yalta Conference, p. 52; The USSR: Institutions and People, pp. 110-111.

48. Fenno, *The Yalta Conference*, p. 40.

49. Ibid., p. 44.   Fenno writes of an unidentified senior U.S. official who commented on Roosevelt's health:

> The President looked physically tired at Casablanca; but his mind worked well.   At Teheran there were signs of loss of memory.   At Yalta he could neither think consecutively nor express himself coherently. (Ibid., p. 48).

50. U.S. Senate, Committees on Armed Services and Foreign Relations, *Hearings on the Military Situation in the Far East* (Washington, D.C.: U.S. Government Printing Office, 1951), quoted in Fenno, The Yalta Conference, p. 57.

Following Yalta, the State Department issued the following statement on 4 March 1945:

As far as the United States are concerned, the status of the Baltic
States has not altered in any way, not even after the Yalta
conference....The Baltic States -- Lithuania, Latvia, and Estonia --
were still acknowledged by the State Department (emphasis added).

Budreckis, "Liberation Attempts," p. 393. The emphasized portion implies the State
Department's grave interpretation of Yalta with regard to the Baltic States. See
also Bruno Chevrier, "The International Status of the Baltic States," Baltic Review,
1, 6 (November 1946), p. 271.

51. Budreckis, "Liberation Attempts," p. 379.

52. Harry S. Truman, *Memoirs I* (Garden City, NY: Doubleday, 1955), p. 378.

53. Povilas Zadeikis, letter to U.S. Acting Secretary of State Dean Acheson,
no. 1237, 29 July 1946, pp. 1-2.

54. Vizulis, "Diplomacy of the Allied Powers," p. 57.

55. Schnorf, "The Baltic States...1943-1946," p. 74.

56. Leonas Sabaliunas, "Baltic Perspectives: The Disillusionment with the
West and the Choices Ahead," *Lituanus*, 14, 2 (Summer 1968), p. 11. See also
Harold Nicolson, Diplomacy, 2d ed. (London: Oxford University Press, 1960), pp.
51-54.

57. "Kremlin Tactics in Converting the Baltic States into Satellites," *Baltic
Review*, 7 (16 June 1956), 13.

58. Padvaiskas, "Russian-American Relations," p. 9.

59. Vizulis, "Diplomacy of the Allied Powers," p. 59.

60. Schnorf, "The Baltic States...From Truman to Johnson," p. 59.

7

Extended Implementation
of Nonrecognition

EXECUTIVE ACTION

As noted in the previous chapter, the nonrecognition policy did indeed survive the trying times of World War II. On various occasions, the U.S. government has reaffirmed the policy by way of public statements made by presidents and secretaries of state, official certifications, and formal policy statements. Baltic affairs are monitored in the U.S. State Department not by the Soviet desk but by a separate Baltic desk. This is the official governmental watchdog over the nonrecognition policy.

In addition, the Baltic chiefs of mission receive national-day greetings from the secretary of state to coincide with their respective countries' independence days. This is the custom followed toward all accredited ministers in Washington. An example of such a greeting is the 8 February 1968 letter of Secretary of State Dean Rusk to Joseph Kajeckas, the Lithuanian envoy:

> On the occasion of the fiftieth anniversary of Lithuania's independence, I am very pleased to extend to you best wishes on behalf of the Government and people of the United States.
>
> Throughout its long and proud history, the Lithuanian nation has endured with fortitude many periods of trial and alien rule. Unhappily, in our own time, Lithuania's re-establishment as an independent state was followed only twenty-two years later by its forcible incorporation into the Soviet Union. The Lithuanian people have responded to this situation through the years with unyielding courage and unfaltering hope for freedom and national independence. The firm purpose with which the Lithuanians both at home and abroad have struggled to preserve their national heritage is the best assurance of their survival as a nation.
>
> Americans look with understanding and sympathy upon the just aspiration of the Lithuanian people to determine freely their own

destiny. The United States Government, by its continued non-recognition of the forcible incorporation of Lithuania, affirms its belief in Lithuania's right of self-determination.[1]

It is interesting to note that although each successive administration since Roosevelt has explicitly supported the nonrecognition policy, its particular interpretation has been different depending upon who sits in the Oval Office. This is reflected in the national-day greetings. Secretary of State Cyrus Vance's letter to Lithuanian Charge Dr. Stasys Backis of 9 February 1978 reveals a human rights-oriented pre-Afghanistan approach of President Jimmy Carter. The letter talks of courage, perseverance, national consciousness, and the maintenance of traditions. Secretary of State George Shultz's letter of 15 February 1983 condemns outright the Soviet actions of 1940, a focus more in line with the foreign policy of President Ronald Reagan.[2]

In both 1972 and 1982, Lithuanians in the United States addressed the U.S. government on the subject of official maps and Lithuania's place in them. These encounters resulted in a more favorable depiction of Lithuania and the other Baltic States. Representative Charles Dougherty (R-PA) successfully included the following provision in the Defense Department's authorization for 1983:

> None of the funds appropriated pursuant to an authorization of appropriations in this Act may be used to prepare, produce or purchase any map showing the [USSR] that does not-
>> (1) show the geographic boundaries of Estonia, Latvia, and Lithuania and designate those areas by those names;
>> (2) include the designation "Soviet Occupied" in parenthesis under each of those names; and
>> (3) include in close proximity to the area of the Baltic countries the following statement: "The United States Government does not recognize the incorporation of Estonia, Latvia, and Lithuania into the Soviet Union".[3]

The nonrecognition note is now placed near Latvia between Leningrad and Moscow; before it had been in the Indian Ocean. Concurrently, the U.S. State Department began listing the Baltic States within the East European section. They had been omitted before.

The first Lithuanian broadcast over the Voice of America was made on 16 February 1951. The Washington bureau began with 12 broadcasts daily, and the Munich bureau with 3. At the request of Senator Charles Percy (R-IL), chairman of the Senate Foreign Relations Committee, an announcement was made on 2 October 1984 that altered the European service. The U.S. Board for International Broadcasting unanimously voted to transfer the Baltic Language Services Division from Radio Liberty, which broadcasts to the Soviet Union, to Radio Free Europe, which transmits to East Europe. The changes in the flowchart and on-air identification were designed to better conform with U.S. policy.[4]

CONGRESSIONAL ACTION

Of course, it has not only been the executive branch that has taken steps to reaffirm the nonrecognition policy. Indeed, in the days following the Soviet invasion of Lithuania, which coincided with German adventurism in the West, Congress passed a joint resolution geared to withholding recognition of forcible territorial transfers in the western hemisphere.[5]

Legislators most often speak of Lithuania on or about 16 February of each year, which is the Lithuanian independence day. Statements and, more frequently, extensions of remarks submitted in writing following a session abound, in the *Congressional Record* in February. Obviously, these actions serve only to placate constituencies and possess little, if any, practical effect. One commentator is especially severe in her judgment of these rhetorical exercises:

> It is very doubtful that any Lithuanians have ever noticed this practice [of repeating speeches]. On the contrary, they are lovingly grateful for these "forensic" crumbs which fall from the tables of the busy legislators. And the Lithuanian-Americans of Racine and Linden and East St. Louis are voters, too, so the arrangement, though time-consuming, is not without mutual advantage.[6]

Congress has taken other actions on behalf of the Baltic States. At various times, it has passed resolutions commending executive nonrecognition of the incorporation, and has called for the withdrawal of Soviet civilian and military personnel.[7]

In 1961, Leonardas Valiukas, a California Lithuanian, started the group Americans for Congressional Action to Free the Baltic States, which sought passage of a resolution asking the president to raise the Baltic question in the United Nations. Ad hoc committees were established in Baltic communities in the U.S. to raise funds and lobby legislators to this effect. By the first session of the 89th Congress, there were 73 House and Senate resolutions with this purpose in mind. Finally, House Concurrent Resolution 416 passed the House on 23 June 1966. Senator Mike Mansfield (D-MT) asked the Senate to unanimously approve the resolution on 22 October of that year. The Senate consented and called on the president:

> (a) to direct the attention of world opinion at the United Nations and at other appropriate international forums and by such means as he deems appropriate, to the denial of the rights of self-determination for

the peoples of Estonia, Latvia, and Lithuania, and

(b) to bring the force of world opinion to bear on behalf of the restoration of these rights to the Baltic peoples.[8]

This, however, was merely a Sense of the Congress resolution without the force of law. The State Department vaguely responded that the U.S. ambassador to the United Nations would implement the resolution "at an appropriate time."[9]

Congress took more direct action at the October 1970 Interparliamentary Conference at the Hague. One of the U.S. delegates was Representative Edward Derwinski (R-IL). A delegate from the Soviet Union was Justas Paleckis, head of the Lithuanian governmental apparatus since the occupation. When Derwinski pointed out the circumstances surrounding the Baltic incorporation, Paleckis replied:

> Mr. Derwinski's thinking had been too much influenced by the military criminals of the Baltic countries who, together with Hitler's troops, had left their countries. The people there were a thousand times freer than they had ever been under the regimes of fascist dictatorship so strongly defended by Derwinski, who was sick with anti-communism.

By the early 1980s, there was even an Ad Hoc Congressional Committee on the Baltic States and Ukraine in the House, consisting of about 40 members. The first cochairmen were Representative Charles Dougherty (R-PA) and Representative Brian J. Donelly (D-MA). In addition to sponsoring human rights-related resolutions, the committee regularly called in Baltic and Ukrainian representatives for formal consultations.[10] However, by far the most important Baltic congressional committee, both in terms of publicity and substance, was the Kersten Committee of 1953-1954.

In late 1952 and early 1953, an idea began brewing within the Lithuanian American Council that a formal committee with investigative capabilities -- and public relations potential -- be formed to examine the incorporation of Lithuania into the Soviet Union. The group advocating this route was encouraged by the congressional investigation of the Soviet Katyn Forest massacre of Polish officers, and by President-elect Dwight Eisenhower's remarks on the liberation of East Europe. The council, following internal debates as to how to proceed, began lobbying the White House, Congress, the State Department, and the media, seeking support and sponsors.[11]

Representative Charles J. Kersten, a Republican from Milwaukee, had previously expressed his support for the liberation movement in East Europe. He had authored an amendment to the Mutual Security Act providing one hundred million dollars for resistance fighters behind the Iron Curtain. When Mary Kizis, director of the Lithuanian Information Center, a subsidiary of the Lithuanian American Council, asked if Kersten would take the lead in the establishment of a special committee, he immediately agreed.

On 26 March 1953, a council delegation met with President Eisenhower. The matter of the special committee was raised during the proceedings. When the president asked if such a committee had operated before, Kersten replied no. When the president inquired about a sponsor for the legislation, Kersten announced that he would take the lead. He subsequently drafted a resolution and dispatched it to the State Department for its comments. By mid-April 1953, the undersecretary had approved the resolution and pledged his department's cooperation.

Representative Kersten introduced House Resolution 231 on 7 May 1953, but it was soon bogged down in the Rules Committee, whose chairman, Representative Leo E. Allen (R-IL), appeared uncertain as to its utility. Following further lobbying by Lithuanian-American groups, Speaker Joseph Martin (R-MA) agreed to find the right moment to move the resolution out of committee. By July, however, no progress had been achieved and the session was drawing to a close. More lobbying was unleashed on Capitol Hill. At a White House ceremony on 11 July marking the one-year anniversary of Eisenhower's nomination to the presidency, Representative Allen approached Kersten, informed him of consultations with Speaker Martin, and promised to place the resolution on the committee's agenda.

However, when Rules Committee member Representative Hugh Scott of Pennsylvania moved to consider the legislation, Allen appeared to change his position, reasoning that this was a matter for the United Nations to consider. He also noted that it was already 13 years since the events of 1940, and questioned the need for an investigation following such a lapse of time. Majority Leader Rep. Charles A. Halleck (R-IN) added that the legislation should first go to the Foreign Affairs Committee. By the morning of 20 July, telegrams began pouring into the offices of key congressional members from Lithuanian-Americans urging swift action on the resolution. Representative Allen was also contacted by the Republican National Committee to end the delay. Finally, after a conference of Martin, Halleck, and Kersten, it was agreed to place the resolution on the agenda immediately.

Due to revisions that had been made in the interim, the legislation was now known as House Resolution 346. It was considered in the Rules Committee on 23 July, which later unanimously recommended it to the full House. Consideration in the House had to come quickly, for money would still have to come from the Appropriations Committee to avoid delaying the hearings until the start of the next session. It was placed on the House's agenda for 27 July. At 6:30 A.M., after considering the Korean armistice, Hugh Scott was finally able to sponsor the motion. Halleck seconded it, and Kersten spoke on its behalf. After a half hour of statements from 13 members of Congress, HR 346 was unanimously approved. It read, in part,

Whereas the Government of the United States... maintains diplomatic relations with the Governments of...Lithuania, Latvia, and Estonia and consistently has refused to recognize their seizure and forced "incorporation" into the [USSR]: Now, therefore, be it

Resolved, That there is hereby created a select committee to be composed of seven Members of the House...to be appointed by the Speaker, one of whom he shall designate as chairman....[12]

The committee is authorized and directed to conduct a full and complete investigation and study of said seizure and forced "incorporation" of Lithuania, Latvia, and Estonia by the [USSR] and the treatment of the said Baltic peoples during and following said seizure and "incorporation".[13]

Thirty thousand dollars was appropriated to the special committee over a two-year period. Three hundred thirty-five witnesses testified before the committee, which also collected over two hundred documents, lists, and signed items of testimony.[14] The committee ultimately produced two major reports on the Baltic summer of 1940.[15] The Kersten Committee hearings gave an opportunity to fully present, for the first time, the ultimate reason for the existence of the U.S. nonrecognition policy, namely an objective account of the events in question directed and compiled by non-Baltics. In his own testimony, Secretary of State John Foster Dulles gave perhaps the most eloquent summary of both the hearings and the policy:

Some may say that it is unrealistic and impractical not to recognize the enforced incorporation of Estonia, Latvia, and Lithuania into the Soviet Union....We are not prepared to seek illusory safety for ourselves by a bargain with their masters which would confirm their captivity....We do not look upon the conference table as a place where we surrender our principles, but rather as a place for making our principles prevail.[16]

NONRECOGNITION AND U.S.-USSR RELATIONS

Nonrecognition is not merely a piece on the chessboard of domestic politics, as outlined above. Its primary focus is outside the country as a message to the nations of the world community, specifically the Soviet Union, of the U.S. attitude toward aggression in the Baltic. The policy has certainly affected domestic political and legal affairs in the U.S.[17] It has also affected U.S.-Soviet relations.

Of course, the Soviets fought against the nonrecognition policy from its inception, stating that it would sour the course of U.S.-USSR relations. The continued presence of the Baltic diplomats in the U.S., as well as the problems surrounding vessels in U.S. territorial waters, were the most obvious manifestations of the policy against which the Soviets directed their attacks. Undersecretary of State Sumner Welles and Soviet Ambassador Constantine A. Oumansky discussed these matters on 27 February 1941. Welles noted that the U.S. would not back down from its position, and that certain issues would have to remain in the realm of "unsolvable problems"; this is where the Baltic States were placed. Oumansky found this unacceptable.[18]

Public U.S. proposals and statements regarding the Baltic States have always brought vehement reaction from the Kremlin.[19] Two general responses have been charges of U.S. interference in Soviet internal affairs, and the contention that the Baltic States joined the Soviet Union voluntarily. A third response began surfacing in the 1960s in an attempt to turn the tables on the United States and the morality of its actions. Writing of respect for sovereignty and territorial integrity, Victor Karpov notes:

> This principle should be strictly observed; and its observance is, of course, incompatible with some resolutions that have from time to time been adopted by the American Congress, as those calling for "liberation" of some integral parts of [the] Soviet Union- of...Lithuania...I would say this is roughly the same as if the parliament of Mexico, for example, would have passed a resolution demanding that Texas, Arizona, and California be "liberated from American slavery."[20]

Following the completion of World War II, the first forum where the nonrecognition policy became a factor in terms of foreign affairs was Nuremberg. On 6 October 1945, U.S., British, French, and Soviet representatives signed the indictments of German war criminals before the International Military Tribunal. Among the charges were atrocities committed in the "Lithuanian Soviet Socialist Republic," the "Latvian Soviet Socialist Republic," and the "Estonian Soviet Socialist Republic." Supreme Court Justice Robert H. Jackson, the U.S. prosecutor at Nuremberg, signed the indictment, but also deposited a reservation with the Tribunal's secretary:

> Reference is made to Estonia, Latvia, Lithuania and certain other territories as being within the area of the U.S.S.R. This language is proposed by Russia and is accepted to avoid delay....The indictment is signed subject to this reservation and understanding:
> I have no authority either to admit or to challenge, on behalf of the United States, the Soviet claims to sovereignty over such territories. Nothing, therefore, in this indictment is to be construed as a recognition by the United States of such sovereignty.[21]

Jackson's letter was made public in Berlin on 15 October 1945.

The liberation espoused by President Eisenhower and Secretary of State John Foster Dulles was welcomed by those who viewed George Kennan's containment policy as one of tacitly recognizing spheres of influence between East and West. However, those who thought that liberation was to be applied literally toward Lithuania, Latvia, and Estonia were sorely disappointed. U.S. inaction during the East German and Hungarian uprisings of the 1950s demonstrated that liberation would not come easily.[22]

Be that as it may, the Eisenhower administration lost no opportunities to criticize the Kremlin for its behavior. At the Four Power Conference in Berlin in February 1954, consisting of the U.S., U.K., USSR, and France, Secretary Dulles cited the illegal tactics used in incorporating the Baltic States, which were replicated in Eastern Europe at the close of World War II.[23]

July of the following year saw the Big Four gather at Geneva, where the West desired to place the Baltic on the agenda. The proposal was rejected by the Soviets, though there were press reports that the matter was discussed aside from the formal talks. It was announced that the matter was postponed until the October 1955 conference, where it was once again blocked by the Kremlin's foreign minister. It is interesting to note that Stasys Lozoraitis, chief of the Lithuanian Diplomatic Service, went to Geneva in case Lithuania would require formal representation, although this turned out to be a wasted -- and idealistic -- effort on his part.[24]

Greater controversy was generated during the ratification process for a new U.S.-Soviet consular convention. Negotiations commenced in 1959 and the treaty was signed at Moscow on 1 June 1964. Among the provisions of the convention was Article VII, paragraph 3, which allowed consular officials to register nationals of the sending state residing in the receiving state. Other provisions included the customary notarial, commercial, and custodial functions of consulates.[25]

The Senate Foreign Relations Committee considered the convention the following year, and on 30 July 1965 voted 7 to 1 to recommend it to the full Senate, which failed to ratify it. The Johnson administration brought it up again in 1967, and the Foreign Relations Committee began considering it on 23 January of that year.[26]

Lithuanians in the United States were concerned over seemingly vague passages and possible double meanings that could indirectly destroy the nonrecognition policy. When hearings commenced for the second time, Lithuanian-American groups began lobbying senators for its defeat, and collected documentation to back up their claims. Anthony J. Rudis, president of the Lithuanian American Council, testified against the treaty because it did not explicitly grant an exception to the Baltic States. He was especially concerned that the Soviet Union could claim Baltic nationals as nationals of the USSR under Soviet citizenship decrees. The convention would also have granted immunity to consular staffers, something that was usually granted only to embassy staff. Indeed, Representative Edward J. Derwinski (R-IL) pointed out the implications of this provision regarding Americans with relatives in Soviet-occupied territory: "The possibility of coercion, bribery, even blackmail are evident if Soviet consular officials have the freedom to roam throughout the United States."[27]

In an exchange between Rudis and committee member Senator Eugene McCarthy (D-MN), McCarthy pointed out that no treaty with the USSR distinguished the Baltic States; this was done in separate statements. Rudis conceded this point, but added that he was concerned about possible harassment from staffers, for example, Vytautas Zenkevicius, who was second secretary at the Soviet embassy and who possessed immunity. McCarthy replied that the convention would not change this arrangement, but noted that the matter could be helped if only ethnic Russians were allowed to assume immune diplomatic and consular positions. Rudis agreed, adding that it would be improper for the U.S. to open a consulate in the Baltic States.[28]

The U.S. State Department's legal adviser assured the committee that ratification of the convention would have no effect on nonrecognition. Furthermore, in a 2 February 1967 letter to the committee's chairman, Senator J. William Fulbright (D-AR), Assistant Secretary for Congressional Relations Douglas MacArthur II asserted:

> Recognition of the incorporation of Estonia, Latvia and Lithuania into the USSR would, like all cases of diplomatic recognition, require a positive statement or positive act by the United States. This Convention contains no such statement and provides for no such act....The ratification of this treaty will not change this [nonrecognition] policy -- any more than did the signing of the more than 105 bilateral and multilateral agreements which we have entered into with the USSR.[29]

However, the State Department did acknowledge one problem, namely the establishment of U.S. consular offices in the Baltic, and its potential for de facto recognition. In his testimony, Secretary of State Dean Rusk said, "We do have a bit of a dilemma there, Senator."[30] Nonetheless, the issue of nonrecognition did not sufficiently overshadow the convention to cause its amendment or to prevent its passage. The Senate ratified it on 16 March 1967 by a vote of 66 to 28.[31]

The United States and Soviet Union have grappled not only bilaterally, but also in the United Nations. U.S. ambassadors to the U.N. have addressed U.N. bodies several times on the topic of Lithuania and the other Baltic States. Ambassador Adlai Stevenson utilized the Baltic as an example of Soviet colonialism. Ambassador Arthur Goldberg carried this point further on 31 August 1967 when he reiterated the U.S. policy of nonrecognition. On 24 November 1976, Ambassador William Warren Scranton addressed the U.N.'s Third Committee on the denial of freedom and religious expression in the Baltic. The Soviet representative replied that the Baltic States had a rightful place in the Soviet Union. Finally, Ambassador

Jeane J. Kirkpatrick delivered to U.N. Secretary-General Javier Perez de Cuellar the text of a 26 July 1983 statement by President Ronald Reagan, which gave an overview of the occupation of the Baltic and reaffirmed nonrecognition.[32]

While such instances are somewhat routine and uneventful, an incident of greater consequence occured when Mrs. Leokadia Pilyushenko arrived at the 1967 fall session of the U.N. along with the rest of the Soviet delegation. This, in and of itself, meant nothing. However, Pilyushenko identified herself as Soviet Lithuania's foreign minister. When speaking before the Third Committee, she stated that she represented the Lithuanian Soviet Socialist Republic and went on to disparage Lithuania during the period of independence. The U.S. representative to the committee, Patricia Roberts Harris, replied that Pilyushenko had no right to speak on behalf of Lithuania.

Despite requests from Congress,[33] however, neither the U.S. nor any other member has ever sought to place the Baltic issue on the U.N.'s formal agenda.[34] The U.S. has, in fact, consciously done this in order to avoid embarassment:

> The question has been raised on various occasions about the desirability of United States initiatives in the United Nations calling for the restoration of independence to the Baltic countries....At the present time, however, the great majority of the UN members do not adhere to the position of the US Government on this issue. We must recognize that any failure of such an initiative in the United Nations would be a severe rebuff to the United States and would seriously prejudice our position in the matter before the world.[35]

In addition to the explicit rejection of U.S. action in the U.N., the above statement went on to say that the U.S. could do no more on behalf of the Baltic than it had already done: "Any US initiatives in the United Nations of the nature described above could well be misleading in suggesting that more can be done than we are already doing in behalf of the Baltic peoples."[36] In other words, the U.S. government continues to embrace the policy of nonrecognition-but also notes its practical limits. This is nothing new, for, as the previous chapter on wartime diplomacy described, the U.S. recognized the policy's limitations almost from its inception.

THE BALTIC AND IMPLICATIONS FOR U.S.-USSR RELATIONS

Sometimes, the routine of international intercourse forces the United States to deal fairly directly with Lithuania and the other Baltic States. Particular cases regarding individuals must be addressed, as well as those of family reunification, special visits, and other topics.[37] U.S. government personnel have been in the Baltic and have dealt with the Soviet regimes there. Effective foreign relations do not allow absolute isolation from even an unrecognized government. This, however, does not violate the nonrecognition policy. Gerhard von Glahn offers an explanation:

> It is quite possible for a given state to have dealings (*relations officienses*) with an unrecognized government without proceeding to recognition, *provided* the absence of intent to recognize is made clear. Thus the United States maintained agents in several Latin American republics before recognizing the latter as states independent from Spain, a course of action also pursued by Great Britain at the time. During the American Civil War, Great Britain sent a number of official agents to the Confederate States, yet did not recognize the latter as an independent entity. Many other governments have acted similarly in modern history.[38]

Nevertheless, although the U.S. ambassador in Moscow and cabinet-level officers of the U.S. government, as a matter of principle, do not visit the Baltic, there has been some concern when other senior U.S. officials have done so.[39] On 14 September 1972, a Lithuanian American Community delegation lodged a protest with the State Department after U.S. Consul General designate Culver Gleysteen visited Vilnius and met with Soviet Lithuanian officials.[40] In a 28 October 1972 letter to Senator Hugh Scott, National Security Adviser Henry Kissinger assured skeptics that this did not violate the nonrecognition policy:

> This visit in no way alters the United States' policy of not recognizing the forcible incorporation of Lithuania into the Soviet Union. Our proposed Consulate General in Leningrad includes Vilnius in its area of consular jurisdiction. Mr. Gleysteen visited the city to familiarize himself with it and to meet the local officials with whom our consular officials will have to deal in facilitating contacts between Americans and Lithuanians. Mr. Gleysteen's visit was thus in keeping with our desire to maintain ties with the Lithuanian people without recognizing Lithuania's forcible incorporation into the Soviet Union.[41]

This, of course, occured during the period of detente. The mood of U.S.-Soviet relations under President Reagan was considerably different when the U.S. ambassador in Moscow, Jack Matlock, refused to receive a delegation from the Supreme Soviet of the Latvian SSR in December 1987. The delegation was protesting a U.S. House of Representatives resolution on Latvia's independence day. The Latvians were kept waiting in the street for about an hour until the embassy's second secretary informed them that they could be received only as private citizens. When a similar resolution was passed for Lithuania's independence day two months later on 16 February 1988, Ambassador Matlock again refused a delegation from the Lithuanian SSR, which was protesting U.S. interference in Lithuania's affairs.

Since the espousal of the policy of nonrecognition, both the Congress and the Executive have sought to keep it alive. Much of this activity, in the form of statements, resolutions, and conferences, has been geared toward consumption by domestic groups, specifically Lithuanians, Latvians, and Estonians residing in the United States. However, exceptions such as the Kersten Committee hearings, which cost substantial money and effort, are indications that the policy is taken seriously, at least by those familiar with the circumstances surrounding it.

The policy has also affected U.S.-Soviet relations. Initially, the Kremlin declared that the Baltic issue would create a permanent rift between the two countries. Of course, a rift still exists, but the effect of the nonrecognition policy here is minimal, despite Soviet rhetoric aimed against it. Granted, the policy has caused Washington and Moscow to grapple between themselves and on the floor of the United Nations, but successful wartime diplomacy in the early 1940s -- and even detente in the 1970s -- were carried out in spite of it.

Chapter five of this study demonstrated that the policy possessed concrete political and legal consequences. The previous chapter, however, showed that it also has limitations. When expedient, the policy was temporarily shelved during wartime. This chapter has expanded on the limitations. First, the U.S. can go only so far in helping the Baltic States. There are relatively few tools for action in the hands of U.S. policymakers. Second, it is unavoidable to unofficially deal with the Soviet regimes in the Baltic. Indeed, in many cases involving individuals it is beneficial. The next chapter will address several specific instances where implementation of the nonrecognition policy has been problematic -- or nonexistent.

NOTES

1. Reproduced in Lithuanian Council of Chicago (LCC), Lietuvos nepriklausomybes atkurimo ir 717 metu karalystes isteigimo minejimas (Commemoration of Lithuania's Independence and the 717th anniversary of the establishment of the Lithuanian kingdom) (Chicago: LCC, 1968), p. 14. For similar greetings, see Estonia, Consulate General, Policy of the United States of America toward Estonia, (New York: Consulate General of Estonia, n.d.), p. 12; Leonardas Simutis, *Amerikos Lietuviu Taryba: 30 metu Lietuvos laisves kovoje 1940-1970* (Lithuanian American Council: 30-year struggle for the liberation of Lithuania 1940-1970) (Chicago: LAC, 1971), pp. 164-165.

2. U.S. Department of State, letter of Secretary of State Cyrus Vance to Lithuanian Minister Dr. Stasys Backis, 9 February 1978; U.S. Department of State, letter of Secretary of State George P. Shultz to Lithuanian envoy d'Affaires Dr. Stasys Backis, 15 February 1983.

3. Public Law 97-252, Department of Defense Authorization Act, 1983, 8 September 1982, section 1134.

4. Algirdas Budreckis, "Liberation Attempts from Abroad," in *Lithuania 700 Years, 2d rev. ed., ed. Albertas Gerutis (New York: Manyland, 1969), pp. 402-403; U.S. Senate, Committee on Foreign Relations, "Baltic Radio Service to be Transferred to Radio Free Europe at Percy Request," media notice, 2 October 1984, p. 1.*

5. U.S. Congress, House Joint Resolution 556, Senate Joint Resolution 271, 76th Congress, 3rd session. See Robert Langer, *Seizure of Territory: The Stimson Doctrine and Related Principles in Legal Theory and Diplomatic Practice* (Princeton, NJ: Princeton University Press, 1947), p. 82.

6. Norma Krause Herzfeld, "The Persistent Lithuanians: A Government without a Country," *The Catholic Reporter, 9 June 1961, section 2, p. 1.*

7. U.S. Senate Resolution, 29 April 1954, quoted in Estonia, Consulate General, *Policy of the United States*, pp. 9-10; U.S. House of Representatives, House Concurrent Resolution 57, 4 February 1981, pp. 2-3.

8. U.S. Congress, House Concurrent Resolution 416, 22 October 1966. See Budreckis, *Lithuanians in America, pp. 135-136.*

9. Budreckis, "Liberation Attempts from Abroad," pp. 420-421.

10. Vytautas Kutkus, *JAV Lietuviu Bendruomenes krasto valdybos veikla nuo 1979 m. gruodzio men. 15 d. iki 1982 m. spalio men. 23 d.* (Activity of the Lithuanian American Community from 15 December 1979 to 23 October 1982), (n.p.: LAC, 1982), pp. 14-15.

11. Unless otherwise indicated, the passage on the Kersten Committee is taken from Lithuanian American Council, *Kersteno rezoliucija ir pastangos ja pravesti JAV Kongrese* (The Kersten Resolution and efforts for its passage in the U.S. Congress) (n.p.: Lithuanian American Council, c. 1953), pp. 1-10.

12. C. J. Kersten (R-WI), chairman, A. M. Bentley (R-MI), E. J. Bonin (R-PA), F. E. Busbey (R-IL), T. J. Dodd (D-CT), T. M. Machrowicz (D-MI), R. J. Madden (D-IN).

13. House Resolution 346, 27 July 1953 (legislative day). See also Simutis, *Amerikos Lietuviu Taryba, pp. 180-181.*

14. Antanas Kucas, *Lithuanians in America*, trans. Joseph Boley (Boston: Encyclopedia Lituanica, 1975), pp. 279-280.

15. U.S. House of Representatives, Select Committee to Investigate the Incorporation of the Baltic States into the U.S.S.R., *Baltic States Investigation I* (Washington, D.C.: U.S. Government Printing Office, 1953); U.S. House of Representatives, Third Interim Report of the Select Committee on Communist Aggression, Report of the Select Committee to Investigate Communist Aggression and the Forced Incorporation of the Baltic States into the U.S.S.R. (Washington, D.C.: U.S. Government Printing Office, 1954).

16. U.S. House of Representatives, *Baltic States Investigation I*, p. 4.

17. See chapter 5.

18. U.S. Department of State, *Foreign Relations of the United States*, Diplomatic Papers, 1940, Volume I, General (Washington, D.C.: U.S. Government Printing Office, 1959), pp. 708-712. See also p. 785.

19. Richard A. Schnorf, "The Baltic States in U.S.-Soviet Relations: From Truman to Johnson," *Lituanus, 14, 3 (Fall 1968), 54.*

20. Victor P. Karpov, "The Soviet Concept of Peaceful Coexistence and Its Implications for International Law," in *The Soviet Impact on International Law*, ed. Hans W. Baade (Dobbs Ferry, NY: Oceana, 1965), p. 20.

21. "Jackson Avoided Stand on Baltic," *The New York Times*, 20 October 1945, p. 4. The British Foreign Office announced on 19 October that the British signature on the indictments also did not imply recognition. See also Assembly of Captive European Nations, International Agreements and Pledges Concerning East-Central Europe (New York: ACEN, 1960), p. 45.

      The U.S. government has usually been fairly scrupulous when discussing the Baltic States. In April 1950, a U.S. military aircraft allegedly flew over Baltic territory, which prompted a protest from the Kremlin that Soviet territory had been violated. The U.S. State Department responded that "the United States Navy Aircraft in question...did not fly over any Soviet or Soviet-occupied territory or territorial waters adjacent thereto." Quoted in Krystyna Marek, *Identity and Continuity of States in Public International Law* (Geneva: Librairie E. Droz, 1968), p. 403 (Marek's emphasis).

22. Schnorf, "The Baltic States...From Truman to Johnson," p. 46ff.

23. Antanas Trimakas, "Satellite Status for the Baltic States-A Possible Opening for Freedom," *Baltic Review*, 7 (16 June 1956), 7-8.

24. Schnorf, "The Baltic States...From Truman to Johnson," p. 49; Trimakas, "Satellite Status," pp. 8-9.

25. U.S. Senate, Committee on Foreign Relations, *Consular Convention with the Soviet Union, Hearings on Executive D (Washington, D.C.: U.S. Government Printing Office, 1967), pp. 283-292.*

26. Simutis, *Amerikos Lietuviu Taryba*, p. 423.

27. Edward J. Derwinski, "Remarks in the House of Representatives on Proposed Consular Convention with the Soviet Union," press release, 9 August 1965, p. 4. See also Simutis, *Amerikos Lietuviu Taryba*, pp. 423-424; U.S. Senate, Consular Convention with the Soviet Union, p. 242.

28. Ibid., pp. 250-252.

29. Ibid., p. 139. See also p. 248.

30. U.S. Senate, *Consular Convention with the Soviet Union*, p. 331. See also Derwinski, "Remarks...on Proposed Consular Convention," p. 1.

31. Simutis, *Amerikos Lietuviu Taryba*, p. 426.

32. Edgars Dunsdorfs, *The Baltic Dilemma II: The Case of the Reversal of the De Jure Recognition by Australia of the Incorporation of the Baltic States into the Soviet Union* (Melbourne: Baltic Council of Australia, 1982), p. 425; Bronis J.

Kaslas, ed. *The USSR-German Aggression against Lithuania* (New York: Robert Speller & Sons, 1973), p. 468; Schnorf, "The Baltic States...From Truman to Johnson," p. 53; U.S. Mission to the United Nations, "The United States Reaffirms Recognition of Independence of Estonia, Latvia and Lithuania," press release, 29 July 1983, pp. 1-3.

33. For example, see Edward J. Derwinski, "Derwinski Introduces New Baltic States Resolution," news release, 18 November 1977, p. 1.

34. Schnorf, "The Baltic States...From Truman to Johnson," p. 48.

35. U.S. Department of State, "United States Policy toward the Baltic States," *Public Information Series*, no. P-317-870, c. 1970, p. 1.

36. Ibid., p. 1.

37. U.S. Department of State, statement by Robert L. Barry, Assistant Secretary of State for European Affairs before the Subcommittee on International Organizations, House Foreign Affairs Committee, 26 June 1979, pp. 2-3.

38. Gerhard von Glahn, *Law among Nations: An Introduction to Public International Law*, 4th ed. (New York: Macmillan, 1981), p. 104.

39. U.S. Department of State, "US Policy: The Baltic Republics," *Gist*, August 1984, p. 2.

40. Budreckis, *Lithuanians in America*, p. 63.

41. Henry M. Kissinger, letter to Sen. Hugh Scott, 28 October 1972.

8

Problems of Implementation: Case Studies

POSTWAR BALTIC REPATRIATION

While, by and large, the U.S. government has stood by the nonrecognition policy in both word and deed, there have been instances where the policy has been undermined, either perceptually or in fact. The first major transgression against it was the forced postwar repatriation of Lithuanians, Latvians, and Estonians to their native lands, now under Moscow's control.

Following the conclusion of hostilities, several hundred thousand Baltic persons found themselves in the western occupation zones of the defeated Germany. They had fled as the Red Army swept westward back across the continent. If Baltic citizens were not considered citizens of the Soviet Union, they would not have been in any danger of forced repatriation to the USSR, for the Western powers did not recognize the citizenship decree of the presidium of the Supreme Soviet issued on 7 September 1940:

> (1) In accordance with Section 1, the Law on Nationality of the USSR of August 19, 1938, it is hereby established that nationals of the Lithuanian, Latvian, and Estonian Soviet Socialist Republics shall be USSR nationals from the day when these Republics are received into the USSR.
> (2) Nationals of the Lithuanian, Latvian, and Estonian [SSRs] who at the time of the promulgation of the present decree are outside of the confines of the USSR and were not deprived of nationality by the Soviet governments of these Republics must register on or before November 1, 1940, as Soviet Nationals at diplomatic missions and consultants [sic] of the USSR by means of a personal appearance or by mailing a special application with their passports.[1]

In addition, the Western allies possessed moral and legal traditions of ready asylum for political exiles:[2]

The international practice after World War I shows that no prisoners of war were forcibly extradited to their countries of origin. At that time, the problem arose only between certain powers and Soviet Russia. From 1918 to 1921, the Soviets signed twenty-seven international treaties and agreements concerning the repatriation of prisoners of war *and civilians*. All were based upon the principle of voluntary repatriation only and contained almost identical clauses explicitly precluding any forced repatriation.[3]

These sentiments were echoed in postwar declarations by individual governments, as well as the United Nations. The Geneva Convention Relating to the Status of Refugees, signed on 28 July 1951, explicitly prohibits forced repatriation to a person's native land if he or she will face persecution there.[4]

In order to establish procedures for processing displaced persons, U.S. and Soviet military authorities signed an agreement regarding liberated prisoners of war and civilians at Yalta on 11 February 1945. The document contains no reference to the use of force, though it sees repatriation as the only solution.[5] Furthermore, the U.S. and the USSR defined a displaced person as one who was a Soviet citizen on or before 1 September 1939, and who was displaced on or after 21 June 1941. Finally, a 12 May 1945 order from the Supreme Commander of the Allied Expeditionary Force, General of the Army Dwight D. Eisenhower, stated that Baltic citizens could not be forcibly repatriated because they did not meet the former criterion, and neither the U.S. nor the United Kingdom recognized subsequent political and territorial changes there.[6]

Nonetheless, the U.S. government did not strictly adhere to a policy of voluntary repatriation for citizens not charged with war crimes or collaboration with the Nazis. Even while negotiators were attempting to safeguard Russian and Baltic people who did not wish to return to their homelands, policy was beginning to shift inside government circles. As early as the autumn of 1944, a memorandum was written by Bernard Guffler, Special War Problems Division of the U.S. State Department, to Charles Bohlen, chief of the East European Affairs Division, which indicated the change:

> The new policy toward Soviet nationals differs from the policy hitherto followed with regard to them and with the policy which it is proposed to continue to follow with regard to other Allied nationals. The most notable difference is that no persons claimed by other Allied Governments are delivered to the custody of those Governments against their wills. The adoption of this new policy towards the Soviets will result in the delivery to the Soviet authorities of persons hitherto withheld from them because they were unwilling to return to the Soviet Union.[7]

Bohlen "signified his approval" on 20 October 1944.[8]

The U.S. Army began activating what one writer has identified as Operation Keelhaul, a secret repatriation plan that called for the return, forced if necessary, of approximately two million prisoners of war and displaced persons into Soviet hands.[9] The plan was partially implemented from 1944 to 1947, not because of ignorance of the Eisenhower directive, but because of the way the Displaced Persons Branch of the U.S. Army handled the matter. The same month that Eisenhower sought to protect Baltic citizens, this army branch issued the following instruction: "After identification by Soviet Repatriation Representatives, Soviet displaced persons will be repatriated regardless of their individual wishes."[10] The loophole in this order was that Soviet representatives could point to a person who originated in what subsequently became Soviet territory. The individual then had no recourse, and protests meant little.

The Soviets were also conducting a campaign for the return of Lithuanians, Latvians, and Estonians. Soviet diplomats attacked them as fascists and war criminals who were conducting reactionary anti-Soviet campaigns in displaced persons camps. Furthermore, according to the Kremlin, they were aided by the Western allies, who sought to continue German war policy by searching for inexpensive labor. Specifically, the Soviets stated that as of 1 January 1947, 221,500 of the 827,000 refugees in Germany were Soviet citizens, and demanded free access to them. The Soviet criminal code labeled flight abroad as treason, which was punishable by death. Relatives remaining behind could also be punished, regardless of whether they assisted in the escape. Ironically, although the Soviets claimed Baltics as Soviet citizens, Soviet law automatically abolished Soviet citizenship for an individual who departed the country without the knowledge of the authorities.[11]

The Soviet campaign was also carried out closer to the displaced persons. Repatriation officers began supplying the camps with booklets and brochures extolling life in the Lithuanian SSR. However, more direct measures were also employed. Secret Order 199 of the United Nations Relief and Rehabilitation Administration (UNRRA) noted that displaced persons' leaders who were opposed to repatriation should be transferred to other camps containing individuals not slated for repatriation. The International Refugee Organization (IRO), which succeeded UNRRA on 1 July 1947, issued a secret *Manual for Eligibility Officers*, all copies of which were destroyed upon IRO's liquidation. That manual stated that a displaced person must give sufficient information why he or she should not be repatriated. Though a political and not an economic reason had to be given, arguments against communism had to be "plausible." For example, the absence of religious freedom was not sufficient to avoid repatriation.

In 1946, the Lithuanians of the Reutlingen camp were invited to the assembly hall of an elementary school to listen to the presentation of a Soviet officer. He warned that they would not possess the right of repatriation indefinitely. Those who did not return would lose their Soviet citizenship.[12] Swettenham humorously writes of the cool reception accorded to Soviet repatriation missions:

"Soviet literature was distributed in the camps, but usually found its way into numerous toilets! Repatriation for Balts at any rate was a washout."[13] Not all incidents, however, were humorous. On 6 September 1945, when UNRRA and U.S. personnel attempted to repatriate individuals -- Ukrainians in this case -- from the Mannheim and Kempten camps, violence broke out. From then on, U.S. authorities barred the forcible repatriation of Ukrainians, and forbade UNRRA from utilizing U.S. personnel in any repatriation efforts.[14]

Needless to say, the specter of repatriation caused anxiety among Lithuanians. Several publications appeared that voiced this concern, along with booklets geared to call favorable attention to their plight. Some even proposed that Baltic national committees be allowed to perform consular functions in Germany in order to guarantee the personal status of Lithuanians, Latvians, and Estonians. Fears were reinforced when letters describing the unfavorable situation in the Baltic were smuggled back to the West from repatriated persons.

While the displaced persons in Germany were struggling to remain in the West, a battle was being fought on the other side of the Atlantic to the same end. As early as 9 April 1944, Lithuanian Minister Povilas Zadeikis dispatched a note to the State Department on this issue. He received assurances that no persons in the U.S. zone of occupation would be repatriated against their will. Zadeikis also directed the United Lithuanian Relief Fund of America to inform the displaced persons to firmly maintain their claims to Lithuanian citizenship. Despite the efforts of Lithuanian-American organizations, and the intercession of Eleanor Roosevelt, the U.S. promises were not fully kept.[15]

By 1947, Operation Keelhaul had ceased and Secretary of State George C. Marshall said that "It is the fixed policy of the United States Government to oppose any forced repatriation of displaced persons."[16] Unfortunately, this came too late for several thousand Baltic citizens who were removed to their countries against their will among the approximately 2,100,000 persons repatriated to the Soviet Union.[17] This was despite the fact that the U.S. had not recognized the regimes functioning in Lithuania, Latvia, and Estonia since 1940. Indeed, it was only in 1950 that the U.S. government legislatively recognized a special category of refugee who could not return to his country for fear of political or religious persecution. This was in the form of amendments to the Displaced Persons Act of 1948.[18] It is interesting that the nonrecognition policy was able to protect Baltic property from falling into the hands of the Soviets -- but not Baltic persons.

THE SIMAS KUDIRKA INCIDENT

This chapter has discussed the forced repatriation of several thousand Lithuanians, Latvians, and Estonians. We now turn to the forced repatriation of one Lithuanian, Simas Kudirka, a sailor in the Soviet merchant marine.

On 23 November 1970, the US Coast Guard cutter *Vigilant* and the Soviet fishing trawler *Sovetskaya Litva* (Soviet Lithuania) met in U.S. waters off Martha's Vineyard, Massachusetts. There a U.S. delegation was to meet with the Soviets to discuss problems of interest to the New England fishing industry, specifically the Soviet's illegal use of tightly woven nets, which were also dropped to excessive depths. The delegation consisted of three fishing-industry civilians, a Coast Guard legal adviser, and two officials from the U.S. Commerce Department's National Marine Fisheries Service. The *Vigilant* (WMEC-617) was a 210-foot medium-endurance cutter based in New Bedford, Massachusetts. The *Sovetskaya Litva* (M-26402) was a 509-foot refrigerated trawler, based in Klaipeda, Lithuania, which operated along the east coast of the United States.

At some point during the proceedings, Simas Kudirka, a radio operator on board the trawler, managed to leap undetected onto the deck of the *Vigilant*. Kudirka hid below and informed a U.S. sailor of the circumstances. The sailor, in turn, reported to the vessel's commanding officer, Commander Ralph Eustis. Eustis was a 1954 graduate of the Coast Guard Academy and the U.S. Naval Postgraduate School. His previous assignments had included tours in Maine, Japan, California, and Coast Guard Headquarters. When Eustis went below to interrogate Kudirka, Kudirka informed him that he was Lithuanian and not Russian. Kudirka also requested political asylum.

This information made its way back to one of the civilian delegates, Robert M. Brieze, president of the New Bedford Seafood Producers Association. Ironically, Brieze was a Latvian whose entire family had been deported to Siberia in 1941, and who had fled the Soviets in 1944. Brieze had earlier expressed anger that a ship named *Soviet Lithuania* was sailing into U.S. waters, despite the nonrecognition policy. Brieze went to see Commander Eustis and informed him of the policy, the presence of the Baltic desk at the State Department, and the danger to Kudirka were he returned to Soviet officials. He also advised that the Lithuanian Legation in Washington should be contacted.[19]

The incident, however, took a different course. The commander of the First Coast Guard District in Boston, Rear Admiral William B. Ellis, was recovering from an illness, and had relinquished district command to his chief of staff, Captain Fletcher W. Brown, Jr. Technically, Ellis was not in command and could issue no binding directives. Nonetheless, Brown informed Ellis of the situation and sought his advice. Admiral Ellis and other officers began displaying an appalling lack of historical knowledge. Ellis was unaware of the nonrecognition policy, and confused the concepts of defection and desertion. One of the officers thought that Brieze had escaped the Soviets in order to avoid the draft.[20] A radio conversation between Ellis and Commander Eustis was indicative of these attitudes:

> "In order to protect the fisheries talks," Ellis said, "you should notify the Soviets of the defection. You must also return the defector if they so desire. But if they choose to do nothing, keep him on board."

"But if the defector jumped overboard while the ships were unmooring," Eustis remarked, "The Vigilant could make an attempt to pick him up."

"In this case, too," Ellis replied, "the Soviet ship should be given the first opportunity. Make sure you don't preempt them in taking that action."[21]

When testifying after the incident, Ellis stated: "I'm not sure if [Captain Brown] said the man was a Lithuanian. I don't think it would have meant anything if he had. He was still a Soviet citizen."[22] Furthermore, although Ellis was formally not in command, his advice to subordinates acquired the ring of an order.[23]

By then the U.S. State Department had been drawn into the matter. Edward L. Killham was the officer in charge of bilateral affairs in the Office of Soviet Union Affairs. This was his third tour at the bilateral section of the Soviet desk. Killham was a senior foreign service officer with 18 years of experience. The initial report had been phoned to him by Captain Wallace C. Dahlgren, chief of the Intelligence Division in the U.S. Coast Guard Office of Operations. As a country officer, Killham possessed the authority to order a defector held by U.S. officials. However, he viewed this not as a genuine defection but rather as a possible Soviet attempt at provocation. In any event, U.S. officials appeared more concerned with the success of the negotiations than with the political ramifications of the incident.[24]

Not only were officials failing to address the basic issues of asylum and nonrecognition, the system itself was beginning to break down. Communications problems delayed transmissions. Bureaucratic procedures and chains of command were blurring among different actors at the Coast Guard and State Department. While Ellis and Killham appeared to be advocating one course of action, the Coast Guard district's legal officer, Commander Flanagan, advised that Kudirka should be detained, brought ashore, and transferred to either the State Department or the Immigration and Naturalization Service. Finally, the entire matter should have been handled at the Baltic, not the Soviet, desk.[25]

> The path of inquiry was becoming overgrown with the dense vegetation of bureaucracy. The problem itself had become distorted and reduced to a technical detail of a Search and Rescue operation with some potential political nuances.[26]

By now, the Soviets had discovered Kudirka's presence on board the *Vigilant* and demanded his return. The *Sovetskaya Litva's* commander, Captain Popov, lodged a maritime protest to the *Vigilant*, contending that Kudirka had stolen three thousand rubles from the safe in Popov's stateroom -- though rubles are worthless outside the Soviet Union.[27]

Brieze later testified:

> At approximately 11 p.m., Captain Eustis said that he had orders
> from above to give back the Lithuanian defector to the Russians.
> I then pleaded with Captain Eustis to save the defector's life and
> keep him aboard the Vigilant. Captain Eustis said he had no choice
> as he had received his orders. At this time Captain Eustis was
> crying. He said that the orders had come from the Boston office.[28]

Soon thereafter, Soviet sailors were allowed to board the *Vigilant*, and to capture, beat, and transport Kudirka back to the *Sovetskaya Litva*. Though distraught, Commander Eustis reportedly ordered the crew to remain silent regarding the incident. However, the three civilian fishermen aboard the *Vigilant* at the time made the story public. New Bedford shopkeepers refused service to Coast Guard personnel, who were also jeered in the town's streets. The *Vigilant* was placed under guard following bomb threats. Commander Eustis's home was placed under surveillance and his phone number was changed to an unlisted one. His two sons were harrased in the local school, including once by a teacher.[29]

The media response, in both liberal and conservative quarters, was critical. Although President Richard Nixon was informed only two days later, the story had already been nationally broadcast. International response was also harsh. One week following the Kudirka incident, the U.N. Commissioner for Refugees, Prince Sadrunin Khan, called on U.S. Ambassador Charles Yost and presented a protest addressed to Secretary of State William Rogers. Lithuanian-Americans staged massive demonstrations in major cities, protesting U.S. actions and demanding Kudirka's return.[30] President Nixon could not ignore the response, and stated at his news conference of 10 December 1970: "I can assure you it will never happen again.   The [U.S.] for 190 years has had a proud tradition of providing opportunities for refugees and guaranteeing their safety, and we are going to meet that tradition."[31]

Investigations conducted by Congress and the Coast Guard followed the much-publicized incident. During congressional hearings, Representative Edward Derwinski (R-IL) stated:

> The fact that the seaman involved was a Lithuanian, it is
> incomprehensible to me that anybody at a reasonable level in the
> Department of State, or anybody who had reached a captain's or
> admiral's rank in the Coast Guard, would not understand that the
> Soviet Union is made up of many captive peoples and a Lithuanian
> is not a Russian.[32]

During Robert Brieze's testimony, Representative John Buchanan (R-IL) added:

> It would appear, Mr. Brieze, that you have a better understanding
> of international law and of United States foreign policy than either

the Coast Guard or the State Department, since we do not recognize
that the Soviet Union has any right under Heaven to a Lithuanian
citizen seeking asylum.[33]

Indeed most official U.S. discussion of the Kudirka incident speaks of mistakes in
implementing asylum-granting procedures.   There is usually no mention of the
nonrecognition policy, indicating that a great many personnel are either unaware of
it or do not fully understand its implications in practical matters.   For example,
Louis F. E. Goldie, a professor at the U.S. Naval War College, writes that the
Kudirka incident "was merely an illegality [foreigners exercising authority on U.S.
territory] aided and abetted by an officer of the U.S. Coast Guard."[34]

Admiral Ellis, Captain Brown, and Commander Eustis were suspended
pending investigation. A Coast Guard board of investigation recommended general
courts-martial for Ellis and Brown. Secretary of Transportation John Volpe did not
concur with this decision, and provided the officers with the opportunity to retire
with punitive letters of reprimand; they took this route. Volpe did, however, concur
in Eustis's' reassignment. Eustis was transferred to Executive Base, Governor's
Island, New York, where he served as executive officer. He was passed over for
promotion to the rank of captain in May 1972.[35] Finally, the State Department
issued a policy directive dealing with asylum requests on 4 January 1972.
Guidelines were also issued to the Coast Guard.[36]

As for Kudirka, he was tried in secret and on 20 May 1971 he was
sentenced to ten years in a Siberian labor camp for high treason. At his trial, he
was allowed to speak for four hours, where he denied being a Soviet subject and
demanded independence for Lithuania. Lithuanian-American organizations, along
with a number of politicians, continued to work for his cause.   It was later
discovered that Kudirka's mother had been born in Brooklyn, New York, and had
later emigrated to Lithuania. Under U.S. law, since she was an American citizen,
Kudirka too could claim U.S. citizenship. Although the USSR does not recognize
dual citizenship, President Gerald Ford was able to strike a bargain with Soviet
General Secretary Leonid Brezhnev and won Kudirka's release. On 5 November
1974, a Soviet plane carrying Kudirka and his wife, daughter, and mother landed at
New York City's Kennedy Airport, almost four years after the incident off Martha's
Vineyard.[37]

As far as senior foreign service and naval officers were concerned, the
Kudirka incident revolved around the issue of political asylum. The matter only
incidentally involved a Lithuanian sailor. Nonrecognition here played a secondary
role in terms of bureaucratic decision making in a short-term situation, as well as
in long-term official analyses. Beyond the issuance of new asylum guidelines for
U.S. personnel and a pro forma reaffirmation of the policy, it was largely ignored.
Forced repatriation once again occured, but this time on a U.S. naval vessel in U.S.
territorial waters.   Had the incident not taken place in a politically charged
atmosphere, it might never have come to light, indicating the passive role of the

nonrecognition policy in official circles. As an announced policy, it has withstood the test of time. However, in a real world situation, it fell through the bureaucratic cracks.

THE HELSINKI ACCORDS

The Final Act of the Conference on Security and Cooperation in Europe was signed at Helsinki, Finland, on 1 August 1975. It climaxed a decade-long effort on the part of the Soviet Union to win confirmation of the territorial and political status quo on the continent. The act consisted of three "baskets" dealing with military confidence building, broad-based cooperation, and human rights. The Declaration on Principles Guiding Relations Between Participating States included provisions on sovereign equality, respect for the rights inherent in sovereignty, avoidance of the threat or use of force, territorial integrity, nonintervention in internal affairs, and the right of self-determination.[38]

Already three years prior to the signing of the Helsinki Accords, Americans of Eastern European descent were warning that the agreement could recognize the status quo in Europe, that is, Soviet domination of Eastern Europe, including the Baltic States. A Lithuanian-American delegation presented a memorandum to U.S. Secretary of State Henry Kissinger urging "that the international status of the Baltic states not be compromised" at the conference. U.S. officials, in turn, maintained that the U.S. advocated peaceful territorial changes and continued nonrecognition of the Baltic annexation.[39]

As the signing of the final act drew near, more activity was taking place between Congress and the State Department regarding the status of the nonrecognition policy. On 11 April 1975, Representative Thomas E. Morgan (D-PA), chairman of the House Committee on International Relations, received assurances from the State Department that nonrecognition would not be bargained away at Helsinki:

> The Department affirms that it remains the policy of the United States not to recognize the forcible annexation of the Baltic States by the USSR.
> The Department of State agrees...that the United States delegation to the Conference should not agree to the recognition by the Conference of the Soviet Union's forcible annexation of Estonia, Latvia and Lithuania. We expect that the Conference will adopt a declaration of principles which will include respect for "frontier inviolability" but in our view this will not involve recognition.[40]

On the very eve of the signing of the accords, President Gerald Ford, Secretary Kissinger, and congressional representatives received a delegation of

Americans of Eastern European descent in the White House. President Ford noted that the U.S. was not abandoning East Europe:

> We have acted in concert with our free and democratic partners to preserve our interests in Berlin and Germany, and have obtained the public commitment of the Warsaw Pact governments to the possibility of peaceful adjustment of frontiers -- a major concession which runs quite contrary to the allegation that present borders are being permanently frozen....
>
> Specifically addressing the understandable concern about the effect of the Helsinki declarations on the Baltic nations, I can assure you...that the United States has never recognized the Soviet incorporation of Lithuania, Latvia and Estonia and is not doing so now. Our official policy of non-recognition is not affected by the results of the European Security Conference.
>
> There is included in the declaration of principles on territorial integrity the provision that no occupation or acquisition of territory in violation of international law will be recognized as legal.[41]

In and of itself, the Helsinki signing did not violate the nonrecognition policy, especially in view of repeated U.S. pronouncements to this effect. What was disturbing were reports that Secretary Kissinger, the National Security Council, and the State Department sought to dilute the policy for the sake of detente. Bill Anderson reported in the *Chicago Tribune* on 15 March 1975 that:

> President Ford is getting advice to drop United States diplomatic recognition of Lithuania, Latvia, and Estonia....
>
> Opinion is so strong...that some officials in the White House initially tried to conceal from the press a [February] meeting by Ford with supporters of freedom for the Baltic States....
>
> It was felt that the highly motivated Baltic supporters would generate publicity and damage "delicate" dealings with Russia....
>
> This time Kissinger's staff lost to Ford's staff, although there was a compromise: The NSC wanted the Baltic group to talk only about "domestic" American matters and to see Ford without advertising the meeting. . . .
>
> Further compounding the NSC-State Department problem is the fact that Ford for some time has shown a higher-than-average Presidential interest in the Baltic situation.[42]

Anderson later reported that certain White House staffers prevented the Voice of America from broadcasting news of the visit, censored photographs, and attempted to have Representative Edward Derwinski, who had organized the meeting, reprimanded.[43]   When these disclosures were made, the State Department was subjected to "a rolling avalanche of outraged telephone calls, telegrams, and letters."[44]

About the time of the February delegation to the White House, the U.S. consul in Leningrad, Joseph V. Neubert, and his deputy, Garry L. Mathews, visited the Baltic States and met with senior communist officials.[45] The *New York Times* reported:

> The United States through its consulate [in Leningrad] is diluting a 35-year-old policy of refusing to recognize the incorporation of Lithuania, Latvia and Estonia into the Soviet Union.
>
> Western diplomats [in Leningrad] feel that there is a gradual but unmistakable American movement toward de facto, if not formal, recognition of the Soviet Baltic republics....
>
> [Consul General Neubert] acknowledged that in effect he was now the United States Ambassador to the three republics....
>
> Mr. Neubert adheres to American policy protocol by not making direct contacts with the highest party and government officials in the Baltic republics, but he has met with their deputies....
>
> The consulate, rather than the embassy in Moscow, has responsibility for reporting on the Baltic region to the State Department.[46]

Such developments only served to increase anxiety among those who clung to the policy as an important moral statement on the part of the United States.

Months after the signing of the Helsinki Accords, when the controversy would have been expected to settle, the House of Representatives saw fit to address the issue once again in terms of the nonrecognition policy. House Resolution 864 was approved by the House Subcommittee on International Political and Military Affairs on 18 November 1975, and was debated by the full House on 2 December. HR 864 stated, in part:

> Whereas the Soviet Union appears to interpret the Final Act of the Conference on Security and Cooperation in Europe, signed at Helsinki, as giving permanent status to the Soviet Union's illegal annexation of Estonia, Latvia, and Lithuania,...Now, therefore, be it
>
> *Resolved*, That notwithstanding any interpretation which the Soviet Union or any other country may attempt to give to the Final Act... it is the sense of the House of Representatives (1) that there has been no change in the longstanding policy of the United States on nonrecognition of the illegal seizure and annexation by the Soviet Union of the three Baltic nations..., and (2) that it will continue to be the policy of the United States not to recognize in any way the

annexation of the Baltic nations by the Soviet Union.[47]

During the debate, Representative Edward Koch (D-NY), tried to frame the resolution relative to detente:

> Detente is an admirable goal, but we need not -- and should not -- forsake the truth or acquiesce in oppression in our quest for better relations with the Soviet Union. If we acquiesce in the illegal incorporation of the Baltic States, are we not as guilty of cynical expediency as Russia and Germany were when they originally divided up this area of Eastern Europe in their pact of 1939?[48]

Koch went on to say that the nonrecognition policy in particular, and U.S. foreign policy in general, were designed to be definite statements to the world community: "What is the purpose of our foreign policy if it is not to encourage self-determination and democracy around the world?"[49] Representative Edward P. Boland (D-MA), too, emphasized that foreign policy addresses not merely domestic interest groups, but a broader international audience, as well: "We do not consider this resolution merely for those citizens of Latvian, Lithuanian, and Estonian descent. We mean by this resolution to express to the world that this body does not waiver in its commitment to freedom throughout the world."[50] House Resolution 864, directed mainly to the Kremlin's attention, was unanimously approved the same day. The Senate passed a similarly worded resolution, Senate Resolution 406, on 5 May 1976.[51]

Helsinki did not end with the signing of the accords in August 1975. The "Helsinki process" consists of follow-up review meetings and reports focusing on adherence to the political commitments made in 1975. Critics of the accords assert that continued meetings sanctify Soviet hegemony in Europe with nothing in return. Others say that the Helsinki process focuses attention on Soviet human-rights violations.[52]

The first review occured in Belgrade, Yugoslavia in 1977-1978. On 25 November 1977, Senator Robert Dole (R-KS) and Ambassador Arthur Goldberg of the U.S. delegation spoke of the Baltic States during addresses to the conference. The second review occured in Madrid in 1980-1981. On 15 December 1980, Warren Zimmerman, deputy chairman of the U.S. delegation, reaffirmed the nonrecognition policy, adding that the Soviet incorporation violated Principle Eight of the Helsinki Accords. Zimmerman also noted that territorial acquisition contrary to international law as listed in Principle Four was applicable to the Baltic.[53] For the Madrid conference, President Jimmy Carter appointed Rimas Cesonis as a public member of the U.S. delegation. Cesonis was a member of the public affairs committee of the Lithuanian American Community. The Vienna conference took place in 1986-1987. At the conference, the U.S. delegation repeated Washington's position on the Baltic.

The U.S. State Department and the U.S. Commission on Security and Cooperation in Europe, which is a mixed executive-legislative entity, issue periodic reports on the monitoring of the Helsinki process. They routinely reaffirm the nonrecognition policy, and chronicle the progress of human rights in the Baltic States under the equal rights and self-determination provisions of Principle Eight. However, at least in the State Department reports, the section dealing with Principle Eight usually repeats itself every year. In other places where activities are broken down by nation, the Baltic States are included in the Soviet Union.

It must be noted that the Final Act is not a treaty under international law, but rather a nonbinding declaration of intentions. The act explicitly states that it is not eligible for registration under Article 102 of the United Nations Charter.[54] The U.S., however, considers the 10 principles of the Helsinki Declaration to be "solemn moral and political undertakings drawn from the body of established international law."[55] Washington's position notwithstanding, the USSR claims that the Helsinki Declaration of Principles applies between East and West, but not necessarily between the Soviet Union and other Socialist states. Thus, as far as the Kremlin is concerned, the Final Act justifies behavior such as the 1968 invasion of Czechoslovakia.[56]

Finally, a number of commentators have addressed the supposed recognition of the Lithuanian occupation implicit in the Helsinki Accords. In retrospect, most advise against a defeatist interpretation of the Final Act, citing repeated U.S.-government pronouncements reaffirming nonrecognition. Indeed, they caution that concessions of recognition at Helsinki psychologically play into the hands of Soviet leaders. The signatories of the Final Act possessed no authority to determine the status of the Lithuanian state. Thus, regardless of what occured in Helsinki in 1975, the legal status of Lithuania remains unchanged.[57]

It appears that the status of Europe as a whole also remains unchanged. On 19 October 1977 at Belgrade, Ambassador Albert W. Sherer, deputy chairman of the U.S. delegation, conceded:

> The Europe envisaged by the Declaration of Principles is one in which each state feels secure in its basic interests without the need to assert special hegemonic rights or intra-alliance reservations. We have not yet reached that day. We must continue to work toward it.[58]

THE U.S. OFFICE OF SPECIAL INVESTIGATIONS

In 1975, Rep. Elizabeth Holtzman (D-NY) began planning legislation to amend the 1952 Immigration and Naturalization Act, which contained no specific provision excluding Nazi war criminals from the U.S. The amendment sought to identify, exclude, and deport persons who, under the Nazi regime, "engaged or assisted in or incited or ordered any other person to engage or assist in the persecution of any person on account of such person's race, religion or national origin." The act was signed by President Jimmy Carter in October 1978.[59] September of the following year saw the creation of the Office of Special Investigations (OSI) within the Justice Department's Criminal Division. Its task was the location and deportation of Nazi war criminals living in the United States.

Several months later, in January 1980, Walter S. Rockler, OSI director, and his deputy, Allan A. Ryan, Jr., traveled to Moscow to secure Soviet cooperation in identifying and prosecuting Eastern European war criminals. Most relevant documentation and witnesses were located in Soviet-controlled territory. Rockler and Ryan met with Soviet Procurator General Roman Rudenko. Though Ryan and others have termed the cooperative agreement reached a "handshake," Zumbakis writes that "a statement that no formal agreement or report was ever executed or exchanged is implausible, at best. The stakes were too important, the bureaucratic level too high, for a handshake agreement."[60] Zumbakis contends that there are documents related to the Moscow Agreement, but that the OSI objects to their release by the State Department.[61]

The OSI's activities have generated discussion over several issues beyond the scope of this study, including the presence of Nazi war criminals in the United States, utilization of Soviet evidence in American trials, the use of civil procedures without juries, Nazi activities in the Baltic States during World War II, discrimination against Americans of East European descent, and alleged Soviet machinations in tandem with the OSI. What is important here is the impact of the OSI on the nonrecognition policy. This was dramatically brought out during the deportation proceedings of Karl Linnas.

Karl Linnas was a retired 67-year-old land surveyor who lived with his wife and three daughters on Long Island, New York, in 1987. He was tried in absentia in his native Estonia in January 1962, and was sentenced to death for war crimes in connection with his alleged administration of a concentration camp during the German occupation of his country.[62] Following proceedings in the United States, Linnas's U.S. citizenship was revoked in 1981, and several federal courts ruled that he could be deported for lying on his 1951 visa application, where he wrote that he had been a student during the war. The U.S. Supreme Court cleared the way for Linnas's deportation on 27 January 1987. His family approached approximately 50 countries trying to find one -- other than the Soviet Union -- that would accept him. However, they all rejected Linnas's entry, and he was deported from New York City to Estonia on 20 April 1987.[63] He died, according to Soviet reports, of heart failure several months later.

In addition to the objections noted above, the Linnas deportation raised questions of nonrecognition as applied to Baltic citizenship. As noted at the beginning of this chapter, the presidium of the USSR Supreme Soviet issued a decree on 7 September 1940 converting Lithuanian, Latvian, and Estonian nationality to Soviet nationality. Those who recognize the incorporation of the

Baltic States into the Soviet Union regard Baltic refugees as stateless persons not entitled to diplomatic protection. The U.S., however, recognizes such persons as possessing their original Baltic citizenship, unless they have been naturalized as U.S. citizens.[64]

Linnas was naturalized and, later, denaturalized. At this point he came within the jurisdiction of the Immigration and Naturalization Service (INS). Because Linnas had lost his citizenship, he no longer possessed the right to remain in the U.S. An INS administrative law judge, along with the Board of Immigration Appeals, determined his deportability. Once this stage has been completed, a defendant can choose the country to which he or she wishes to be deported, provided the country in question agrees. In regard to the OSI trials, the only country that has been willing to accept deportees has been the Soviet Union.[65]

Presumably, when the U.S. deported Linnas to Soviet-occupied Estonia, it was violating the nonrecognition policy. However, Washington has not interpreted events in such a manner, but has focused more narrowly on deportation proceedings. In the first place, when a defendant is found guilty in an OSI trial, he or she is not guilty of war crimes per se, but of entering the United States illegally, for example, by lying on visa and citizenship applications. As such, the matter is a domestic one, completely divorced from events that may have taken place outside the U.S.

Then, deportation occurs under section 243 (a)(7) of the Immigration and Nationality Act, which deports a person to any country willing to accept him or her, and not on the basis of country of nationality or citizenship.[66] When Linnas went to Estonia, he was not going as an Estonian as far as the U.S. was concerned. In general terms, deportation:

> to the Soviet Union would not, as a matter of law, contravene the long-standing and firmly held U.S. policy of non-recognition of the forcible incorporation of Estonia into the Soviet Union. [US officials] strongly adhere to that policy and believe it is unaffected by [Linnas's] deportation.[67]

One group has cynically commented that "this response, although acknowledging the non-recognition policy, amounts to little more than lip service."[68]

Indeed, while the U.S. asserts that such deportations do not legally violate nonrecognition, the USSR politically may interpret them as a form of de facto recognition. Thus Washington may be looking at the matter much too narrowly, without considering the practical implications.[69] Furthermore, it is not known whether the nonrecognition policy was ever discussed in conjunction with the Moscow agreement.[70] While as a matter of principle, the director of OSI is barred from entering the Baltic, his or her subordinates may do so with an escort from the U.S. embassy in Moscow or the consulate in Leningrad.[71]

As of this writing, only one person of Baltic origin, Karl Linnas, has been deported to Soviet-occupied territory in the Baltic. With the strict, procedural U.S. interpretation of this and possibly other deportations, the OSI cases are not glaring legal examples of violation of nonrecognition, as were postwar repatriation and the Simas Kudirka incident. Realistically, however, it is difficult to reconcile deportation with nonrecognition. The punishment of war criminals is a vital task that must be vigorously pursued. However, perhaps a formula could be constructed whereby punishments would be served in the U.S., rather than the Baltic. Otherwise, a contemporary version of Operation Keelhaul may be underway.

CONCLUDING REMARKS

Chapter five of the present study examined the very real legal, political, diplomatic, and economic consequences of the nonrecognition policy. Chapters six and seven, on the other hand, saw that the policy could be circumvented. The case studies in this chapter recounted four instances of factual or perceptual violation of nonrecognition.

Postwar repatriation, the Kudirka incident, and the activities of the OSI impacted on individuals turned over to authorities not recognized as possessing legitimate jurisdiction over Lithuanian, Latvian, and Estonian nationals. In these cases, nonrecognition was either unknown or simply ignored. In any event, the policy was, at best, a secondary factor. Only at Helsinki did it assume greater importance. In fact, there its importance grew to the point of two rival bureaucracies, Ford's and Kissinger's, fighting over its appropriateness in that context -- as well as its viability at all. Interestingly, where the policy took center stage, at Helsinki, it was not violated despite the harsh rhetoric emanating from conservative and ethnic groups. Nonrecognition was only perceptually violated by the signing of the Helsinki Accords.

The U.S. government formally does not recognize the occupation and its logical consequences, that is, mass naturalization and the abandonment of sovereignty. These cases deal with Washington's commitment to that stand. However, there were other issues involved besides nonrecognition. For example, in repatriation and the Kudirka incident, matters of asylum and political persecution were also in play. Diplomacy, too, was a factor, for repatriation was executed in the afterglow of successful East-West wartime diplomacy, while Kudirka was handed back at the threshold of detente. The OSI presents another dilemma; namely, how to reconcile the policy with denaturalization proceedings while properly crusading against war criminals.

A student of nonrecognition cannot afford to ignore the limited practical role of Baltic diplomats in these cases. While they successfully operated to protect national interests in the legal and economic realms, the needs of diplomacy, coupled with bureaucratic ignorance or sabotage, limit their powers. The only guarantee that Baltic diplomats can expect under the nonrecognition policy is a courteous reception.

Nonrecognition hangs by a thread, as demonstrated in Kissinger's actions during Helsinki, the words of a U.S. consul (the pseudo-ambassador to the Baltic), and the legal tightrope walked by the OSI. Indeed, one human being was sacrificed for the sake of successful fishing talks. This is compounded by the occasional incompetence of those individuals seeking to preserve the policy, as seen in the fatalistic declarations of those convinced that the West sold out the Baltic States at Helsinki.

Be that as it may, the policy has not been forgotten. The controversy surrounding the Kudirka incident, as well as questions focused on the OSI, are indicative of this. The post-Helsinki declarations -- as always, bipartisan -- are also applicable here. The problem is not that the policy is never invoked, but rather that it is invoked after it has been violated. This is especially obvious in the most flagrant violations, repatriation and Kudirka. Ultimately, the policy exists to protect a group of people -- a task that has not always proved successful.

NOTES

1. U.S. Senate, Committee on Foreign Relations, *Consular Convention with the Soviet Union*, Hearings on Executive D (Washington, D.C.: U.S. Government Printing Office, 1967), p. 345.

2. Julius Epstein, *Operation Keelhaul: The Story of Forced Repatriation from 1944 to the Present* (Old Greenwich, CT: Devin-Adair, 1973), p. 21.

3. Ibid., p. 14 (author's emphasis).

4. Article 33, Section 1. See also U.N. General Assembly Resolution, 12 February 1946. Quoted in Epstein, pp. 16-17.

5. Epstein, *Operation Keelhaul*, pp. 25-26; U.S. Department of State, Foreign Relations of the United States, Diplomatic Papers, The Conferences at Malta and Yalta, 1945 (Washington, D.C.: U.S. Government Printing Office, 1955), pp. 985-987.

Some individuals maintained a suspicion that there was a secret protocol attached to the Yalta document regarding forced repatriation. See "Secret Yalta Displaced Persons Clauses," Baltic Review, 1, 4-5 (July-August 1946), 238-240.

6. Juri Piiroja, Eugen Ulk, Karlis Kundzins, Arvedis Schvabe, Pranas Rudinskas, Leopoldas Balsys, *Baltic Refugees and Displaced Persons* (London: Boreas, 1947), pp. 15-16. See also Janis Skrundens, Latvia 1918-1968 (New York: American Latvian Association, 1968), p. 22.

7. U.S. Department of State, *Foreign Relations of the United States*, Diplomatic Papers, 1944, Volume IV, Europe (Washington, D.C.: U.S. Government Printing Office, 1966), p. 1258.

8. U.S. Department of State, *Foreign Relations of the United States*, 1944, IV, p. 1260.

9. Epstein, *Operation Keelhaul*, pp. 1ff. Epstein writes that he was not allowed access to the secret U.S. files on Operation Keelhaul.

10. Allied Expeditionary Force, Supreme Headquarters, G-5 Division, Displaced Persons Branch, *Guide to the Care of Displaced Persons in Germany*, revised May 1945.

11. Piiroja, et al., *Baltic Refugees*, pp. 10, 14.

12. Alseika, *Trys desimtmeciai emigracijoje*, p. 71. U.S. officers also urged Baltics to return to their homelands. Pp. 71-72 describe a visit to the Hanau camp by a Captain Moses on 10 June 1947. He told the Lithuanians there that their future was uncertain. Lithuania was in need of people for administration and industry. He claimed that those who had returned were writing positive letters about their postrepatriation experiences. See also Stasys Mingaila, Neapkenciamo zmogaus uzrasai (Writings of an intolerable person) (Western-occupied Germany: Author, 1948), p. 61.

13. John Alexander Swettenham, *The Tragedy of the Baltic States: A Report Compiled from Official Documents and Eyewitnesses' Reports* (New York: Praeger, 1954) p. 177.

14. Antanas Kucas, *Amerikos lietuviu istorija* (American Lithuanian history) (South Boston: Lithuanian Encyclopedia Press, 1971), p. 567.

15. Watson Kirkconnell, "Eclipse of Baltic Freedom," *Baltic Review*, 1, 4-5 (July-August 1946), 221; Kucas, Amerikos lietuviu istorija, p. 567; Swettenham, Tragedy, p. 180.

16. Epstein, *Operation Keelhaul*, p. 1. Secretary of State James F. Byrnes wrote: "We support [the displaced persons] and will not force them to return...as long as there is reason to believe they would be punished for political reasons." See his Speaking Frankly (New York: Harper and Brothers, 1947), p. 168.

17. Grzybowski, *Soviet Public International Law*, p. 239.

18. Public Law 555, An Act to Amend the Displaced Persons Act of 1948, 16 June 1950, section 2(d). See also Public Law 203, Refugee Relief Act of 1953, 7 August 1953.

19. Jurgis Gliauda, *Simas*, trans. Kestutis Ciziunas and J. Zemkalnis (New York: Manyland, 1971), pp. 3, 53-54; Algis Ruksenas, Day of Shame: The Truth about the Murderous Happenings aboard the Cutter "Vigilant" during the Russian-American Confrontation off Martha's Vineyard (New York: David McKay, 1973), pp. xv, 15; U.S. House of Representatives, Attempted Defection by Lithuanian Seaman Simas Kudirka, Hearings before the Subcommittee on State Department Organization and Foreign Operations, Committee on Foreign Affairs (Washington, D.C.: U.S. Government Printing Office, 1971), pp. 31ff.

20. Gliauda, *Simas*, pp. 25-26; Ruksenas, Day of Shame, pp. 277-279; U.S. House of Representatives, Attempted Defection by Lithuanian Seaman Simas Kudirka, Report of the Subcommittee on State Department Organization and Foreign Operations, Committee on Foreign Affairs (Washington, D.C.: U.S. Government Printing Office, 1971), pp. 7-9.

21. Gliauda, *Simas*, pp. 51-52.

22. Ruksenas, *Day of Shame*, p. 279.

23. Gliauda, *Simas*, p. 26.

24. Ibid., pp. 37-38; Ruksenas, *Day of Shame*, p. 86.

25. Gliauda, *Simas*, pp. 42-43; Ruksenas, Day of Shame, pp. 190, 192, 198, 276-287; U.S. House of Representatives, Attempted Defection, Hearings, pp. 37, 115.

26. Gliauda, *Simas*, p. 36.   Documents from the Lithuanian Consulate General in Chicago, now located at the Lithuanian Research and Studies Center, indicate that confusion abounded not only during the incident, but following it, as well.   Vague information was being received from U.S. government agencies, including an incorrect rendition of Kudirka's name as Simas Gruze.

27. Ibid., pp. 80-81.

28. U.S. House of Representatives, *Attempted Defection*, Hearings, p. 35. See also Ruksenas, Day of Shame, pp. 173, 225.

29. Kucas, *Amerikos lietuviu istorija*, p. 304; Ruksenas, Day of Shame, p. 275.

30. Kucas, *Amerikos lietuviu istorija*, pp. 303-304; Ruksenas, Day of Shame, pp. 265-266, 270, 272-274.

31. Ibid., p. 275.

32. U.S. House of Representatives, *Attempted Defection*, Hearings, p. 4.

33. Ibid., p. 41.

34. Louis F. E. Goldie, "Legal Aspects of the Refusal of Asylum by U.S. Coast Guard on 23 November, 1970," *Lituanus*, 18, 3 (Fall 1972), 63.

35. Ruksenas, *Day of Shame*, pp. 294-298. For other accounts of the Kudirka incident, see Joanne S. Gowa, U.S. Obligations under International Law Governing the Status of Refugees and the Granting of Asylum: The Case of Simas Kudirka. Monograph Series in Public Affairs No. 6 (Princeton, NJ: Woodrow Wilson School of Public and International Affairs, Princeton University, 1975); Clyde R. Mann, "Asylum Denied: The Vigilant Incident," Lituanus, 18, 3 (Fall 1972), 13-57; Lieutenant Commander Paul M. Regan, USCG, "International Law and the Naval Commander," US Naval Institute Proceedings, 107, 8 (August 1981), 51ff.

36. Gerhard von Glahn, *Law among Nations: An Introduction to Public International Law*, 4th ed. (New York: Macmillan, 1981), pp. 276-277.

37. Kudirka wrote his memoirs after arriving in the United States. See Simas Kudirka and Larry Eichel, *For Those Still at Sea: The Defection of a Lithuanian Sailor* (New York: Dial, 1978).

38. U.S. General Accounting Office, *Helsinki Commission: The First 8 Years*. Report to the Chairman of the Commission on Security and Cooperation in Europe. GAO/NSIAD-85-57, 1 March 1985 (Washington, D.C.: U.S. Government Printing Office, 1985), pp. i, 1-2; U.S. House of Representatives, Conference on Security and Cooperation in Europe, Part II.   Hearings   before   the   Subcommittee   on

International Political and Military Affairs of the Committee on International Relations (Washington, D.C.: U.S. Government Printing Office, 1976), pp. 121-124.

39. Baltic Committee in Scandinavia (BCS), *Memorandum Regarding the European Security and Cooperation Conference* and the Baltic States (Stockholm: BCS, 1972), p. 2; Budreckis, Lithuanians in America, p. 64; U.S. Department of State, letter of Acting Assistant Secretary for Public Affairs John Richardson, Jr. to Ilmar Pleer, president of the Estonian-American National Council, 21 September 1973.

40. U.S. House of Representatives, Subcommittee on International Political and Military Affairs, Committee on International Relations, *Conference on Security and Cooperation in Europe* (Washington, D.C.: U.S. Government Printing Office, 1975), p. 11.

41. U.S. Department of State, *Department of State Bulletin*, 73, 1885, 11 August 1975, pp. 204-206. West German Foreign Minister Hans-Dietrich Genscher on 25 July 1975, and British Prime Minister Harold Wilson on 5 August 1975 declared to their respective parliaments that the Helsinki Accords did not recognize the status quo in Europe as final. See Kaslas, The Baltic Nations, pp. 277-278.

42. Bill Anderson, "Ford Is Urged to Cut Our Baltic Ties," *Chicago Tribune*, 15 March 1975, sec. 1, p. 10.

43. Bill Anderson, "New Stress over the Baltic Lands," *Chicago Tribune*, 18 March 1975, sec. 2, p. 2.

44. "Forgive Them Their Helplessness," editorial, *Chicago Tribune*, 5 April 1975, sec. 1, p. 12.   See also William I. Bacchus, "Multilateral Foreign Policy Making: The Conference on Security and Cooperation in Europe," in The Politics of Policy Making in America: Five Case Studies, ed. David A. Caputo (San Francisco: Freeman, 1977), pp. 132-165.

45. U.S. House of Representatives, *Conference on Security*, p. 37.

46. James F. Clarity, "U.S. Eases Policy on Baltic States," *The New York Times*, 18 May 1975, p. 16.

47. U.S. Congress, *Congressional Record*, 2 December 1975, p. H 11587. See also U.S. House of Representatives, Conference on Security, Part II, pp. 1-2.

48. U.S. Congress, *Congressional Record*, 2 December 1975, p. H 11589.

49. U.S. Congress, *Congressional Record*, 2 December 1975, p. H 11589.

50. U.S. Congress, *Congressional Record*, 2 December 1975, p. H 11589.

51. U.S. Senate, Senate Resolution 406, 5 May 1976, section 5, pp. 4-6.

52. U.S. General Accounting Office, *Helsinki Commission*, p. 2. See also Zinta Arums, Joint Baltic American National Committee (JBANC) 1986 Annual Report (Rockville, MD: JBANC, 1987), pp. 7-9; John B. Genys, "The Joint Baltic American Committee and the European Security Conference," Journal of Baltic Studies, 9 (1978), 245-258.

53. Edgars Dunsdorfs, *The Baltic Dilemma II: The Case of the reversal of the De Jure Recognition by Australia of the Incorporation of the Baltic States into the*

Soviet Union (Melbourne: Baltic Council of Australia, 1982), pp. 382-383; U.S. Commission on Security and Cooperation in Europe, The Belgrade Followup Meeting to the Conference on Security and Cooperation in Europe: A Report and Appraisal, transmitted to the Committee on International Relations, U.S. House of Representatives (Washington, D.C.: U.S. Government Printing Office, 1978), p. 23.

54. Kaslas, *The Baltic Nations*, pp. 277-278; U.S. Commission on Security and Cooperation In Europe (USCSCE), Report to the Congress of the United States on Implementation of the Final Act of the Conference on Security and Cooperation in Europe: Findings and Recommendations Two Years after Helsinki (Washington, D.C.: USCSCE, 1977), p. 4.

55. U.S. Department of State, *The Belgrade Followup Meeting to the Conference on Security and Cooperation in Europe*. October 4, 1977-March 9, 1978 (Washington, D.C.: U.S. Government Printing Office, 1978), p. 13.

56. U.S. Department of State, *Belgrade Followup Meeting*, pp. 13-14.

57. Kazys Sidlauskas, *Amerikos Lietuviu Tarybos veiklos penkmetis* (Lithuanian American Council: Five year summary of activity) (Chicago: LAC, 1980), pp. 8, 10; Petras Stravinskas, Ir sviesa ir tiesa: Rastai ir credo I (And light and truth: Writings and credo I) (Chicago: Valerijonas Simkus, 1978), pp. 74-78.

58. U.S. Department of State, *Belgrade Followup Meeting*, p. 14.

59. Public Law 95-549, 30 October 1978. 92 Stat. 2065, 8 U.S.C. 1251 (a)(19)(1978). See also Silvia Kucenas, "OSI Collaborates with KGB," *Lituanus*, 30, 1 (Spring 1984), 85; U.S. House of Representatives, House Report No. 95-1452 (Washington, D.C.: U.S. Government Printing Office, 1978); S. Paul Zumbakis, Soviet Evidence in North American Courts: An Analysis of Problems and Concerns With Reliance on Communist Source Evidence in Alleged War Criminal Trials (Woodhaven, NY: Americans for Due Process, 1986), pp. 5-6.

60. Ibid., p. 30.   Ryan was appointed OSI director in 1980, and was succeeded by Neal Sher in 1983.

> Rudenko represented the Soviet Union as a prosecutor in the Nuremberg trials, during which he personally attempted to have a "confession" entered into evidence, which the tribunal at Nuremberg discovered had been signed by the witness after several months in solitary confinement and in which all questions and answers had been prepared by Moscow interrogators. In 1952, General Rudenko was personally in command of the slaughter of inmates in a Ural gulag (Ibid., p. 29n).

61. Ibid., p. 30.

62. Though he was formally tried in January 1962, the guilty verdict had already appeared in the 7 December 1961 issue of *Socialist Legality*, published in the USSR.

63. Arums, *Annual Report*, p. 23. See also Charles R. Allen, Jr., Nazi War Criminals among Us (New York: Jewish Currents, 1963), pp. 29-32; Richard Lacayo, "Problems of Crime and Punishment," Time, 20 April 1987, p. 60.

64. N. Kaasik, "The Legal Status of Baltic Refugees," *Baltic Review*, 1, 1 (December 1945), 23-24.

65. Lithuanian American Community, "Memorandum of Concerns Regarding the Conduct of the Office of Special Investigations," *Lituanus*, 31, 4 (Winter 1985), p. 70.

66. 8 U.S.C. 1253 (a)(7).

67. U.S. Department of State, letter of Acting Assistant Secretary for Public Affairs and Acting Spokesman Alan D. Romberg to Jonas Urbonas, chairman, Public Affairs Council, Lithuanian American Community, 18 January 1985, quoted in Lithuanian American Community, "Memorandum of Concerns," p. 71.

68. Ibid. See also "Karl Linnas' Deportation and USA Nonrecognition Policy," *Lituanus*, 31, 4 (Winter 1985), 91.

69. Lithuanian American Community, "Memorandum of Concerns," p. 72.

70. Zumbakis, *Soviet Evidence*, p. 32.

71. Balys Raugas, ed., *JAV LB trys desimtmeciai* (Three decades of the Lithuanian American Community) (Brooklyn: LAC, 1982), p. 290. This notwithstanding, it is interesting to note that a former OSI director frequently utilizes quotation marks when refering to the nonrecognition policy, implying that he does not consider it important, valid, or both. For example, see Allan A. Ryan, Jr., Quiet Neighbors: Prosecuting Nazi War Criminals in America (San Diego: Harcourt Brace Jovanovich, 1984), p. 68.

9

Conclusion

LITHUANIAN DIPLOMATIC CONTINUITY

As the nonrecognition policy entered the 1970s, concern began to mount over the diplomatic continuity of the Republic of Lithuania in the United States. Since the incorporation, diplomatic and consular personnel had remained on duty, supported from the assets frozen by Washington on 15 July 1940. They had also been able to appoint successors when needed. Thus, when Minister Povilas Zadeikis died in 1957, his counselor, Juozas Kajeckas, succeeded him. In turn, Kajeckas's assistant, Dr. Stasys Backis, succeeded him in 1977 following a long illness.[1] However, while honorary consuls could be appointed with little difficulty, the representation at the legation could not be replaced as easily.[2] The U.S. ruled that only individuals commissioned in the Lithuanian foreign service at the time of the occupation could serve at the legation. The problem for continuity was obvious.[3]

Funds to support Lithuanian diplomatic and consular activities in the U.S. and abroad were also dwindling at this time. Representative Charles Dougherty (R-PA) and Senator John Heinz (R-PA) decided to address this issue. After considering several alternatives, such as allowing the U.S. government to cover financial shortfalls not met by Lithuanian-American donations and having Congress establish a large, permanent trust fund, Dougherty and Heinz proposed legislation in which the U.S. government would provide $250,000 annually to the Lithuanian legation as of 1981:

> (a) there is authorized to be appropriated for fiscal year 1981 to the legation of Lithuania in the United States, $250,000.
> (b) The Charge d'Affaires of the legation...is authorized to receive, on behalf of such legation, any funds appropriated under this Act to such legation, and is authorized to administer such funds. Such funds may only be used for the maintenance of the operations of such legation. The Charge d'Affaires may use such funds to pay the compensation of personnel which the Charge d'Affaires may appoint

to be in the diplomatic corps of the legation, except that all such personnel must be of Lithuanian parentage and may not be United States citizens. Such personnel shall be entitled to all the privileges and immunities of diplomatic personnel of comparable rank from other countries.[4]

The State Department, however, did not agree with that manner of financial support:

The sponsors of H.R. 5407 [Rep. Dougherty's bill] believe that after having recognized the Legations's diplomatic status for more than 39 years, it would be inappropriate for the United States to permit the Lithuanian Charge d'Affaires and the small and dwindling corps of Lithuanian diplomats and their families to face a bleak future.

The Department thoroughly shares this view. However, the Department also believes that to provide direct U.S. Government financial assistance to the Lithuanian Legation would degrade the valid and important degree of independence which the Lithuanian Charge d'Affaires, an accredited foreign diplomatic representative, now possesses from the U.S. Government and from U.S. domestic politics and related considerations....

I am pleased to inform you that we are in the final stages of working out an arrangement which will provide for the continuing financial requirements of the Lithuanian Legation.[5]

The arrangement to which the State Department was referring was the pooling of the resources of all three Baltic countries, the bulk of which came from Latvian funds. This was accomplished in 1980.

While the financial security of the Lithuanian diplomatic corps was assured for the near future, the rule that only officers commissioned as of June 1940 could serve would practically invalidate that victory. This problem, however, would soon be resolved as well. In what was probably the most important victory for proponents of the nonrecognition policy since the promulgation of the policy itself, Dr. Stephen Aiello, special assistant to President Jimmy Carter for ethnic affairs, announced in October 1980:

Up until now, we have accepted as diplomatic representatives of the Baltic countries only individuals who were in 1940 commissioned officers of the diplomatic services of the last independent governments. With the passage of time, the number of individuals accreditable under this standard has dwindled to a handful. In view of the important symbolic role of Baltic diplomatic representation, we...are prepared, in response to their request, to coordinate closely with the three present Baltic Charges d'Affaires on designation of their successors in order to provide for continued representation when the present corps of Baltic diplomats is no longer able to function.[6]

This opened the door for a successor to the aging minister in Washington, Dr. Stasys Backis. Backis had been charge since 1 January 1977 and deputy chief of the Lithuanian Diplomatic Service since 20 August 1978. He succeeded to the post of chief upon the death of Stasys Lozoraitis, Sr., on 24 December 1983, and continued to serve as minister in Washington. Meanwhile, on 6 December 1983, Stasys Lozoraitis, Jr., had been confirmed as Backis' counselor. On 15 November 1987, Backis retired as Lithuania's envoy and was succeeded by Lozoraitis, Jr. Backis continues to serve as chief of the service, while officially listed as counselor of legation in Washington. Lozoraitis, Jr., who was not a commissioned officer in 1940, is now Lithuanian representative to both the U.S. and the Vatican.

The Lithuanian legation periodically presents its credentials to the U.S. State Department, disseminates information on the current situation in Lithuania, and sees to it that the status of diplomatic and consular personnel is maintained. Because new appointments are not made by a head of state, the Lithuanian representative is officially a charge d'affaires accredited to the U.S. Secretary of State. In the State Department's *Diplomatic List*, charges are listed in order of their precedence immediately after ambassadors. The senior charge d'affaires in Washington at this writing is Latvian envoy Dr. Anatol Dinbergs, who has served since 1 October 1970. Up until his retirement, Stasys Backis was second charge in order of precedence. The last individual on the list is Ernst Jaakson, Estonian consul general in New York City in charge of legation since 15 December 1965.

As indicated above, honorary consular personnel in the U.S. had been appointed for a number of years, replacing retiring or deceased officers. Mrs. Mary Krauchunas served as vice consul in Chicago from 1983 to 1985. Mr. Vytautas Cekanauskas was appointed consul general in Los Angeles in 1977. Mrs. Josephine Dauzvardis was appointed consul general in Chicago in 1972, and was succeeded by Mr. Vaclovas Kleiza in 1985. There are currently three Lithuanian consuls general in the U.S.: Cekanauskas, Kleiza, and Anicetas Simutis in New York City. Simutis is the only Lithuanian consul general who can provide full consular services to Lithuanian citizens, including the issuance of Lithuanian passports. His jurisdiction encompasses the entire United States, including its territories and possessions. He is not an honorary consul because he was on duty as a consular officer in New York at the time of occupation. He became vice consul in 1951, consul in 1965, and consul general in 1967.

As honorary, and not career, consuls, and as naturalized U.S. citizens, Cekanauskas and Kleiza are subject to the tax laws of the United States, except for fees accepted for consular services.[7] As far as Washington is concerned,

As a matter of U.S. policy, honorary consular officers recognized by the

U.S. Government are American citizens or permanent resident aliens who perform consular services on a part-time basis. The limited immunity afforded honorary consular officers is specified in Article 71 of the [Vienna Convention on Consular Relations]. However, such individuals do not enjoy personal inviolability and may be arrested pending trial if circumstances should otherwise warrant. However, appropriate steps must be provided to accord to such officers the protection required by virtue of their official position. In addition, the consular archives and documents of a consular post headed by an honorary consular officer are inviolable at all times and wherever they may be, provided they are kept separate from other papers and documents of a private or commercial nature relating to the other activities of an honorary consular officer or person working with that consular officer.[8]

LITHUANIA AND THE PHILOSOPHY OF STATEHOOD

As historians often point out, Lithuania was not a state fabricated during the twentieth century, but a nation that had achieved statehood in the thirteenth century. Though formal statehood and the exercise of sovereignty have occasionally been interrupted, the essence of statehood has been alive within the Lithuanian nation for over seven hundred years.

A renewed consciousness of Lithuanian statehood and citizenship appeared before the formal reconstitution of the Lithuanian state during the national renaissance of the late nineteenth century. Statehood manifested itself during various rebellions, the Vilnius Conference of 1905, the 1918 declaration of independence, the wars of independence and, finally, governmental activity until the occupation of 1940. Statehood also manifested itself during the 1941 national revolt, which attempted to reconstitute the Lithuanian state following the Soviet retreat and, after the return of the Red Army, in underground and overt partisan activity.[9]

A century of national revival, culminating in the establishment of an independent state, produced among the Lithuanians strong commitments to national ideas and to the national state. The younger generation especially, sensitive to the medieval traditions of Lithuanian statehood, took modern Lithuania's independence as an axiomatic fact and therefore refused to reconcile itself to its loss.[10]

Statehood is as much a subjective factor of consciousness as it is an objective factor of formal governmental apparatus. The consciousness of a state's goals and tasks leads to a consciousness of duty and obligations toward the state, that is, laboring for and defending it. One commentator stresses the importance of civic consciousness and education during the course of a national occupation. This entails the study of a state's past, democratic principles, legal foundations, and civil-legal goals. In addition to this, however, a citizen of an occupied state must develop new ideas and look to an independent future. If this is not done, statehood itself will be in jeopardy.[11]

This is especially valid when applied to smaller nations. In this regard, V. V. Sveics is quoted here at length:

> Many Big Power ideologists condemn nationalism, and a number of scholars habitually use the term *nationalism* only in a negative sense. However, small nations must recognize and rely on nationalism as a primary source of their strength.
>
> ...Nationalism has become an expression of a nation's will to live and its individualism. It has become a symbol of the dignity of peoples. It is the feeling of belonging to a national brotherhood. In many instances it is the strongest and most durable social bond.
>
> From the point of view of...defense and survival, nationalism -- a product of patriotic loyalty and uniting cohesion -- is the main source of strength. It fixes the basic loyalty, the political objectives, the strategy, and many techniques in the struggles to defend a nation.
>
> Nationalism, adequately mobilized, is an impressive force. In situations of political and social conflict, it enhances national strength in various ways: (a) rallies the nation's forces, (b) unifies them, (c) clarifies the issues of the struggle, distinguishes friend from foe, and (d) provides a guiding philosophy, a sense of direction, an understanding of the goals to be achieved.
>
> Small states and nations that do possess the precious inheritance of nationalism should recognize its value as a foundation of national survival. They should build their future on it.[12]

Lithuanian Minister Dr. Stasys Backis has written that, along with the use of atomic energy, the fight against colonialism is the most distinctive feature of the postwar world.[13] Those fighting for independence in Asia and Africa over the past four decades have realized that an independent state is the most desirable vehicle for the refinement of a nation's social, economic, and cultural progress. Some have gone so far as to assert that the supppression of a nation's progress toward those goals, as well as the forced subjugation of a state, are violations of international law. The mere existence of a state is enough to grant it the right to survival; recognition by other states is unnecessary. As such, all nations, regardless of size and strength, are morally and juridically equal.[14]

Be that as it may, Alfred Cobban has pointed out the practical difficulties in such an approach. He notes that the will of struggling populations has played less of a role in decolonization than the will of the major powers. Thus, while admitting the rights of nationality, the power of a state -- or lack thereof -- cannot be ignored. Such limitations mean that the greater states will, perhaps necessarily, exert the most power on the global stage.[15] Cobban goes on to ask:

> How do these [realities] affect the prospects of national self-determination? Local autonomy may solve the problems of some of the smaller communities, but there are a considerable number of small nations which, because of their history as separate political entities, or their experience of national oppression in the past, will not be satisfied with anything short of political independence and the rank of state. ...On the other hand...we cannot avoid the conclusion that the smaller nations or states are dependent for their economic well-being on the policies of the great world powers. Economic resources mean military power, and the concentration of the one in the modern world has as its concomitant a concentration of the other.[16]

Obviously, as Cobban indicates, sovereignty without an adequate economic or military defense is an oxymoron. In 1940, Lithuania was forced to bend to superior force, although the country and its citizens were never released from their rights and obligations in the international community.[17] Practically speaking, in order to lift the suspension of sovereignty, the lack of resistance in 1940 has presented problems:

> Their surrender of national sovereignty can be both understood and regretted. With no expectation of assistance, they were powerless to withstand Soviet aggression. Yet, in retrospect, it is clear that the cause of independence would have been served better in the eyes of the world through resistance. Finland's stout but futile resistance evoked widespread admiration. No one could have expected the Baltic States to defeat the Soviet Union but even token opposition would have been remembered in a more favorable light than was the almost docile submission.[18]

In the end, however,

> the conception of equality belongs not to the field of power but to that of rights. If we are saying anything that is worth saying when we talk of national equality, we must mean an equality of rights. We come back then to a fundamental question of political philosophy. If it is agreed that the rights of a nation are to be interpreted not in terms of power or prestige, but in terms of the interests of its citizens, then, when we say that all nations are equal we mean that they all have

equal rights to economic, cultural and spiritual well-being.[19]

Evidently, through the nonrecognition policy, the United States still recognizes the existence of the independent Lithuanian state, and the fact that its organs are competent to discuss and represent Lithuania's affairs, although with certain practical limitations.[20] However, as William Hough notes, the de facto presence of Soviet power in that country cannot be forever ignored and, without an international coercive authority, Moscow cannot be compelled to leave. He cites three possibilities of legalization of territorial title: prescription, or the continuous and undisturbed exercise of sovereignty; validation by the injured party; and a quasi-legal action by the international community. As far as Lithuania is concerned, the first method has been disturbed, the second has come by way of spurious plebiscites and installed regimes, and the third has not occured and is not likely to.[21] He concludes that Lithuania does indeed juridically still exist, for

> in light of historical and legal precedents, it must be concluded that the
> only truly legal validation of an illegal annexation remains the genuine
> approbation by the injured party or total and complete acquiescence
> in the face of overwhelming force by the indigenous population and
> third party members.[22]

Thus, Washington is not being unreasonable in asserting its policy of nonrecognition.

Lithuania may juridically still exist as far as the United States is concerned and, as previous chapters have noted, this possesses concrete legal and political consequences. Practically, however, she lives only as the Lithuanian SSR, a union republic of the USSR. According to Article 80 of the Soviet constitution, "A Union Republic has the right to enter into relations with other states, conclude treaties with them, exchange diplomatic and consular representatives, and take part in the work of international organizations."[23] However, under nonrecognition, the U.S. has rejected any overtures from the Lithuanian SSR foreign ministry.

April 1956, however, saw rumors and news reports that Lithuania, Latvia, and Estonia might be granted satellite status as "people's democracies." There was even a report that the 20th congress of the Soviet Communist Party had secretly resolved to have Moscow formally relinquish sovereignty over the Baltic States.[24]

A new People's Democracy of Lithuania, if recognized as a legitimate government by Washington, would then be the heir to the claims of its predecessor, that is, the prewar Lithuanian government. The government in Vilnius would receive title to the assets of procedure located in the U.S. This would include deposits, investments, facilities, and the contents of offices. The Lithuanian diplomats currently stationed in this country presumably would be made to vacate the premises by the new government, and Washington would have no choice but to acquiesce. Lithuania would also most likely be successful in a claim to a seat in the United Nations. While this is obviously sheer speculation, satellite status for

Lithuania and the other Baltic States would present a dilemma for the U.S. and other nations espousing a nonrecognition policy.[25] As of 1990, Lithuania's statehood survives in a different form.

NORMATIVE DIMENSIONS OF NONRECOGNITION

Hough writes that two principles have been at odds in interstate relations for over five thousand years: Machiavelli's *La forza fa giustizia* (Might makes right) and the legal maxim *Ex iniuria ius non oritur* (Legal rights will not arise from illegality).[26]

The U.S. government and interested parties have long stressed the normative nature of the nonrecognition policy, which seeks to apply law, not Machiavellian politics, to the Lithuanian situation. Some commentators have stated that normative goals have little if anything to do with nonrecognition. Algirdas Gustaitis, for example, writes that the U.S. political establishment tries to keep matters related to the policy in a secondary position, not going beyond occasional formalities. He contends that Lithuanians should not be naive as to Washington's intentions toward a small nation. As far as he is concerned, votes and publicity are of primary concern here.[27] Historian Constantine Jurgela wrote that nonrecognition "is not an active policy."[28]

Gerard Mangone correctly points out that international values, or lack thereof, are at the foundation of the nonrecognition policy's effectiveness:

International law, now or in the future, cannot be substituted for international politics. Nevertheless, a substantial improvement in international lawmaking must be made soon if legal definitions, procedures, and judgements ever hope to bridle a few of the startling changes in international relations today that threaten to jar the universe. Lawmaking cannot proceed more rapidly than the shared values of a community, and these, in turn, depend on a rough harmony of economic, ideological, aesthetic, and other interests. International law can be no better than the international political system that nurtures it.[29]

Von Glahn correctly adds "that individual or multilateral declarations concerning the invalidity of conquest as a source of territorial titles have been more than counterbalanced by the contrary practices of states."[30]

This is the crux of the impotence of the nonrecognition policy, for if the nations that make up the global community refuse to obey international law, there can be no hope of collective enforcement:

It is inaccurate and dangerous to assimilate a declaration of this sort to a sanction. Inaccurate, because the only effective sanction is that which is applied collectively in fulfillment of their common obligations by those in a position to bring the aggressor back to respect for the law. Dangerous, because the egoism of States easily induces them to limit to such declarations their resistance to aggression.[31]

If no action is taken, "time is hard on 'theoretical' nations. In an exile of more than 20 years [at that time], the operation becomes diplomacy by petition, a paper diplomacy of words while the deeds behind the words fade away and are conveniently forgotten."[32]

While it is true that pursuit of "good relations" with the Soviet Union may obscure normative goals regarding the Baltic States in particular, and East-West issues in general,[33] Lithuanian Minister Dr. Stasys Backis urges both scholars and laypersons to combine sentiment and jurisprudence with the realities of foreign policy.[34] It was clear from the very enunciation of the nonrecognition policy that the U.S. would not wage war to liberate Lithuania, Latvia, and Estonia. On the other hand, Washington has not abandoned the idea of independence for the three countries.

Indeed, in a sense the U.S. has done more for the Baltic States in terms of her national existence than for other countries. For example, Lithuanian diplomats in Berlin and Moscow believed that Germany and the Soviet Union were the sources of Lithuania's salvation, yet in the last few years of independence, during the course of ultimatums presented by Poland, Germany, and the USSR, those two powers did not offer even symbolic support. The U.S., in its continuing condemnation of the incorporation, stands out as a leader in the international cause for the liberation of the Baltic.

The United States has long infused morality and idealism into her foreign policy. This mentality as applied to the incorporation of the Baltic was, in Senator Charles J. Kersten's words, "in the true American spirit."[35] When viewing the normative character of U.S. foreign policy,

> it cannot be said, although at times it has been so stated, that all these purposive principles, charters, and declarations were only empty words. Standing alone, neither the moral tenets nor the qualities of power and interest define the totality of political endeavor. Rather, that totality contains both.[36]

Thus morality, although it cannot stand alone, is an integral component of Washington's policy toward other nations. While power could not realistically be applied toward liberating the Baltic States, morality certainly has not been ignored. Richard Schnorf, for example, is of the opinion that although nonrecognition was, and is, a politically sound policy, it was not undertaken in response to political expedience, the U.S. ethnic electorate, or the pleas of Baltic diplomats in the United States. U.S. diplomats in the Baltic correctly interpreted the nature of the occupation, elections, and subsequent annexation as staged and illegal. The diplomats reported the immorality of the process to Washington, which responded with a policy "solidly based on moral grounds" and disapproval of Stalin's actions.[37]

As seen in Chapter 6, the course of wartime diplomacy did witness some dilution of the nonrecognition policy. However, one cannot ignore the instances when Washington has reaffirmed its stand. President Roosevelt, Undersecretary Welles, and other staff at the State Department faced incredible pressure from London to ignore the policy during the spring of 1942, when Britain was fighting a desperate battle against Germany and seeking Moscow's support. Though it could have helped inter-Allied relations, the U.S. government did not back down from the policy at a time when the future of the war hung in the balance. Eventually, the Soviets relented and signed a treaty that did not compromise the status of the Baltic.[38]

More recently, the U.S. reaffirmed the nonrecognition policy on another occasion when political expedience and diplomatic courtesy would have warranted its suppression. On 15-19 September 1986, a town meeting-style conference took place in Jurmala, Latvia. It was sponsored by the Chautauqua Institute of Jamestown, N.Y., and attended by approximately 270 U.S. government officials and private citizens. U.S. officials -- wearing lapel pins depicting the U.S. and independent Latvian flags -- reaffirmed the policy for the first time ever on Baltic soil. Indeed, a Soviet official traveled from Moscow to denounce the policy, which was receiving great attention inside the conference as well as outside. This reportedly had a positive impact on the Latvian citizenry. The effect of the policy on morale in the Baltic is a significant factor, although average citizens often do not fully know of or understand it.[39]

While the nonrecognition policy is far from perfect in achieving its goals, the United States' continued adherence to it is primarily based in the morality advocated by the tenets of international law.[40] In the final analysis, normatively, "non-recognition is the most pertinent manifestation of the postulate that a unilateral tour de force should not be allowed to bring about a valid change in the existing territorial order."[41]

A POLICY AWAITING COMPLETION

Of course, ultimately the status of Lithuania and the Baltic States under international law is determined by foreign governments. For many, the Baltic States have ceased to exist as separate political and juridical entities. Although the Soviet Union is guilty according to the letter of the law, no practical action has been taken to redress the grievance.

Does a state exist through recognition or by fulfilling certain conditions of statehood? For Lithuania, statehood, as granted by the U.S. government, is limited and honorary -- a hollow statehood. For, as Raymond Aron writes:

Major historical events, those by which the states are born and die, are external to the juridical order. The Baltic States have ceased to exist, they are no longer subjects of law; nothing the Soviet Union does on the territories that, in 1939, were subject to the Estonian or Lithuanian sovereignty any longer relates to international law, at least in the eyes of those of the states that have ceased to "recognize" Estonia, Lithuania, and Latvia (that is, almost every state). When a state is crossed off the map of the world, it is the victim of a violation of international law. If no one comes to its aid, it will soon be forgotten and the state that has delivered the *coup de grace* will be no less welcome in the assemblies of so-called peaceful nations.[42]

On the other hand, at least in the United States, the political and juridical impact of nonrecognition is quite real. If sovereignty is once again able to be effectively exercised, it will be done by the prewar, though reconstituted, governments of the Baltic. New states will not be created.[43] This is true regardless of the time it takes to achieve restoration, for as Krystyna Marek writes:

In the case of the Baltic States the finality of Soviet annexation cannot be admitted at the present time. The Soviet claim to the domination of the Baltic States continues to be rejected by the international community. No general post-war international instrument has confirmed the existing state of affairs in the Baltic. No general peace-making in Europe has taken place and no foundations of any new international delimitation have been laid. This does not mean that a constitutive and validating effect would attach to such settlements *per se*. It merely means that nothing even approximately final has taken place which would totally destroy any *reasonable chance* of an *ad integrum restitutio* of the Baltic States.

It is precisely the persistence of this reasonable chance of restitution which determines the time-limit up to which the international legal system can withstand a divorce between validity and effectiveness.[44]

Many say that the occupation and incorporation are past history and should be accepted, albeit reluctantly. Nonrecognition is only a fiction with no practical effect. On the other hand, it could be asserted that the matter is important to this day, not only because of the fact that the Baltic States are strategically located with implications for international power politics, but also precisely because of the symbolic value, with symbolism not used as a synonym for trivia.[45] Is public policy merely a practical instrument, or does it also possess some normative dimension? Obviously, Washington has long been concerned with such issues.

Despite the pessimism often attending discussions of nonrecognition, this study has pointed out concrete legal and political effects involving citizenship, restrictions on U.S. government officials, and millions of dollars of assets. One cannot say that Moscow is pleased with the policy, although it has learned to live with it. One cannot ignore the positive effect of the policy on morale in the Baltic. The people living in that region know that they have not been forgotten, and that the events of 1940 have not been erased from history books on the western side of the Iron Curtain.[46] It has also been claimed that:

> the uncertain international status of these nations discourages a great many Soviet citizens from settling in the Baltic countries. Thus it reduces the flow of colonists and considerably hinders Soviet genocidal policies of colonization, ethnic dilution, Russification and effective absorption of Baltic nations into the Soviet Union.
>
> There are indications that this non-recognition of annexation has also had a restraining effect on Soviet repressive policies since their authorities have to consider the possibility that extreme measures of repression in the Baltic countries might not be regarded as an internal matter of the Soviet Union and could provoke protests in the United Nations and elsewhere.[47]

It is probably most accurate to state that the nonrecognition policy has yet to reach its logical conclusion, namely the restoration of practical sovereignty to Lithuania, Latvia, and Estonia. This is the practical, albeit long-term, goal of the policy. While this possibility is kept alive by nonrecogniton, the specific -- and realistic -- moral goals of the policy's founders are achieved. Hence, it is a successful policy. *Ex iniuria ius non oritur*, which does not allow valid title to arise from an invalid act, is precisely what the policy asserts. Washington's continuous reaffirmation of the policy reflects a refusal to confer a title that does not conform to international standards of law and morality, regardless of how imperfectly enforced. The Soviet Union continues to be regarded as a mere occupant in the Baltic, and the Stimson Doctrine remains a vital and viable component of the law. Martin Brakas asserts:

> To a great degree, non-recognition is to be qualified as a kind of intervention against the annexing state....Negative as this intervention by non-recognition may be, it throws a dark shadow of immorality and delinquency on the annexing state's status, brands that state as a law-breaker in the eyes of the world, and interferes with its political and diplomatic freedom of action....Even in this world of imperfect justice in international relations, arbitrariness of states, no matter how mightily and supreme, has its limits where the existence of law *qua* law is endangered.[48]

While asserting the nonrecognition policy, the U.S. government does not practically alter U.S.-Soviet relations, but it nevertheless makes a statement emanating from the very principles on which it stands. It may not be a powerful force against practical exigencies, but it is an important one, for it represents not only the aspirations of Lithuanians, Latvians, and Estonians, but of Americans as well.

NOTES

1. Kajeckas died the following year. See Norma Krause Herzfeld, "The Persistent Lithuanians: A Government without a country," *The Catholic Reporter*, 9 June 1961, sec. 2, p. 1.

2. Mrs. Josephine J. Dauzvardis succeeded her late husband, Dr. Petras Dauzvardis, as consul general in Chicago on 12 November 1972, although in an honorary capacity. Vytautas Cekanauskas succeeded the late honorary Consul General Dr. Julius J. Bielskis in Los Angeles on 6 October 1977. Indeed, the Chicago consulate was upgraded to a consulate general on 11 August 1961. See C. Surdokas, "Lietuvos diplomatine ir konsularine tarnyba II" (Lithuania's diplomatic and consular corps II), *Karys*, 9 (November 1987), 410.

3. The pessimistic tone regarding this matter can be seen in John Sherwood, "The Keeper of Lithuania's Fading Flame," *Chicago Tribune*, 13 July 1978, sec. 2, pp. 1, 4.

4. Senate Resolution 2257 in U.S. Congress, *Congressional Record*, 4 February 1980. Rep. Dougherty had introduced similar legislation in the House on 26 September 1979. See House Resolution 5407.

5. U.S. Department of State, letter of Assistant Secretary for Congressional Relations J. Brian Atwood to Rep. Clement J. Zablocki, chairman, House Committee on Foreign Affairs, 8 February 1980, pp. 1-2. See also U.S. Department State, Statement by Robert L. Barry, Assistant Secretary for European Affairs, before the Subcommittee on International Organizations, House Foreign Affairs Committee, 26 June 1979, p. 5.

6. Stephen Aiello, White House Office of Public Affairs, draft statement, reprinted in *Draugas*, 28 October 1980, p. 1. Aiello, along with his deputy, Victoria Mongiardo, delivered this statement at the annual meeting of the board of directors of the Lithuanian American Community in Chicago just before the November election.

7. John R. Wood and Jean Serres, *Diplomatic Ceremonial and Protocol: Principles, Procedures and Practices* (New York: Columbia University Press, 1970), p. 76.

8. U.S. Department of State, *Foreign Consular Offices*, February 1988, pp. i-ii.

9. Petras Stravinskas, *Ir sviesa ir tiesa: Rastai ir credo. Pirma knyga* (And light and truth: Writings and credo. A first book) (Chicago: Valerijonas Simkus, 1978), pp. 33-35.

10. Zenonas Ivinskis, "The Lithuanian Revolt against the Soviets in 1941," *Lituanus*, 12, 2 (Summer 1966), 5-6.

11. Stasys Backis, "Lietuvos valstybes tarptautine teisine ir politine padetis" (The international legal and political status of the Lithuanian state), in *Lietuva okupacijoje* (Lithuania under occupation), ed. Jonas Balkunas (New York: World Lithuanian Community Congress, 1958), p. 124; Stravinskas, Ir sviesa ir tiesa, pp. 32-33, 37-38.

12. V. V. Sveics, "Nationalism: A Source of Strength for Small Nations," in *Fourth Conference on Baltic Studies: Summaries of Papers* (Brooklyn: Association for the Advancement of Baltic Studies, 1974), p. 69.

13. Stasys Backis, "Kataliku baznycios doktrina apie tautu apsisprendimo teise" (The Catholic Church's Doctrine on Self-Determination), in *Suvaziavimo darbai IV* (Proceedings IV), ed. A. Liuima (Rome: Lithuanian Catholic Academy of Sciences, 1961), p. 52.

14. Konstantinas Rackauskas, "Power Politics vs. International Law," *Baltic Review*, 14 (1 August 1958), 64-65; Antanas Trimakas, "The Soviet Disregard of the Right of Peoples to Self-Determination," Baltic Review, 16 (April 1959), 37.

15. Alfred Cobban, *The Nation State and National Self-Determination* (New York: Crowell, 1970), pp. 289, 301.

16. Cobban, *The Nation State*, p. 284.

17. Backis, "Lietuvos valstybes tarptautine teisine ir politine padetis," p. 123; Cobban, *The Nation State*, p. 285.

18. Richard A. Schnorf, "The Baltic States in U.S.-Soviet Relations: From Truman to Johnson," *Lituanus*, 14, 3 (Fall 1968), 57.

19. Cobban, *The Nation State*, p. 305.

20. See Backis, "Kataliku baznycios doktrina," p. 55.

21. Hough, "Annexation," pp. 468ff.

22. Ibid., p. 480. William L. Tung writes:

If a territory is under the suzerainty of a state which later incorporates it as an integral part of the country, the validity of the action depends upon the wishes of the majority of the population and the international status of the incorporated territory. The detachment of part of the territory of one state by another through conquest followed by the establishment of a puppet regime is really annexation under disguise.

See his *International Law in an Organizing World* (New York: Crowell, 1968), p. 165.

23. *Constitution (Fundamental Law) of the Union of Soviet Socialist Republics.* Adopted at the Seventh (Special) Session of the Supreme Soviet of the USSR, Ninth Convocation, on October 7, 1977 (Moscow: Novosti, 1977), article 80.

24. Antanas Trimakas, "Satellite Status for the Baltic States-A Possible Opening for Freedom," *Baltic Review*, 7 (16 June 1956), 3-4.

25. "Kremlin Tactics In Converting the Baltic States Into Satellites," *Baltic Review*, 7 (16 June 1956), 14-15; Gerhard von Glahn, Law among Nations: An Introduction to Public International Law, 4th ed. (New York: Macmillan, 1981), p. 103.

26. Hough, "Annexation," pp. 303-304.

27. Algirdas Gustaitis, *Simas Kudirka Nobelio taikos premijai* (Simas Kudirka for the Nobel Peace Prize) (n.p.: Europos lietuvis/European Lithuanian, 1971), pp. 8, 11. For an example of symbolism with regard to the nonrecognition policy, one can note that the flags of the independent Baltic States were planted on the moon in May 1972 by the crew of Apollo 16. They were later presented to Baltic diplomats. See statement of Senator Charles H. Percy (R-IL), 21 March 1972, p. 1. The flags are also permanently hung in the Kennedy Center for the Performing Arts in Washington. See Robert Keatley,"Homeless Diplomats: Their Lands Are Gone, Their Mission Remains," The Wall Street Journal, 20 March 1973, p. 1. p. 1.

28. Constantine R. Jurgela, letter to Robert A. Vitas, 22 May 1986. Povilas A. Mazeika writes:

During times of peaceful relations (including the period of the Cold War) the Baltic nations cannot, of course, count on any significant moral or political help from outside the Soviet Russian empire. The question is then whether there are forces within the empire leading to eventual liberation.

See his "Russian Objectives in the Baltic Countries," in *Problems of Mininations: Baltic Perspectives*, eds. Arvids Ziedonis, Jr., Rein Taagepera, and Mardi Valgemae (San Jose, CA: Association for the Advancement of Baltic Studies, 1973), p. 124.

29. Gerard J. Mangone, *The Elements of International Law*, rev. ed. (Homewood, IL: Dorsey Press, 1967), p. 526. Mangone writes: "The eye of the student, scholar, and statesman, therefore, should be fixed on ways to make the current practice of international law contribute to a desirable future for mankind. Put another way, they should be prepared to engage in a battle for values (p. v)."

30. Von Glahn, *Law among Nations*, p. 325.

31. Charles de Visscher, *Theory and Reality in Public International Law*, rev. ed., trans. P. E. Corbett (Princeton, NJ: Princeton University Press, 1968), p. 329.

32. Herzfeld, "The Persistent Lithuanians," p. 1.

33. Trimakas, "The Soviet Disregard," p. 9, writes: "Western pressure on the Kremlin has been mild, although embarassing to the Soviet leaders." Cf. Richard Pipes, *Survival Is Not Enough: Soviet Realities and America's Future* (New York: Simon and Schuster, 1984); Jean-Francois Revel, How Democracies Perish (New York: Doubleday, 1984).

34. Backis, "Lietuvos valstybes tarptautine teisine ir politine padetis," p. 117.

35. Charles J. Kersten, *Self-Determination of the Enslaved Nations-The Only Basis for True Peace*, address before the Lithuanian Chamber of Commerce of Illinois (LCCI), Bismarck Hotel, Chicago, 17 May 1953 (Chicago: LCCI, c. 1953), p. 1.

36. Leonas Sabaliunas, "Baltic Perspectives: The Disillusionment with the West and the Choices Ahead," *Lituanus*, 14, 2 (Summer 1968), 13.

37. Richard A. Schnorf, "The Baltic States in U.S.-Soviet Relations, 1939-1942," *Lituanus*, 12, 1 (Spring 1966), 36-38; Schnorf, "The Baltic States...From Truman to Johnson," 58. In "The Baltic States...1939-1942," p. 36, Schnorf writes:

It is doubtful whether the Baltic diplomats alone could have caused the United States to refer to the proceedings in the Baltic States as "devious processes." Even with the backing of a much larger ethnic group, the Polish Ambassador in 1945 was not able to convince the United States to maintain recognition of the legitimate Polish Government in London.

38. Edmund R. Padvaiskas, "World War II Russian-American Relations and the Baltic States: A Test Case," *Lituanus*, 28, 2 (Summer 1982), 22.

39. Hough, "Annexation," p. 481; *In Re Linnas*, U.S. Immigration Court, New York City, case A8 085 628, 5 April 1985; U.S. House of Representatives, Subcommittee on International Political and Military Affairs, Committee on International Relations, Conference on Security and Cooperation in Europe (Washington, D.C.: U.S. Government Printing Office, 1975), p. 27.

40. Robert Langer, *Seizure of Territory: The Stimson Doctrine and Related Principles in Legal Theory and Diplomatic Practice* (Princeton, NJ: Princeton University Press, 1947), p. 119, writes: "In the field of political life there are no best, only second-best solutions." Cf. David Braybrooke and Charles E. Lindblom, A Strategy of Decision: Policy Evaluation as a Social Process (New York: Free Press, 1970).

41. Langer, *Seizure of Territory*, p. 288.

42. Raymond Aron, *Peace and War: A Theory of International Relations*, trans. Richard Howard and Annette Baker Fox (Garden City, NY: Doubleday, 1966), p. 108. See also Philip C. Jessup, Transnational Law (New Haven, CT: Yale University Press, 1956), p. 62.

43. Marek, p. 416; Alexander Shtromas, "Political and Legal Aspects of the Soviet Occupation and Incorporation of the Baltic States," *Baltic Forum*, 1, 1 (Fall 1984), 38.

44. Marek, *Identity and Continuity*, p. 415. See also U.S. Displaced Persons Commission, Second Semiannual Report to the President and the Congress, 1 August 1949 (Washington, D.C.: U.S. Government Printing Office, 1949), pp. 12-13

45. E. Krepp, *Security and Non-Aggression: Baltic States and U.S.S.R. Treaties of Non-Aggression* (Stockholm: Estonian Information Centre, Latvian National Foundation, 1973), p. 5.

46. Langer, *Seizure of Territory*, p. 288; Schnorf, "The Baltic States...From Truman to Johnson," p. 59.

47. U.S. House of Representatives, *Conference on Security*, p. 27.

48. Martin Brakas, "Lithuania's International Status: Some Legal Aspects 2," *Baltic Review*, 38 (August 1971), 12-13.

10

Epilogue:
Entering the 1990s

When the research for, and writing of, this study commenced, the new political winds initiated by Soviet leader Mikhail Gorbachev had just begun to blow across the face of the Soviet Union, including Lithuania and the other Baltic States. As the work neared its completion, radical changes were occuring in Lithuania.

Two organizations in that country, the Lithuanian Reorganization Association (*Lietuvos Persitvarkymo Sajudis*) and the Lithuanian Freedom League (Lietuvos Laisves Lyga) were created and openly operated, demanding sociopolitical changes in Lithuania.

In terms of religious liberty, St. Casimir Church had been reopened, mass had been said in the Vilnius Cathedral, Bishop Vincentas Sladkevicius had been elevated to cardinal, and Bishop Julijonas Steponavicius had been allowed to return from internal exile to the Vilnius diocese.

Politically, the chief of Lithuania's Communist Party, Ringaudas Songaila, resigned in October 1988 after only one year in office. He was replaced by Algirdas Brazauskas. The country has also witnessed environmental demonstrations and mass political rallies, culminating in the legalization of independent Lithuania's tricolor and its raising on the fortress of Grand Duke Gediminas in the capital of Vilnius, over which the flag of the Lithuanian SSR had flown for four decades. Discussions continue over the creation of separate Lithuanian currency and postage stamps. Finally, several leaders of Lithuanian exile organizations were invited to participate in political organization within Lithuania.

Discussion over the possibility of autonomy within the Soviet Union has increased. Although no prominent Lithuanians have called for independence, the logical culmination of current events, even if it took several decades, would indeed be the restoration of complete Lithuanian political independence. In historical parallel, Lithuania today stands in the same position as during the national renaissance, which occured at the turn of the present century. At that time, autonomy was the goal of Lithuanian leaders, with independence emerging as a viable option only shortly before the declaration of independence on 16 February 1918. Of course, there is a difference in that the Lithuanian population today is a more educated one, not having been subject to the long-term russification efforts that had been practiced by the czars.

In terms of the U.S. nonrecognition policy, it appears that morality and reality may occasionally converge. As was mentioned in Chapter 6 of the present study, the United States stayed the nonrecognition course and took the moral high ground at a time when it would have been politically expedient to repudiate the policy. Certain State Department diehards, Loy Wesley Henderson among them, were of the opinion that nonrecognition possessed long-term implications for Lithuania's international personality, in addition to the practical effects as denoted in Chapter 5. Washington has not abandoned the idea of independence for Lithuania.

It has been this author's contention that the Roosevelt administration never intended nonrecognition to commit the U.S. to actually liberate Lithuania. This task would have to be accomplished by the Lithuanians themselves. The events of 1988-1989 are bearing this out. The policy crafted in Washington is now awaiting completion in Vilnius. Lithuanians there are not going to allow the legitimization of the Soviet presence there by way of unopposed prescription or formal plebiscitary validation. Statehood exists not solely through recognition, but by an active manifestation of state consciousness. This exists in Lithuania, without yet possessing the formal apparatus of statehood.

In terms of future U.S. policy, those who wish to push nonrecognition along to its intended conclusion would do best to subtly exercise political leverage toward Moscow and inter-republic cooperation in the Soviet Union. For example, a leader of the Armenian national movement has visited Kaunas to discuss common issues and goals with Lithuanians.

Indeed, both Americans and Lithuanians must be subtle and reasoned in their approach to the new political freedoms. A backlash from the Soviets must be avoided. The Lithuanian Reorganization Association, which is made up of leading intellectuals, has not referred to itself as a party, and is more cautious in its dealings with the Kremlin than is the Lithuanian Freedom League, which has a more emotional base of support. If the Lithuanians do not restrain themselves from making excessive demands, Moscow could take away the freedoms and changes won in the past year. Organizations and activities could once again be declared anti-Soviet manifestations, martial law could be declared, and the Red Army could easily stage extended military maneuvers in the country, as it did during the Polish unrest in the early 1980s. The harsh Soviet reaction to Georgian demonstrations in the early part of 1989 is a more recent example.

The same caution must be exercised in Washington as well. Demagoguery and unreasonable demands would not serve the nonrecognition policy well, although nonrecognition is itself a form of active intervention. Indeed, the U.S. can now take advantage of citizen exchanges between this country and Lithuania to gain information as well as to exert political influence and encourage the current process in Lithuania. The U.S. effort must be private and adroit, and not subject to needless publicity.

If an independent Lithuanian republic is restored, it will be the legal continuation of the regime extinguished in the summer of 1940. Practically, as mentioned in the study, it will be socioeconomically very different from its predecessor. However, it will still be considered the legitimate heir to the mantle of the Lithuanian government reconstituted at the conclusion of World War I, and will be able to make the legal and financial claims of its predecessor.

What of Lithuania's diplomats in the U.S.? Their status was extended under President Carter. A future independent Lithuanian republic could retain and augment the already existing network of envoys and consuls, or it could replace it. In any event, the Lithuanian government would have the advantage of possessing international representation and continuity, an advantage that did not exist in 1918. Indeed, there have already been calls for separate membership for Lithuania in the United Nations.

The debate over the utility of nonrecognition continues to this day, and is probably not fully embraced by U.S. policymakers. However, it continues to exist and it cannot be denied that it has had a positive impact on its target country. The U.S. has maintained Lithuania's legal personality in the courts and in treaties, as well as in the maintenance of the Lithuanian Diplomatic Service and independent Lithuania's assets. The nonrecognition process is now being furthered in Lithuania. If the process is not halted or mismanaged, the policy will arrive at its logical conclusion -- and thus will one day no longer be necessary.

Editor's Note: This epilogue reflects the author's thinking at the end of 1989, prior to Lithuania's independence movement in the spring of 1990.

Bibliography

Books

Abend, Hallett. *Half Slave, Half Free: This Divided World*. Indianapolis: Bobbs-Merrill, 1950, 304 pp., figures.

Aizenas, Cahaimas. "Istorinis posukis" (Historic turn). In *Uz ateiti sviesia: Is atsiminimu I 1918-1940* (For a brighter Future: Reminiscences I 1918-1940). Eds. K. Kalniuviene and D. Melyniene. Vilnius: Mintis, 1980, pp. 193-205.

Akademiia nauk SSSR, Institut gosudarstva i prava. *International Law: A Textbook for Use in Law Schools*. Trans. Dennis Ogden. Moscow: Foreign Languages Publishing House, 1961, 477 pp.

Akehurst, Michael. *A Modern Introduction to International Law*. Winchester, MA: Unwin Hyman, 1987, 320 pp.

Alantas, Vytautas, ed. *Antanas Vanagaitis*. Sodus, MI: J. J. Baciunas, 1954, 192 pp., ill.

Alexiev, Alex. *Soviet Nationalities in German Wartime Strategy, 1941-1945*. Report R-2772-NA. Santa Monica, CA: Rand, 1982, 39 pp.

Alilunas, Leo J., ed. *Lithuanians in the United States: Selected Studies*. San Francisco: R & E Research Associates, 1978, 185 pp.

Allen, Charles R., Jr. *Nazi War Criminals among Us*. New York:Jewish Currents, 1963, 42 pp., ill.

Alseika, Vytautas. *Trys desimtmeciai emigracijoje: Nuo Roitlingeno iki Niujorko* (Three decades of emigration: From Reutlingen to New York). Vilnius: Mintis, 1977, 320 pp., ill.

Ambrose, Aleksas. *Chicagos lietuviu istorija 1869-1959* (History of Lithuanians in Chicago 1869-1959). Chicago: Lithuanian-American Historical Society, 1967, 664 pp., ill.

Amerikos Lietuviu Misija ir jos darbai (The American Lithuanian Mission and its activity). Detroit: Viktoras Petrikas, 1945, 32 pp., ill.

Aron, Raymond. *Peace and War: A Theory of International Relations.* Trans. Richard Howard and Annette Baker Fox. Garden City, NY: Doubleday, 1966.

The Atlantic Charter or the Lifeboat of Millions of People Who Lost Their Homes. Amberg, Sweden: C. Mayr, 1941, 7 pp.

Audenas, Juozas. "The Activities of the Supreme Committee for Liberation of Lithuania." In *Twenty Years' Struggle for Freedom of Lithuania.* Ed. Juozas Audenas. New York: ELTA, 1963, pp. 40-92, ill., map.

_____. Paskutinis posedis: Atsiminimai (Final conference: Reminiscences). New York: Romuva, 1966, 278 pp.

Audrunas, Jonas, and Petras Svyrius. *Lietuva tironu panciuose I: Bolseviku okupacija* (Lithuania in the bonds of tyrants I: Bolshevik occupation). Cleveland: Lietuvai vaduoti sajunga/Association to Liberate Lithuania, 1946, 312 pp., ill.

Augustaitis, Jonas. *Dvieju pasauleziuru varzybos* (The contest of two worldviews). Chicago: Author, 1977, 159 pp., ill.

Ausrotas, Bronius. *Sunkiu sprendimu metai* (Year of difficult decisions). Chicago: Lithuanian Book Club, 1985, 237 pp., ill.

Baade, Hans W., ed. *The Soviet Impact on International Law.* Dobbs Ferry, NY: Oceana, 1965, 174 pp.

Bacchus, William I. "Multilateral Foreign Policy Making: The Conference on Security and Cooperation in Europe." In *The Politics of Policy Making in America: Five Case Studies.* Ed. David A. Caputo. San Francisco: Freeman, 1977, pp. 132-165, ill., figures.

Bachunas, J. J.. *Antanas Olis.* Sodus, MI: Author, 1953, 20 pp., ill.

_____. *Vincas S. Jokubynas.* Sodus, MI: Author, 1954, 12 pp., ill.

Backis, Stasys. "Lietuvos valstybes tarptautine teisine ir politine padetis" (The international legal and political status of the Lithuanian state). In *Lietuva okupacijoje* (Lithuania under occupation). Ed. Jonas Balkunas. New York: World Lithuanian Community Congress Committee, 1958, pp. 117-127.

Bailey, Bernardine. *The Captive Nations: Our First Line of Defense.* Chicago: Chas. Hallberg, 1969, 191 pp., ill.

Baltic Humanitarian Association. *The Baltic Refugees.* Stockholm: Baltic Humanitarian Association, 1946, 20 pp., figures, map.

Baltutis, Viktoras, ed. *Australijos lietuviu metrastis II* (Australian Lithuanian yearbook II). Adelaide: Australian Lithuanian Community, Australian Lithuanian Foundation, 1983, 496 pp., ill.

Balys, Jonas, ed. *Lithuania and Lithuanians: A Selected Bibliography.* New York: Lithuanian Research Institute, Praeger, 1961, 190 pp.

Baras, K. *Tremtinio pergyvenimai keliaujant is pavergtos Lietuvos, per ivairius krastus, i laisves sali* (An emigrant's experiences traveling from occupied Lithuania, through various countries, to the land of freedom). Chicago: Draugas, 1942, 80 pp.

Barkauskas, Antanas. *Manoji Respublika* (My republic). Vilnius: Mintis, 1980, 190 pp., ill.

Barron, Bryton. *Inside the State Department*. New York: Comet, 1956.

Beitz, Charles R. *Political Theory and International Relations*. Princeton, NJ: Princeton University Press, 1979, 212 pp.

Berzinsh, Alfreds. *I Saw Vishinsky Bolshevize Latvia*. Washington, D.C.: Latvian Legation, 1948, 56 pp., ill., figures, map.

Bilmanis, Alfred. *What Latvia Wishes From This War? Background, Actual Situation, Hopes for Future*. Washington, D.C.: Latvian Legation, 1943, 23 pp., ill.

_____. *The Baltic States in Post-War Europe*. Washington, D.C.: Latvian Legation, 1943, 86 pp., figures, maps; 2d ed. 1944, 48 pp., ill., figures, maps.

_____. *Baltic Essays*. Washington, D.C.: Latvian Legation, 1945.

_____. *Latvia as an Independent State*. Washington, D.C.: Latvian Legation, 1947, 405 pp., ill., figures, maps.

_____. *The Problem of the Baltic in Historical Perspective*. Heidelberg, West Germany: Scholar, 1948, 12 pp.

_____. *A History of Latvia*. Princeton, NJ: Princeton University Press, 1951, 441 pp., ill., maps.

Bimba, Antanas. *Naujoji Lietuva faktu ir dokumentu sviesoje* (New Lithuania in the light of facts and documents). Chicago: Lietuvos Draugu Komitetas/Friends of Lithuania Committee, 1940, 201 pp.

_____. *Prisikelusi Lietuva: Tarybu Lietuvos liaudies ir vyriausybes zygiai ekonominiam ir kulturiniam salies gyvenimui atstatyti* (Risen Lithuania: Steps taken by the masses and leadership of Soviet Lithuania to restore economic and cultural life). New York: Amerikos lietuviu darbininku literaturos draugija/American Lithuanian Workers Literary Society, 1946, 224 pp., ill., maps.

Blieka, J., et al., eds. *Tarybu Lietuvos valstybes ir teises dvidesimtmetis (Two decades of state and law in Soviet Lithuania)*. Vilnius: State Political and Scientific Press, 1960, 304 pp.

Bot, B. R. *Nonrecognition and Treaty Relations*. Leyden, the Netherlands: A. W. Sijthoff, 1968, 286 pp.

Braybrooke, David, and Charles E. Lindblom. *A Strategy of Decision: Policy Evaluation as a Social Process*. New York: Free Press, 1970.

British League for European Freedom. *The Baltic States*. Edinburgh: British League for European Freedom, Scottish Section, 1945, 27 pp.

Buchan, John, ed. *The Baltic and Caucasian States: The Nations of To-day. A New History of the World*. Boston: Houghton Mifflin, 1923, 269 pp., figures, maps.

Budreckis, Algirdas. *The Lithuanian National Revolt of 1941*. South Boston: Lithuanian Encyclopedia Press, 1968, 147 pp., maps.

_____. *Soviet Occupation and Annexation of the Republic of Lithuania June 15-August 3, 1940*. New York: American Lithuanian National Association,

1968, 31 pp.

_____. "Liberation Attempts from Abroad." In *Lithuania 700 Years*, 2d rev. ed. Ed. Albertas Gerutis. New York: Manyland, 1969, pp. 378-425.

_____, ed. *The Lithuanians in America 1651-1975: A Chronology and Fact Book*. Dobbs Ferry, NY: Oceana, 1976, 174 pp., figures.

Bullitt, William C. *The Great Globe Itself*. New York: Scribner's, 1946.

Byrnes, James F. *Speaking Frankly*. New York: Harper, 1947, 324 pp., ill., map.

Campbell-Johnson, Alan. *Eden: The Making of a Statesman*. New York: Ives Washburn, 1955.

Cantril, Hardley, ed. *Public Opinion 1935-1946*. Princeton, NJ: Princeton University Press, 1955.

Caputo, David A., ed. *The Politics of Policy Making in America: Five Case Studies*. San Francisco: Freeman, 1977, 189 pp., ill., figures.

Chamberlin, William Henry. *America's Second Crusade*. Chicago: Henry Regnery, 1950.

_____. *Beyond Containment*. Chicago: Henry Regnery, 1953.

Chambon, Henry de. *La Tragedie des Nations Baltiques* (The tragedy of the Baltic Nations). Paris: Editions de la Revue Parlementaire, 1946, 227 pp.

Channon, Henry. *Chips: The Diaries of Sir Henry Channon*. Ed. Robert Rhodes James. London: Weidenfeld and Nicolson, 1967.

Chase, Thomas G. *The Story of Lithuania*. New York: Stratford House, 1946, 392 pp., figures, maps.

Chen, Ti-Chiang. *The International Law of Recognition, with Special Reference to Practice in Great Britain and the United States*. Ed. L. C. Green. New York: Praeger, 1951.

Churchill, Winston S. *Blood, Sweat, and Tears*. New York: Putnam, 1941, 462 pp.

_____. *The Grand Alliance*. Boston: Houghton Mifflin, 1950.

_____. *The Hinge of Fate*. Boston: Houghton Mifflin, 1950.

_____. *Closing the Ring*. Boston: Houghton Mifflin, 1952.

_____. *Triumph and Tragedy*. Boston: Houghton Mifflin, 1953.

Ciechanowski, Jan. *Defeat in Victory*. Garden City, NY: Doubleday, 1947.

Clute, Robert E. *The International Legal Status of Austria 1938-1955*. The Hague: Martinus Nijhoff, 1962, 157 pp.

Coates, William Peyton, and Zelda K. Coates. *A History of Anglo-Soviet Relations*. London: Lawrence and Wishart, 1944.

Cobban, Alfred. *The Nation State and National Self-Determination*. New York: Crowell, 1970, 318 pp.

Committee for a Free Estonia (CFE). *Estonia: Independent and a Soviet Colony*. New York: CFE, 1961, 56 pp., figures.

Committee for Promotion of Peace. *Falsifiers of History: An Historical Document on the Origins of World War II*. New York: Committee for Promotion of Peace, c. 1948, 64 pp.

Crowe, David Martin, Jr. *The Foreign Relations of Estonia, Latvia, and Lithuania, 1938-1939.* Ph.D. Dissertation, University of Georgia, 1974.

Damusis, Adolfas. *Antinacine lietuviu rezistencija* (Lithuanian anti-Nazi resistance). Toronto: Teviskes ziburiai, 1974.

Danys, Milda. *DP: Lithuanian Immigration to Canada after the Second World War.* Toronto: Multicultural History Society of Ontario, 1986, 365 pp., ill., maps.

Daulius, Juozas. *Komunizmas Lietuvoje* (Communism in Lithuania). Kaunas, Lithuania: Sviesa, 1937, 259 pp.

David, William Morris, Jr. *The Development of United States Policy toward the Baltic States, 1917-1922.* Ph.D. Dissertation, Columbia University, 1962.

Davies, Joseph E. *Mission to Moscow.* New York: Simon and Schuster, 1941.

Davis, Lynn Etheridge. *The Cold War Begins: Soviet-American Conflict over Eastern Europe.* Princeton, NJ: Princeton University Press, 1974, 427 pp.

Davison, W. Phillips. "The Public Opinion Process." In *Policy-Making in American Government.* Ed. Edward V. Scheiner. New York: Basic Books, 1969, pp. 13-23.

De Visscher, Charles. *Theory and Reality in Public International Law,* rev. ed. Trans. P. E. Corbett. Princeton, NJ: Princeton University Press, 1968, 527 pp.

Djilas, Milovan. *The New Class: An Analysis of the Communist System.* New York: Praeger, 1957, 214 pp.

Domasevicius, K. *Tarybinio valstybingumo vystymasis Lietuvoje.* (The development of the Soviet state in Lithuania). Vilnius: Mintis, 1966, 195 pp.

Dovydenas, Liudas. *Mes valdysim pasauli: Atsiminimai II* (We will rule the world: Reminiscences II). New York: Romuva, 1970, 250 pp., ill.

Dubnick, Melvin J., and Barbara A. Bardes. *Thinking about Public Policy: A Problem-Solving Approach.* New York: John Wiley and Sons, 1983, 283 pp., figures.

Dunsdorfs, Edgars. *The Baltic Dilemma: The Case of the De Jure* Recognition by Australia of the Baltic States into the Soviet Union. New York: Speller, 1975, 302 pp., ill.

_____. *The Baltic Dilemma II: The Case of the Reversal of the De Jure Recognition by Australia of the Incorporation of the Baltic States into the Soviet Union.* Melbourne: Baltic Council of Australia, 1982, 172 pp., ill.

Eden, Anthony. *The Reckoning.* Boston: Houghton Mifflin, 1965.

Epstein, Julius. *Operation Keelhaul: The Story of Forced Repatriation from 1944 to the Present.* Old Greenwich, CT: Devin-Adair, 1973, 255 pp., ill.

Fainhauz, David. *Lithuanians in Multi-Ethnic Chicago until World War II.* Chicago: Lithuanian Library Press/Loyola University Press, 1977, 230 pp., ill.

Falk, Richard A. *The Role of Domestic Courts in the International Legal Order.* Syracuse, NY: Syracuse University Press, 1964, 184 pp.

Feis, Herbert. *Churchill-Roosevelt-Stalin: The War They Wage and the Peace They Sought.* Princeton, NJ: Princeton University Press, 1957.

Fenno, Richard F., Jr., ed. *The Yalta Conference*. Boston: D. C. Heath, 1955, 112 pp.

Fenwick, Charles G. *Foreign Policy and International Law*. Dobbs Ferry, NY: Oceana, 1968, 142 pp.

Flannery, Christopher. *The Baltic Question and the Foundation of the "Grand Alliance" 1940-1942*. Ph.D. Dissertation, Claremont Graduate School, 1980.

Franck, Thomas M., and Michael J. Glennon. *Foreign Relations and National Security Law: Cases, Materials and Simulations*. St. Paul, MN: West, 1987, 941 pp.

Frederiksen, Oliver J., ed. *Problems of Soviet Foreign Policy*. Munich: Institute for the Study of the USSR, 1959, 141 pp., figures.

Friedmann, Wolfgand. *The Changing Structure of International Law*. New York: Columbia University Press, 1966.

Gaddis, John Lewis. *The United States and the Origins of the Cold War, 1941-1947*. New York: Columbia University Press, 1972, 396 pp.

Gadolin, Axel. *The Solution of the Karelian Refugee Problem in Finland*. The Hague: Martinus Nijhoff, 1952.

Gaida, Pranas, et al. *Lithuanians in Canada*. Ottawa: Canada Ethnic Press Federation, 1967, 370 pp., ill., figures, maps.

Galloway, L. Thomas. *Recognizing Foreign Governments: The Practice of the United States*. Washington, D.C.: American Enterprise Institute for Public Policy Research, 1978, 191 pp., figures.

Galva, Gediminas. *Ernestas Galvanauskas: Politine biografija* (Ernestas Galvanauskas: Political biography). Chicago: Academic Press, 1982, 440 pp., ill.

Gardner, Richard N. "The Soviet Union and the United Nations." In *The Soviet Impact on International Law*. Ed. Hans W. Baade. Dobbs Ferry, NY: Oceana, 1965, pp. 1-13.

Gasparavicius, K., ed. *Mokslininku zodis* (Scholars' word). Kaunas: State Encyclopedia, Dictionary and Scientific Press, 1948, 72 pp., ill.

_____, ed. *Tevyneje* (In the motherland). Kaunas: State Encyclopedia, Dictionary and Scientific Press, 1948, 107 pp., ill.

Gaucys, Povilas, Jonas Dainauskas, and Tomas Remeikis, eds. *Lietuviu iseivijos spaudos bibliografija 1970-1974* (Bibliography of the emigre Lithuanian press 1970-1974). Chicago: Institute of Lithuanian Studies Press, 1977, 300 pp.

Gaucys, Povilas, and Jonas Dainauskas, eds. *Lietuviu iseivijos spaudos bibliografija 1975-1979* (Bibliography of the emigre Lithuanian press 1975-1979). Chicago: Institute of Lithuanian Studies Press, 1984, 414 pp.

Gedvilas, Mecislovas. *Lemiamas posukis: 1940-1945 metai*   (Decisive turn 1940-1945). Vilnius: Vaga, 1975, 389 pp., ill.

Gerutis, Albertas. "Occupied Lithuania." In *Lithuania 700 Years*, 2d rev. ed. Ed. Albertas Gerutis. New York: Manyland, 1969, pp. 257-312, ill.

_____. *Petras Klimas*. Cleveland: Viltis, 1978, 320 pp.

Gliauda, Jurgis. *Simas*. Trans. Kestutis Ciziunas and J. Zemkalnis. New York:

Manyland, 1971, 120 pp., ill.

Gould, Wesley L., and Michael Barkun. *International Law and the Social Sciences.* Princeton, NJ: Princeton University Press, 1970, 338 pp.

Gowa, Joanne S. *U.S. Obligations under International Law Governing the Status of Refugees and the Granting of Asylum: The Case of Simas Kudirka.* Princeton, NJ: Woodrow Wilson School of Public and International Affairs, 1975.

Graham, Malbone W., Jr. *New Governments of Eastern Europe.* New York: Henry Holt, 1927, 826 pp., figures, maps.

_____. *The Diplomatic Recognition of the Border States II: Estonia.* Berkeley: University of California Press, 1939.

_____. *The Diplomatic Recognition of the Border States III: Latvia.* Berkeley: University of California Press, 1941.

Grzybowski, Kazimierz. *Soviet Private International Law.* Leyden, the Netherlands: A. W. Sijthoff, 1965, 179 pp.

_____. *Soviet Public International Law: Doctrines and Diplomatic Practice.* Leyden, the Netherlands: A. W. Sijthoff, 1970, 544 pp.

Gudelis, P. *Bolseviku valdzios atsiradimas Lietuvoje 1918-1919 metais ju paciu dokumentu sviesoje* (Appearance of the Bolshevik government in Lithuania 1918-1919 in light of their own documents). London: Lithuanian Veterans' Association, 1972, 162 pp.

Gustaitis, Algirdas. *Simas Kudirka Nobelio Taikos Premijai* (Simas Kudirka for the Nobel Peace Prize). n.p.: Europos lietuvis, 1971, 11 pp.

_____. *Taikos Lituanika* (Lithuanian peace). Melbourne, Australia: Teviskes aidai, 1974, 38 pp.

Handrack, Hans-Dieter. "The Cultural Policy of the German Administration in the Reichskommissariat Ostland, 1941-44." In *Fourth Conference on Baltic Studies: Summaries of Papers.* Ed. Arunas Alisauskas. Brooklyn: Association for the Advancement of Baltic Studies, 1974, p. 24.

Harmstone, Teresa Rakowska. *Communism in Eastern Europe,* 2d ed. Bloomington: Indiana University Press, 1984, 391 pp., figures, map.

Harrison, E. J. *Lithuania Past and Present.* New York: Robert M. McBride, 1922, 224 pp., ill., maps.

_____. *Lithuania's Fight for Freedom,* 3d ed. New York: Lithuanian American Information Center, 1948, 62 pp.

Hazard, John N. *The Soviet System of Government,* 4th rev. ed. Chicago: University of Chicago Press, 1968, 275 pp., figures.

Henderson, Loy W. *A Question of Trust: The Origins of U.S.-Soviet Relations.* The Memoirs of Loy W. Henderson. Ed. George W. Baer. Stanford, CA: Hoover Institution Press, 1987, 579 pp.

Horecky, Paul L. *Russia and the Soviet Union: A Bibliographic Guide to Western-Language Publications.* Chicago: University of Chicago Press, 1971, 473 pp.

Hull, Cordell. *The Memoirs of Cordell Hull.* 2 vol. Ed. Walter Johnson. New York:

138

Bibliography

Macmillan, 1942, 1948.

Isenberg, Irwin. *The Soviet Satellites of Eastern Europe*. New York: Scholastic, 1963, 160 pp., ill., figures, maps.

Ivanov, Jan. *Les Republiques Baltiques (1938-1958)* (The Baltic republics 1938-1958). Paris: Revue Politique et Parlamentaire, 1958, 11 pp., figures.

Ivask, Ivar, ed. *First Conference on Baltic Studies: Summary of Proceedings*. Tacoma, WA: Association for the Advancement of Baltic Studies, 1969, 128 pp., ill.

Ivinskis, Zenonas. "Lithuania during the War: Resistance against the Soviet and Nazi Occupants." In *Lithuania under the Soviets: Portrait of a Nation, 1940-65*. Ed. V. Stanley Vardys. New York: Praeger, 1965, pp. 61-84.

Jackson, J. Hampden. *Estonia*. London: George Allen and Unwin, 1941, 248 pp., maps.

Jackson, Robert H. *Grundlegende Rede vorgetragen im Namen der Vereinigten Staaten von Amerika* (Keynote address in the name of the United States of America). Frankfurt am Main, West Germany: Das Forum, 1946, 72 pp.

Jacobini, H. B. *A Study of the Philosophy of International Law as Seen in Works of Latin American Writers*. The Hague: Martinus Nijhoff, 1954, 158 pp.

James, Alan. *Sovereign Statehood: The Basis of International Society*. Winchester, MA: Unwin Hyman, 1986, 250 pp.

Jasaitis, Domas, ed. *BALFAS 1944-1969* (United Lithuanian Relief Fund of America 1944-1969). Brooklyn: BALF, 1970, 287 pp., ill.

Jessup, Philip C. *Transnational Law*. New Haven, CT: Yale University Press, 1956.

Jonaitis, Leonas. *They Live in Your Midst*. Vilnius: Gintaras, 1972, 51 pp.

Jurgela, Constantine R. *Lithuania and the United States: The Establishment of State Relations*. Chicago: Lithuanian Research and Studies Center, 1985, 264 pp., ill., maps.

Kajeckas, Joseph. *The Story of Captive Lithuania*. Washington, D.C.: Lithuanian Legation, 1969, 14 pp.

Kalme, Albert. *Total Terror: An Expose of Genocide in the Baltics*. Ed. Walter Arm. New York: Appleton-Century-Crofts, 1951, 310 pp., ill.

Kalpokas, V., ed. *Repatrijuotuju tarybiniu pilieciu teises* (Rights of repatriated Soviet citizens). Vilnius: State Political Press, 1947, 13 pp.

Kancevicius, V. *1940 metu birzelis Lietuvoje* (June 1940 in Lithuania). Vilnius: Mintis, 1973, 111 pp., ill.

_____, ed. *Lithuania in 1939-1940: The Historic Turn to Socialism*. Vilnius: Mintis, 1976, 230 pp., ill.

Kancevicius, V., V. Niunka, R. Sarmaitis, and L. Sepetys, eds. *Atsiminimai apie Antana Sniecku* (Reminiscences about Antanas Snieckus). Vilnius: Mintis, 1982, 251 pp., ill.

Kantautas, Adam, and Filomena Kantautas, eds. *A Lithuanian Bibliography*. Edmonton, Alberta: University of Alberta Press, 1975, 725 pp.

_____, eds. *Supplement to a Lithuanian Bibliography*. Edmonton, Alberta:

University of Alberta Press, 1979, 316 pp.

Karpov, Victor P. "The Soviet Concept of Peaceful Coexistence and Its Implications for International Law." In *The Soviet Impact on International Law*. Ed. Hans W. Baade. Dobbs Ferry, NY: Oceana, 1965, pp. 14-20.

Kaslas, Bronis J., ed. *The USSR-German Aggression against Lithuania*. New York: Robert Speller, 1973, 543 pp., ill., maps.

_____. *The Baltic Nations-The Quest for Regional Integration and Political Liberty*. Pittston, PA: Euramerica, 1976, 319 pp., maps.

Kasulaitis, Algirdas J. *Komunizmo gresme emigracijos kryzkeleje: Diasporos atsakomybe valstybei, tautai ir ateiciai* (The threat of Communism on the crossroads of emigration: The diaspora's duty to state, nation, and the future). n.p.: c. 1969, 24 pp.

_____. *Lithuanian Christian Democracy*. Chicago: Leo XIII Fund, 1976, 244 pp., ill.

Kennan, George F. *Soviet Foreign Policy 1917-1941*. Princeton, NJ: Princeton University Press, 1960, 192 pp.

_____. *Russia and the West under Lenin and Stalin*. Boston: Little, Brown, 1961, 411 pp.

Kerimov, D. A., ed. *Soviet Democracy in the Period of Developed Socialism*. Trans. Barry Jones. Moscow: Progress, 1979, 278 pp.

Kersten, Charles J. *Self-Determination of the Enslaved Nations-The Only Basis for True Peace*. Speech before the Lithuanian Chamber of Commerce of Illinois, Chicago (LCCI), 17 May 1953. Chicago: LCCI, 1953, 13 pp.

Klesment, Johannes. *The Estonian Soldiers in the Second World War*. Stockholm: Estonian National Council, 1948, 35 pp.

Klorys, K. *Liaudziai pakilus: Is atsiminimu 1917-1920 metais* (The masses having risen: Reminiscences 1917-1920). Vilnius: State Literary Press, 1958, 211 pp., ill.

Koncius, Joseph B. *History of Lithuania*. Chicago: Lithuanian American Community, n.d., 142 pp., ill.

_____. *Atsiminimai is BALFo veiklos 1944-1964* (Reminiscences from BALF 1944-1964). Chicago: BALF, 1966, 404 pp., ill.

Kovrig, Bennett. *The Myth of Liberation: East-Central Europe in U.S. Diplomacy and Politics since 1941*. Baltimore: Johns Hopkins University Press, 1973, 360 pp.

Krepp, E. *Security and Non-Aggression: Baltic States and U.S.S.R. Treaties of Non-Aggression*. Stockholm: Estonian Information Centre, Latvian National Foundation, 1973, 64 pp.

Kristian, A. A. *The Right to Self-Determination and the Soviet Union*. London: Boreas, 1952, 80 pp.

Krivickas, Domas. *Soviet-German Pact of 1939 and Lithuania*. Hamilton, Ontario: Federation of Lithuanian-Canadians, 1959, 14 pp., ill., map.

_____. "Lithuania's Struggle against Aggression and Subjugation." In *Twenty Years' Struggle for Freedom of Lithuania*. Ed. Juozas Audenas. New York: ELTA, 1963, pp. 118-146.

_____. "Naciu-sovietu pakto teisines ir politines pasekmes po 40 metu" (Legal and political consequences of the Nazi-Soviet pact after 40 years). In *Lituanistikos instituto 1981 metu suvaziavimo darbai* (1981 proceedings of the Institute of Lithuanian Studies). Ed. Ina C. Uzgiris. Chicago: ILS, 1985, 83-104.

Krupavicius, Mykolas. *Visuomeniniai klausimai* (Social questions). Chicago: Leo XIII Fund, 1983, 488 pp., ill.

Kubilius, V., ed. *Po gimtuoju dangum* (Under native skies). Kaunas: Spindulys, c. 1950, 79 pp., ill.

Kucas, Antanas. *Amerikos lietuviu istorija* (American Lithuanian history). South Boston: Lithuanian Encyclopedia Press, 1971, 639 pp., figures, map.

_____. *Lithuanians in America*. Trans. Joseph Boley. Boston: Encyclopedia Lituanica, 1975, 349 pp., ill.

Kudirka, Simas, and Larry Eichel. *For Those Still at Sea: The Defection of a Lithuanian Sailor*. New York: Dial, 1978, 226 pp.

Kutkus, Vytautas. *JAV Lietuviu Bendruomenes krasto valdybos veikla nuo 1979 m. gruodzio men. 15 d. iki 1982 m. spalio men. 23 d.* (Activity of the Lithuanian American Community from 15 December 1979 to 23 October 1982). N.p.: LAC, 1982, 20 pp.

Kviklys, Bronius. *Lietuviu kova su naciais 1941-1944 m.* (Lithuanians' fight against the Nazis 1941-1944). Memmingen, West Germany: Mintis, 1946, 48 pp., ill., figures.

Langer, Robert. *Seizure of Territory: The Stimson Doctrine and Related Principles in Legal Theory and Diplomatic Practice*. Princeton, NJ: Princeton University Press, 1947, 313 pp.

Langer, William Leonard, and Everett S. Gleason. *The Undeclared War, 1940-1941*. New York: Harper and Bros., 1953.

Laski, Harold J. *Studies in the Problem of Sovereignty*. New Haven, CT: Yale University Press, 1917, 297 pp.

Lauterpacht, H. *Recognition in International Law*. Cambridge: Cambridge University Press, 1947, 413 pp.

Leahy, William D. *I Was There*. New York: Whittlesey House, 1950.

Lerner, Warren. "The Historical Origins of the Soviet Doctrine of Peaceful Coexistence." In *The Soviet Impact on International Law*. Ed. Hans W. Baade. Dobbs Ferry, NY: Oceana, 1965, pp. 21-26.

Lipson, Leon. "Peaceful Coexistence." In *The Soviet Impact on International Law*. Ed. Hans W. Baade. Dobbs Ferry, NY: Oceana, 1965, pp. 27-37.

Lithuanian American Council. *Kersteno rezoliucija ir pastangos ja pravesti JAV Kongrese* (The Kersten Resolution and efforts to gain its passage in the U.S.

Congress). n.p.: Lithuanian American Council, c. 1953, 12 pp.

Lithuanian Committee to Combat Nazism and Fascism (LCCNF). *Do You Know Them?* Chicago: LCCNF, 1964, 9 pp.

Lithuanian Council of Chicago (LCC). *Lietuvos nepriklausomybes atkurimo ir 717 metu karalystes isteigimo minejimas* (Commemoration of Lithuania's independence and the 717th anniversary of the establishment of the Lithuanian crown). Chicago: LCC, 1968, 64 pp., ill.

Lithuanian Information Bureau (LIB). *Lithuanian Recognition*. Washington, D.C.: LIB, c. 1921, 68 pp., figures, map.

Liulevicius, Vincentas. *Lietuvos kaimyniniu krastu istorijos bruozai* (Historical sketches of Lithuania's neighbors), 2d rev. ed. Chicago: Lithuanian Institute of Education, 1980, 78 pp., 31 maps.

_____. *Iseivijos vaidmuo nepriklausomos Lietuvos atkurimo darbe* (Emigres' role in the restoration of Lithuania's independence). Chicago: Lithuanian World Community, 1981, 398 pp., ill.

Lourie, Donald B. "Address to Lithuanian American Congress, 27-28 November 1953." In *Visuotinas Amerikos Lietuviu Kongresas*. Ed. Lithuanian American Congress. Chicago: LAC, 1953, pp. 69-74.

Macijauskas, J. *Saule leidzias, saule teka: Atsiminimai* (The sun sets, the sun rises: Reminiscences). Vilnius: State Literary Press, 1961, 286 pp., ill.

Maciuika, Benedict V., ed. *Lithuania in the Last 30 Years*. Subcontractor's monograph prepared in the Division of the Social Sciences at the University of Chicago. HRAF Subcontract HRAF-1 Chi-1. New Haven, CT: Human Relations Area Files, 1955, 439 pp., figures, maps.

Maciulis, Petras. *Trys ultimatumai* (Three ultimatums). Brooklyn: Darbininkas, 1962, 134 pp.

Magi, Artur. *Conference at Helsinki and Its Aftermath*. Stockholm: Estonian Information Centre, 1977, 15 pp.

Mangone, Gerard J. *The Elements of International Law*, rev. ed. Homewood, IL: Dorsey Press, 1967, 532 pp.

Maniusis, J. *Tarybu Lietuva: Laimejimai ir perspektyvos* (Soviet Lithuania: Victories and perspectives). Vilnius: Mintis, 1977, 134 pp., ill.

Manning, Clarence A. *The Forgotten Republics*. New York: Philosophical Library, 1952, 264 pp., map.

Marek, Krystyna. *Identity and Continuity of States in Public International Law*. Geneva: Librairie E. Droz, 1968.

Mazeika, Povilas A. "Russian Objectives in the Baltic Countries." In *Problems of Mininations: Baltic Perspectives*. Ed. Arvids Ziedonis, Rein Taagepara, and Mardi Valgemae. San Jose, CA: Association for the Advancement of Baltic Studies, 1973, pp. 123-128, figures.

Mazour, Anatole G. *Russia: Tsarist and Communist*. Princeton, NJ: D. Van Nostrand, 1969, 995 pp., ill.

Meiksins, Gregory. *The Baltic Soviet Republic*. New York: National Council of American-Soviet Friendship, 1944, 46 pp.

Meissner, Boris. *Die Sowjetunion, die Baltischen Staaten und das Voelkerrecht* (The Soviet Union, the Baltic States, and international law). Cologne, West Germany: Verlag Politik und Wirtschaft, 1956.

Merkelis, Aleksandras. *Antanas Smetona: Jo visuomenine, kulturine ir politine veikla* (Antanas Smetona: His social, cultural and political activity). New York: American Lithuanian National Association, 1964, 740 pp., ill.

Michelson, S. *Lietuviu iseivija Amerikoje 1868-1961* (Lithuanian emigres in America 1868-1961). South Boston: Keleivis, 1961, 499 pp., ill., figures.

Mickevicius-Kapsukas, V. *Pirmoji Lietuvos proletarine revoliucija ir Sovietu valdzia* (First Lithuanian proletarian revolution and Soviet government). Chicago: American Lithuanian Workers Literary Society, 1934, 240 pp., ill.

Miezelaitis, E., et al., eds. *Kovu puslapiai* (Battle pages). Vilnius: Vaga, 1974, 623 pp., ill.

Millis, Walter, ed. *The Forrestal Diaries*. New York: Viking Press, 1951.

Mingaila, Stasys. *Neapkenciamo zmogaus uzrasai* (Writings of an untolerated person). Western-Occupied Germany: Author, 1948, 119 pp.

Mizara, Rojus. *Zvilgsnis i praeiti* (Glance at the past). Vilnius: State Literary Press, 1960, 335 pp., ill.

Mosely, Philip E. *The Kremlin and World Politics*. New York: Vintage, 1960.

Nathan, James A., and James K. Oliver. *Foreign Policy Making and the American Political System*. Boston: Little, Brown, 1983, 273 pp., figures.

Navickas, Kostas. *TSRS vaidmuo ginant Lietuva nuo imperialistines agresijos 1920-1940 metais* (The role of the USSR in defending Lithuania from imperialist aggression 1920-1940). Vilnius: Mintis, 1966, 336 pp.

_____. *The Struggle of the Lithuanian People for Statehood*. Vilnius: Gintaras, 1971, 175 pp., ill., maps.

Newman, Bernard. *Baltic Background*. London: Robert Hale, 1948, 280 pp., ill., figures, maps.

Nicolson, Harold. *Diplomacy*, 2d ed. London: Oxford University Press, 1960.

Norem, Owen J. C. *Timeless Lithuania*, 2d ed. Cleveland: Viltis, 1967, 299 pp.

Ohloblyn, Alexander P. "Soviet Historiography." In *Academic Freedom under the Soviet Regime*. Ed. Anton A. Adamovich et al. Munich, West Germany: Institute for the Study of the History and Culture of the USSR, 1954, pp. 69-77.

Olis, Antanas A. "JAV uzsienio politika sarysy su Lietuvos klausimu" (U.S. foreign policy relative to the question of Lithuania). In *Amerikos Lietuviu Tarybos suvaziavimas* (Lithuanian American Council Congress). Ed. Lithuanian American Council. Chicago: LAC, 1954, pp. 39-41.

Ornstein, Norman J., and Shirley Elder. *Interest Groups, Lobbying and Policymaking*. Washington, D.C.: Congressional Quarterly Press, 1978, 245 pp., figures.

Page, Stanley W. *The Formation of the Baltic States*. Cambridge: Harvard University Press, 1959, 196 pp.

Pajaujis-Javis, Joseph. *Soviet Genocide in Lithuania*. New York: Manyland, 1980, 246 pp.

Pakstas, Kazys. *The Lithuanian Situation*. Chicago: Lithuanian Cultural Institute, 1941, 62 pp., ill.

_____. *Lithuania and World War II*. Chicago: Lithuanian Cultural Institute, 1947, 80 pp., maps.

Paleckis, Justas. *Kelias i Lietuva atviras* (The road to Lithuania is open). Vilnius: State Political Press, 1947, 35 pp., ill.

_____. *Metu vieskeliais 1917-1972* (On the roads of years 1917-1972). Vilnius: Vaga, 1973, 334 pp., ill.

Paplenas, Jonas. "Antanas A. Olis." In *Tautines Minties Keliu: Lietuviu tautininkijos istoriniai bruozai* (The path of national thought: Historical sketches of the Lithuanian national movement). Ed. Jonas Puzinas and Jonas Pranas Palukaitis. Chicago: American Lithuanian National Association, 1979, pp. 318-321, ill.

Pasilaitis, Juozas. *Hearken Then Judge: Sidelights on Lithuanian DPs*. Tubingen, West Germany: Patria, c. 1948, 48 pp., ill., figures.

Pennar, Jaan, ed. *Report on the Soviet Union in 1956*. Munich, West Germany: Institute for the Study of the USSR, 1956, 218 pp., figures.

Petkeviciene, Leokadija. *Didvyriskos kovos avangarde: JAV lietuviu komunistu veikla 1919-1969 metais* (In the vanguard of a noble struggle: Lithuanian American communist activity 1919-1969). Vilnius: Mintis, 1979, 223 pp.

Petrauskas, Kazimieras. "Antifasistine demonstracija Panevezyje 1940 m. birzelio 16 d." (Anti-fascist demonstration in Panevezys 16 June 1940). In *Uz ateiti sviesia: Is atsiminimu I 1918-1940* (For a brighter future: Reminiscences I 1918-1940). Ed. K. Kalniuviene and D. Melyniene. Vilnius: Mintis, 1980, pp. 190-192.

Piiroja, Juri, et al. *Baltic Refugees and Displaced Persons*. London: Boreas, 1947, 40 pp.

Pipes, Richard. *Survival Is Not Enough: Soviet Realities and America's Future*. New York: Simon and Schuster, 1984.

Pone, Maris. "The Fate of the Baltic Gold Reserves in London." In *Problems of Mininations: Baltic Perspectives*. Ed. Arvids Ziedonis, Jr., Rein Taagepera, and Mardi Valgemae. San Jose, CA: Association for the Advancement of Baltic Studies, 1973, p. 193.

Priests' League. *Amerikos lietuviu kataliku darbai* (Catholic action of Lithuanian Americans). Harrisburg, PA: Priests' League, 1943, 352 pp., ill.

Prunskis, Juozas. *Lithuania's Jews and the Holocaust*. Chicago: Lithuanian American Council, 1979, 48 pp., ill., map.

Pruseika, L. *Teisybe apie Lietuva* (The truth about Lithuania). Chicago: Apsvietos

Fondas/Education Fund, 1940, 32 pp.

Pusta, Kaarel Robert. *The Soviet Union and the Baltic States*. New York: John Felsberg, Inc., 1943, 79 pp., map.

Rackauskas, Konstantinas. *Lietuvos konstitucines teises klausimais* (Questions of Lithuanian constitutional law). New York: Author, 1967, 178 pp.

Raila, Bronys. *Tamsiausia pries ausra* (Darkest before dawn). Chicago: Srove, n.d., 448 pp.

_____. *Bastuno maistas* (Wanderer's riot). Chicago: AM and M Publications, 1977, 499 pp.

Rakunas, A. *Klasiu kova Lietuvoje 1940-1951 metais* (Class struggle in Lithuania 1940-1951). Vilnius: Mokslas, 1976, 216 pp.

Rameliene, A. Butkute. *Lietuvos Komunistu Partijos kova uz Tarybu valdzios itvirtinima respublikoje 1940-1941 m.* (The fight of the Communist Party of Lithuania for a Soviet government in the republic 1940-1941). Vilnius: State Political and Scientific Press, 1958, 208 pp.

Rastikis, Stasys. *Ivykiai ir zmones: Is mano uzrasu* (Events and Personalities: From my notes). Ed. Bronius Kviklys. Chicago: Academic Press, 1972, 616 pp., ill.

_____. *Lietuvos likimo keliais: Is mano uzrasu* (On the roads of Lithuania's destiny: From my notes). Ed. Jonas Dainauskas. Chicago: Academic Press, 1982, 792 pp., ill.

Raugas, Balys, ed. *JAV LB trys desimtmeciai* (Three decades of the Lithuanian American Community). Brooklyn: LAC, 1982, 374 pp., ill., figures.

Rei, August. *Have the Baltic Countries Voluntarily Renounced Their Freedom?* New York: World Association of Estonians, 1944, 47 pp.

_____. *Have the Small Nations a Right to Freedom and Independence?* London: Boreas, 1946, 32 pp.

Remeikis, Thomas. *Opposition to Soviet Rule in Lithuania 1945-1980*. Chicago: Institute of Lithuanian Studies Press, 1980, 680 pp., ill., figures, map.

Revel, Jean-Francois. *How Democracies Perish*. New York: Doubleday, 1984.

Romeris, Mykolas. *Lietuvos konstitucines teises paskaitos I* (Lectures in Lithuanian constitutional law I). Kaunas, Lithuania: Law Faculty of the University of Vytautas the Great, 1937, 527 pp.

Root, Waverly. *The Secret History of the War II*. New York: Charles Scribner's Sons, 1946.

Rossi, Angelo. *The Russo-German Alliance August 1939-June 1941*. Boston: Beacon, 1951.

Royal Institute of International Affairs. *The Baltic States: A Survey of the Political and Economic Structure and the Foreign Relations of Estonia, Latvia, and Lithuania*. London: Oxford University Press, 1938, 194 pp., figures, map.

Rudminas, V. *Melai ir tiesa apie Lietuva* (Lies and truth About Lithuania). Chicago: Lietuviu literaturos draugijos apsvietos fondas/Lithuanian Literary Society Education Fund, c. 1943, 64 pp., ill.

Ruksenas, Algis. *Day of Shame: The Truth about the Murderous Happenings aboard the Cutter "Vigilant" during the Russian-American Confrontation off Martha's Vineyard*. New York: David McKay, 1973, 368 pp., ill.

Ryan, Allan A., Jr. *Quiet Neighbors: Prosecuting Nazi War Criminals in America*. San Diego: Harcourt Brace Jovanovich, 1984.

Sabaliunas, Leonas. *Lithuania in Crisis: Nationalism to Communism, 1939-1940*. Bloomington: Indiana University Press, 1972, 293 pp., figures.

Sapoka, Adolfas. *Vilnius in the Life of Lithuania*. Toronto: Lithuanian Association of the Vilnius Region, 1962, 174 pp., ill.

Sarmaitis, R., ed. *Revoliucijos judejimas Lietuvoje: Straipsniu rinkinys* (Revolutionary movement in Lithuania: Collection of essays). Vilnius: State Political and Scientific Press, 1957, 915 pp., ill., maps.

_____, ed. *Lietuvos Komunistu Partijos istorijos apybraiza I: 1887-1920* (Historical overview of the Communist Party of Lithuania I: 1887-1920). Vilnius: Mintis, 1971, 526 pp., ill., maps.

Savickis, Jurgis. *Zeme dega I* (The ground burns I). Chicago: Terra, 1956, 455 pp., ill.

Schuman, Frederick L. *Europe on the eve: The crises of diplomacy 1933-1939*. New York: Knopf, 1939, 586 pp., maps.

Schwarz, Jordan A. *Liberal: Adolf A. Berle and the Vision of an American Era*. New York: Free Press, 1987.

Schwarzenberger, Georg. *A Manual of International Law*, 5th ed. New York: Praeger, London Institute of World Affairs, 1967.

Scott, John. *Duel for Europe: Stalin versus Hitler*. Boston: Houghton Mifflin, 1941.

Senn, Alfred Erich. *The Emergence of Modern Lithuania*. New York: Columbia University Press, 1959, 272 pp., maps.

Sesplaukis, Alfonsas, ed. *Lituanica Collections in European Research Libraries: A Bibliography*. Chicago: Lithuanian Research and Studies Center, 1986, 215 pp.

Sherwood, Robert E. *Roosevelt and Hopkins*. New York: Harper and Bros., 1950.

Sidlauskas, Kazys. "Supreme Committee for Liberation of Lithuania as Representative of Lithuanian National Interests." In *Twenty Years' Struggle for Freedom of Lithuania*. Ed. Juozas Audenas. New York: ELTA, 1963, pp. 93-117.

_____. *Amerikos lietuviu tarybos veiklos penkmetis* (Five years' activity of the Lithuanian American Council). Chicago: LAC, 1980, 24 pp., ill.

_____. *Svarstybos visuomeniniais ir teisiniais klausimais* (Reflections on social and legal questions). St. Petersburg, FL: Leo XIII Fund, 1987, 216 pp., ill.

Simmonds, George W., ed. *Nationalism in the USSR and Eastern Europe in the Era of Brezhnev and Kosygin*. Detroit: University of Detroit Press, 1977, 534 pp., figures.

Simutis, Leonardas. *Amerikos Lietuviu Taryba: 30 metu Lietuvos laisves kovoje 1940-1970* (Lithuanian American Council: 30-year struggle for the liberation of

Lithuania 1940-1970). Chicago: LAC, 1971, 499 pp., ill.

Sinha, S. Prakash. "Self-Determination in International Law and Its Applicability to the Baltic Peoples." In *Res Baltica*. Ed. Adolf Sprudzs and Armins Rusis. Leyden, the Netherlands: A. W. Sijthoff, 1968, pp. 256-285.

Sirvydas, Vytautas. *Bronius Kazys Balutis: Jo gyvenimas ir darbai* (Bronius Kazys Balutis: His life and work). Sodus, MI: J. J. Bachunas, 1951, 128 pp., ill.

Skerys, Antanas. *Geelongo Lietuviu Bendruomenes kronika 1948-1978* (Chronicle of the Geelong Lithuanian Community 1948-1978). Geelong, Australia: Australian Lithuanian Community, 1980, 295 pp.

Skrundens, Janis. *Latvia 1918-1968*. New York: American Latvian Association, 1968, 78 pp., ill.

Skruodys, K. J. *Tarptautine teise* (International law). Vilnius: Lietuviu mokslo draugija/Lithuanian Scientific Society, 1921, 114 pp.

Slapsiene, Birute Abdulskaite. "Nepamirstamos dienos" (Unforgettable days). In *Uz ateiti sviesia: Is atsiminimu I 1918-1940* (For a brighter future: Reminiscences I 1918-1940). Ed. K. Kalniuviene and D. Melyniene. Vilnius: Mintis, 1980, pp. 206-207.

Sliogeris, Vaclovas. *Antanas Smetona: Zmogus ir valstybininkas. Atsiminimai* (Antanas Smetona: Person and statesman. Reminiscences). Sodus, MI: Juozas J. Bachunas, 1966, 187 pp., ill.

Snell, John L. *Illusion and Necessity*. Boston: Houghton Mifflin, 1963.

Snieckus, Antanas. *Su Lenino veliava I: 1927-1969* (With Lenin's flag I: 1927-1969). Vilnius: Mintis, 1977, 439 pp., ill.

Sodaitis, Antanas. *Pirmieji desimts metu 1944-1954* (First decade 1944-1954). Brooklyn: United Lithuanian Relief Fund of America, 1954, 135 pp., ill.

Spekke, Arnolds. *Latvia and the Baltic Problem*. London: Latvian Information Bureau, 1952.

Sprudz, Adolf. *The Annexation of Latvia by the Union of Soviet Socialist Republics*. Ph.D. Dissertation, University of Louvain, 1953.

Sruogiene, Vanda Daugirdaite. *Lietuvos istorija: Lietuva amziu sukury* (History of Lithuania: Lithuania through the ages). Chicago: Tevynes myletoju draugija/Motherland Society, 1956, 957 pp., ill.

Standley, William H., and Arthur A. Ageton. *Admiral Ambassador to Russia*. Chicago: Regnery, 1955.

Steponaitis, Antanas. *Tevyneje ir pasauly: Prisiminimai ir apybraizos* (In the motherland and the world: Reminiscences and sketches). Brooklyn: Franciscan Press, 1962, 319 pp.

Stettinius, Edward R., Jr. *Roosevelt and the Russians*. New York: Stettinius Fund, 1949.

Stravinskas, Petras. *Ir sviesa ir tiesa* (And light and truth). Chicago: Valerijonas Simkus, 1978, 214 pp.

_____. *Atsiminimai ir pasaulezvalga* (Reminiscences and worldview). Chicago:

Stravinskis Publication Committee, 1982, 216 pp.

Stromas, Aleksandras. *Politine samone Lietuvoje* (Political consciousness in Lithuania). London: Nida, 1980, 104 pp., ill.

Strong, Anna Louise. *The New Lithuania*. New York: Workers Library Publishers, 1941, 64 pp.

Sveics, V. V. "Nationalism: A Source of Strength for Small Nations." In *Fourth Conference on Baltic Studies: Summaries of Papers*. Ed. Arunas Alisauskas. Brooklyn: Association for the Advancement of Baltic Studies, 1974, p. 69.

Swettenham, John Alexander. *The Tragedy of the Baltic States: A Report Compiled from Official Documents and Eyewitnesses' Reports*. New York: Praeger, 1954, 216 pp., figures, maps.

Taracouzio, Timothy A. *The Soviet Union and International Law: A Study Based on the Legislation, Treaties and Foreign Relations of the Union of Soviet Socialist Republics*. New York: Macmillan, 1935, 530 pp.

Tarulis, Albert N. *Soviet Policy toward the Baltic States 1918-1940*. Notre Dame, IN: University of Notre Dame Press, 1959, 276 pp., maps.

_____. *American-Baltic Relations 1918-1922: The Struggle over Recognition*. Washington, D.C.: Catholic University of America Press, 1965.

Tiesa apie musu gyvenima (The truth about our life). Vilnius: Tiesa, 1947, 16 pp., ill.

La Tragedie des Etats Baltes (The tragedy of the Baltic States). Paris: Monde Nouveau, 1952, 83 pp.

Triska, John F., and Robert M. Slusser. *The Theory, Law, and Policy of Soviet Treaties*. Stanford, CA: Stanford University Press, 1962, 593 pp.

Truman, David B. *The Governmental Process: Political Interests and Public Opinion*, 2d ed. New York: Knopf, 1971, 561 pp.

Truman, Harry S. *Memoirs I*. Garden City, NY: Doubleday, 1955.

_____. *Memoirs II*. Garden City, NY: Doubleday, 1956.

Trunk, Isaiah. *Jewish Responses to Nazi Persecution: Collective and Individual Behavior in Extremis*. New York: Stein and Day, 1979, 371 pp., ill., maps.

Tung, William L. *International Law in an Organizing World*. New York: Crowell, 1968.

Tunkin, G. I. *Theory of International Law*. Trans. William E. Butler. Cambridge, MA: Harvard University Press, 1974, 497 pp.

Vaiceliunas, Juozas. *Antrasis pasaulinis karas* (World War II). Sudbury, Ontario: Author, 1960, 350 pp., ill.

Vaitiekunas, Vytautas. *Bendravimas su Lietuva* (Relations with Lithuania). Brooklyn: Lietuviu fronto biciuliu studiju biuras/Lithuanian Front Study Bureau, n.d., 49 pp.

_____. *Lithuania*. New York: Assembly of Captive European Nations, 1965, 48 pp., figures, maps.

Vaitkevicius, B., ed. *Lietuvos TSR istorija IV: 1940-1958 metais* (History of the

Lithuanian SSR IV: 1940-1958). Vilnius: Mokslas, 1975, 366 pp.

_____. *Tarybu Lietuva: Praeities ir dabarties bruozai 1940-1980* (Soviet Lithuania: Sketches of the past and present 1940-1980). Vilnius: Mokslas, 1980, 207 pp.

Vaitkevicius, B., S. Juoniene, and R. Sarmaitis, eds. *Leninas ir Lietuva* (Lenin and Lithuania). Vilnius: Mintis, 1969, 230 pp., ill.

Vaitkevicius, B., et al., eds. *Proletarine revoliucija Lietuvoje: 1918-1919 metu revoliuciniu ivykiu Lietuvoje dalyviu atsiminimai* (Proletarian revolution in Lithuania: Reminiscences of Revolutionaries 1918-1919). Vilnius: State Political and Scientific Press, 1960, 527 pp., ill.

Vaitkus, Mykolas. *Milzinu rungtynese 1940-1944: Atsiminimai* (The race of giants 1940-1944: Reminiscences). London: Nida, 1972, 205 pp.

Valancius, Grigas. *Lietuva ir Karaliauciaus krastas* (Lithuania and Konigsberg). Kirchheim-Teck, West Germany: Author, 1946, 95 pp., map.

Van der Post, Laurens. *A View of All the Russias*. New York: Morrow, 1964.

Vardys, V. Stanley. "Aggression, Soviet Style, 1939-40." In *Lithuania under the Soviets: Portrait of a Nation, 1940-65*. Ed. V. Stanley Vardys. New York: Praeger, 1965, pp. 47-58.

_____. *The Catholic Church, Dissent and Nationality in Soviet Lithuania*. Boulder, CO: East European Quarterly, 1978, 336 pp., figures, map.

Venclova, Antanas. *Vidurdienio vetra* (Midday storm). Vilnius: Vaga, 1969, 653 pp., ill.

Venclova, Tomas. *Lietuva pasaulyje* (Lithuania in the world). Chicago: Academic Press, 1981, 292 pp, ill.

Viliamas, V. *Isikurimo galimybes uzjurio krastuose* (Overseas settlement possibilities). Nordlingen, West Germany: Sudavija, 1947, 112 pp.

Vitas, Robert A. *Civil-Military Relations in Lithuania under President Antanas Smetona 1926-1940*. M.A. Thesis, Loyola University of Chicago, 1986, 259 pp., figures, maps.

Vitols, Hugo, N. Kaasik, J. Kajeckas, and M.W. Graham. *Annexation of the Baltic States*. Stockholm: Baltic Humanitarian Association, 1946, 36 pp.

Von Glahn, Gerhard. *Law among Nations: An Introduction to Public International Law*, 4th ed. New York: Macmillan, 1981, 810 pp.

Welles, Sumner. *The Time for Decision*. New York: Harper and Brothers, 1944, 431 pp., map.

_____. *Seven Decisions That Shaped History*. New York: Harper and Brothers, 1951.

Werth, Alexander. *Russia at War 1941-1945*. New York: Dutton, 1964.

Wood, John R., and Jean Serres. *Diplomatic Ceremonial and Protocol: Principles, Procedures and Practices*. New York: Columbia University Press, 1970.

Woodward, Ernest Llewellyn, Sr. *British Foreign Policy in the Second World War I*. London: H.M. Stationery Office, 1970.

Zeimantas, Vytautas. *Teisingumas reikalauja* (Justice demands it). Vilnius: Mintis,

1984, 109 pp., ill.

Ziedonis, Arvids, Jr., et al., eds. *Baltic History*. Columbus, OH: Association for the Advancement of Baltic Studies, 1974.

Ziedonis, Arvids, Jr., Rein Taagepera, and Mardi Valgemae, eds. *Problems of Mininations: Baltic Perspectives*. San Jose, CA: Association for the Advancement of Baltic Studies, 1973, 214 pp., figures.

Zinkus, J., ed. *Lietuvos TSR* (Lithuanian SSR). Vilnius: Mokslas, 1980, 272 pp., ill.

Ziugzda, J., ed. *Lietuvos TSR istorija nuo seniausiu laiku iki 1957 metu* (History of the Lithuanian SSR from ancient times to 1957). Vilnius: State Political and Scientific Press, 1958, 519 pp., ill.

_____. *Lietuvos TSR istorija III: 1917-1940* (History of the Lithuanian SSR III: 1917-1940). Vilnius: Mintis, 1965, 407 pp., ill.

Zumbakis, S. Paul. *Soviet Evidence in North American Courts: An Analysis of Problems and Concerns with Reliance on Communist Source Evidence in Alleged War Criminal Trials*. Woodhaven, NY: Americans for Due Process, 1986, 168 pp., ill., figures.

Articles

Albinski, Henry S. Review of *The Baltic Dilemma*, by Edgars Dunsdorfs. *Journal of Baltic Studies*, 7, 4 (Winter 1976), 373-374.

"Ambasadorius neprieme Sovietu bendradarbiu" (Ambassador did not receive Soviet associates). *Draugas*, 18 February 1988, p. 1.

"Amerikos Latviu Sajunga apie JAV-SSRS konferencija Latvijoje" (American-Latvian Association on the U.S.-USSR conference in Latvia). *Nepriklausoma Lietuva*, 10 July 1986, p. 1.

Anderson, Bill. "Ford Is Urged to Cut Our Baltic Ties." *Chicago Tribune*, 15 March 1975, sec. 1, p. 10.

_____. "New Stress over the Baltic Lands." *Chicago Tribune*, 18 March 1975, sec. 2, p. 2.

Anderson, Edgar. "Die militarische Situation der Baltischen Staaten" (The military situation in the Baltic States). *Acta Baltica*, 8 (1968), 106-155.

_____. "The Role of the Baltic States between the USSR and Western Europe." *East European Quarterly*, 7 (1973), 286-287.

_____. "Military Policies and Plans of the Baltic States on the Eve of World War II." *Lituanus*, 20, 2 (Summer 1974), 15-34.

_____. "British Policy toward the Baltic States, 1940-41." *Journal of Baltic Studies*, 11, 4 (Winter 1980), 325-333.

Aruja, E. "UNO and the Baltic States." *Baltic Review*, 1, 4-5 (July-August 1946), 236.

Backis, Stasys Antanas. "Kataliku Baznycios doktrina apie tautu apsisprendimo teise"

(The doctrine of the Catholic Church on national self-determination). *Suvaziavimo darbai* (Proceedings of the Lithuanian Catholic Academy of Sciences), 4 (1961), 49-66.

Batten, Jeanne, and Anicetas Simutis. "Is a Small Nation Worth It?" *America*, 76, 25 (22 March 1947), 686-688, figures.

Bilmanis, Alfred. "Baltic States-The Belgium of Eastern Europe." *Social Science*, 21, 1 (January 1946), 31-38.

_____. "Relations between Latvia and Soviet-Russia in the Light of International Law." *Baltic Review*, 1, 6 (November 1946), 277-281, map.

Brakas, Martin. "Lithuania's International Status: Some Legal Aspects 1." *Baltic Review*, 37 (October 1970), 43-59.

_____. "Lithuania's International Status: Some Legal Aspects 2." *Baltic Review*, 38 (August 1971), 8-41.

Briggs, Herbert W. "Non-Recognition in the Courts: The Ships of the Baltic Republics." *American Journal of International Law*, 37, 4 (1943), 585-596.

Budreckis, Algirdas. "Soviet Attempts to Eradicate Lithuanian Sovereignty." *Baltic Review*, 34 (November 1967), 36-42.

Castle, Guy. "The Communist Takeover of the Republic of Lithuania." Transcript of interview with Minister Joseph Kajeckas, 14 August 1960. *Listener's Digest*, Communist Conquest Series IV, WEAM Radio, Arlington, VA, 11 pp.

Chevrier, Bruno. "The International Status of the Baltic States." *Baltic Review*, 1, 6 (November 1946), 270-276, ill.

Clarity, James F. "U.S. Eases Policy on Baltic States." *New York Times*, 18 May 1975, p. 16.

"Courtly defense of a higher law." *Chicago Tribune*, 26 January 1988, sec. 3, p. 3.

Crowe, David M., Jr. "Baltic Resource Material in the National Archives of the United States." *Journal of Baltic Studies*, 7, 1 (Spring 1976), 94-100.

"Daniloff Incident Sours U.S.-Soviet Conference." *Chicago Sun-Times*, 16 September 1986, p. 34.

Dicius, P. "Tarybine zemes reforma Lietuvoje 1940-1941 metais" (Soviet land reform in Lithuania 1940-1941). *Lietuvos TSR Mokslu Akademijos darbai* (Proceedings of the Lithuanian SSR Academy of Sciences), Series A, 1 (1958), 19-30.

"Forgive Them Their Helplessness." Editorial, *Chicago Tribune*, 5 April 1975, sec. 1, p. 12.

Genys, John B. "The Joint Baltic American Committee and the European Security Conference." *Journal of Baltic Studies*, 9 (1978), 245-258.

Gerutis, Albertas. "Kybartu aktai." *Aidai*, 4 (April 1976), 164-171.

Ginsburgs, George. "The Soviet Union and the Problem of Refugees and Displaced Persons 1917-1956." *American Journal of International Law*, 51 (1957), 325.

Goldie, Louis F. E. "Legal Aspects of the Refusal of Asylum by U.S. Coast Guard on 23 November, 1970." *Lituanus*, 18, 3 (Fall 1972), 58-71.

Graham, Malbone W., Jr. "What Does Non-Recognition Mean?" *Baltic Review*, 1, 4-5 (July-August 1946), 171-174.

_____. "Postscript on U.S. Recognition of the Baltic States in 1922." *Lituanus*, 12, 1 (Spring 1966), 90-91.

Hamilton, Kingsley W. "Aspects of the Coming Postwar Settlement." *International Conciliation*, 393 (October 1943), 543-563.

Herzfeld, Norma Krause. "The Persistent Lithuanians: A Government without a Country." *The Catholic Reporter*, 9 June 1961, sec. 2, p. 1.

Hough, William J. H., III. "The Annexation of the Baltic States and Its Effect on the Development of Law Prohibiting Forcible Seizure of Territory." *New York Law School Journal of International and Comparative Law*, 6, 2 (Winter 1985), 300-533, map.

Hudson, George F. "The Lesson of Yalta." *Commentary*, April 1954, pp. 373-380.

Ivinskis, Zenonas. "The Lithuanian Revolt against the Soviets in 1941." *Lituanus*, 12, 2 (Summer 1966), 5-19.

"Jackson Avoided Stand on Baltic." *The New York Times*, 20 October 1945, p. 4.

"JAV pareiskimas del Baltijos diplomatiniu atstovybiu" (U.S. statement regarding Baltic diplomatic representation). *Draugas*, 28 October 1980, p. 1.

Jefremenka, A. "Kolukiu kurimasis Tarybu Lietuvoje 1940-1941 m." (The establishment of collective farms in Soviet Lithuania 1940-1941). *Lietuvos TSR Mokslu Akademijos darbai* (Proceedings of the Lithuanian SSR Academy of Sciences). Series A, 2, 21 (1966), 211-223, figures.

Jennison, Earl W., Jr. Review essay. *Journal of Baltic Studies*, 6, 2-3 (Summer-Fall 1975), 222-224.

Juda, Lawrence. "United States' Nonrecognition of the Soviet Union's Annexation of the Baltic States: Politics and Law." *Journal of Baltic Studies*, 6, 4 (Winter 1975), 272-290.

Jurgela, Constantine R. "Loy Wesley Henderson: Lietuvos, Latvijos ir Estijos gynejas" (Loy Wesley Henderson: Defender of Lithuania, Latvia, and Estonia). *Draugas*, 3 April 1986, p. 3.

Kaasik, N. "The Legal Status of Baltic Refugees." *Baltic Review*, 1, 1 (December 1945), 21-26.

_____. "The Baltic Refugees in Sweden-A Successful Experiment." *Baltic Review*, 2, 1 (December 1947), 55-61.

Kajeckas, Joseph. "The Lithuanian Annexation." *Baltic Review*, 1, 4-5 (July-August 1946), 214-216.

Kancevicius, Vytautas. "Lietuvos istojimas i Tarybu Sajunga" (Lithuania's entry Into the Soviet Union). *Lietuvos istorijos metrastis 1972* (Yearbook of Lithuanian history 1972). Ed. Bronius Vaitkevicius. Vilnius: Mintis, 1973, 119-128.

"Karl Linnas' Deportation and USA Nonrecognition Policy." *Lituanus*, 31, 4 (Winter 1985), 91.

Kaslas, Bronis J. "The Lithuanian Strip in Soviet-German Secret Diplomacy, 1939-

1941." *Journal of Baltic Studies*, 4, 3 (Fall 1973), 211-225.

Keatley, Robert. "Homeless Diplomats: Their Lands Are Gone, Their Mission Remains." *The Wall Street Journal*, 20 March 1973, pp. 1, 20.

Kessler, Felix. "Phantom Diplomats Carry On in Britain-Men with No Country." *The Wall Street Journal*, 12 December 1970, pp. 1, 22.

Kirkconnell, Watson. "Eclipse of Baltic Freedom." *Baltic Review*, 1, 4-5 (July-August 1946), 221-223.

Klesment, Johannes. "The Crime: Seizure and Forced 'Incorporation.'" *Baltic Review*, 1 (December 1953), 5-14.

_____. "New Soviet Position on the Nationality of Estonians Abroad." *Highlights of Current Legislation and Activities in Mid-Europe*, September 1959, 347-348.

_____. "Soviet Theories on the Annexation of Estonia." *Baltic Review*, 24 (March 1962), 40-51.

Klimas, Antanas, et al. "Petras Klimas." *Lietuviu enciklopedija* (Lithuanian encyclopedia), 12 (1957), 120-121.

Klive, Adolfs. "Pacts of Mutual Assistance between the Baltic States and the USSR." *Baltic Review*, 18 (November 1959), 31-40.

Korsts, Voldemars, ed. *Heritage-Nationalities News*. Chicago: Republican State Nationalities Council of Illinois, 1978, 22 pp., ill.

"Kremlin Tactics in Converting the Baltic States Into Satellites." *Baltic Review*, 7 (16 June 1956), 12-22.

Krivickas, Domas.. "Formalities Preliminary to Aggression: Soviet and Nazi Tactics against Lithuania and Austria." *Baltic Review*, 5 (June 1955), 5-22.

_____. "The Evolution of the Soviet Constitution Imposed on Lithuania: One Nation's 'Road to Socialism.'" *Baltic Review*, 6 (March 1956), 41-62.

_____. "Lietuvos tarptautinis status" (Lithuania's international status). *Varpas*, 3-4 (1958), 71-82.

Kucenas, Silvia. "OSI Collaborates With KGB." *Lituanus*, 30, 1 (Spring 1984), 82-90.

Labanauskas, Pov. J. "Sostine atsisveikino su Loy Wesley Hendersonu" (The capital bids farewell to Loy Wesley Henderson). *Draugas*, 15 May 1986, p. 5.

Lacayo, Richard, "Problems of Crime and Punishment." *Time*, 20 April 1987, p. 60.

"'Laisve' nori pabegelius bausti" ('Liberty' ants to punish refugees"). *Musu kryziaus keliai* (Our ways of the cross), 1 (8 September 1945), 24-25.

Laucka, Juozas B. "Nepripazinimo politikos reikalu" (On the nonrecognition policy). *Draugas*, 11 June 1987, p. 4.

"Lietuvos pasiuntinybe prie sv. Sosto veike ir veiks" (The Lithuanian Mission to the Holy See shall continue to operate). *ELTA Information*, 15 January 1959, supplement, 2 pp.

Liivak, Arno. "Soviet Responses to Western Nonrecognition of Baltic Annexation." *Journal of Baltic Studies*, 18, 4 (Winter 1987), 329-348.

Lithuanian American Community. "Memorandum of Concerns Regarding the

Conduct of the Office of Special Investigations." *Lituanus*, 31, 4 (Winter 1985), 47-77.

_____. *Bulletin No. 15*. English summary, 29 December 1987.

"Lithuanian Rally for Sovereignty Clogs Capital." *Chicago Tribune*, 22 November 1988, sec. 1, p. 3.

Loeber, Dietrich A. "Baltic Gold in Great Britain." *Baltic Review*, 36 (October 1969), 11-39.

Lozoraitis, Stasys. "Some Juridical and Moral Aspects of the Occupation of Lithuania." *East and West*, 2, 7 (1956), 29-37.

Mackevicius, Mecislovas. "Lithuanian Resistance to German Mobilization Attempts 1941-1944." *Lituanus*, 32, 4 (Winter 1986), 9-22.

Mann, Clyde R. "Asylum Denied: The Vigilant Incident." *Lituanus*, 18, 3 (Fall 1972), 13-57.

Maziulis, Jonas. Review of Die Sowjetunion, die Baltischen Staaten und das Voelkerrecht, (The Soviet Union, the Baltic States, and international law), by Boris Meissner. *Baltic Review*, 7 (16 June 1956), 73-79.

Melngailis, Nils. "The Chautauqua Conference and Its Meaning for the Baltic Cause." *Lituanus*, 33, 1 (Winter 1987), 83-87.

Middleton, Drew. "Displaced Balts Studied by Allies." *The New York Times*, 19 October 1945, p. 9.

"Mire pabaltieciu draugas" (A Baltic friend dies). *Draugas*, 5 April 1986, p. 4.

Misiunas, Romualdas J. "Sovietu istoriografija, liecianti II-aji pasaulini kara ir Pabaltijo valstybes, 1944-1974 m." (Soviet historiography relative to World War II and the Baltic States 1944-1974). *Suvaziavimo darbai* (Proceedings of the Lithuanian Catholic Academy of Sciences) 10 (1976), pp. 313-342.

"The Missing Countries." *Baltic Review*, 1, 4-5 (July-August 1946), 233.

"Moscow Calls Estonians to Defend Actions." *Chicago Tribune*, 18 November 1988, sec. 1, p. 1.

Mulligan, Timothy P. "The OSS and the Nazi Occupation of the Baltic States, 1941-1945: A Note on Documentation." *Journal of Baltic Studies*, 13, 1 (Spring 1982), 53-58.

Nakas, Victor A. "OSI and the Baltic Community." *Lituanus*, 31, 3 (Fall 1985), 82-85.

"National Flags Fly in Latvia, Lithuania." *Chicago Tribune*, 8 October 1988, sec. 1, p. 4.

Padvaiskas, Edmund R. "World War II Russian-American Relations and the Baltic States: A Test Case." *Lituanus*, 28, 2 (Summer 1982), 5-27.

Pakstas, Kazys. "The Baltic Victims of the Present War." *World Affairs Interpreter*, 12, 1 (April 1941), 33-49, figures.

Pennar, Jaan. "Reflections on Union Republics in the New Soviet Constitution With Special Reference to Their Sovereignty and National Language." *Lituanus*, 25, 1 (Spring 1979), 5-16.

Peters, Charles. "Tilting at Windmills." *The Washington Monthly*, May 1984, p. 10.

Prunskis, Juozas. "In the Memory of Lithuanian Consul General Petras Dauzvardis (1895-1971)." *Lituanus*, 21, 3 (Fall 1975), 34-36.

"Puola popieziu uz okupacijos nepripazinima" (Pope attacked over nonrecognition of occupation). *Draugas*, 11 September 1987, p. 1.

Purre, Arnold. "Why the Baltic Soldiers Fought the Soviets." *Baltic Review*, 2, 2 (June 1948), 23-30.

Pusta, Kaarel Robert. "Estonia and Her Right to Freedom." *Journal of Central European Affairs*, 3, 3 (October 1943), 270-294.

Rackauskas, Konstantinas. "The Problem of the Baltic States." *Baltic Review*, 1, 2-3 (March 1946), 110-111.

_____. "How Has Russia Been 'Rewarded.'" *Baltic Review*, 1, 4-5 (July-August 1946), 235.

_____. "Power Politics vs. International Law." *Baltic Review*, 14 (1 August 1958), 61-79.

_____. "The Political Status of the Baltic Sea and Peace in Northern Europe." *Baltic Review*, 15 (December 1958), 70-80.

Regan, Paul M. "International Law and the Naval Commander." *U.S. Naval Institute Proceedings*, 107, 8 (August 1981), 51 ff., ill.

Remeikis, Thomas. "The Decision of the Lithuanian Government to Accept the Soviet Ultimatum of June 14, 1940." *Lituanus*, 21, 4 (Winter 1975), 19-44.

Rodek, Karl. "The Bases of Soviet Foreign Policy." *Foreign Affairs*, 12 (1934), 193ff.

Roosaare, Evald. "Consular Relations between the United States and the Baltic States." *Baltic Review*, 27 (June 1964), 11-36.

Ruksenas, Kazys. "Del Lietuvos zydu gelbejimo hitlerines okupacijos metais (1941-1945 m.)" (On the rescue of Jews during Hitler's occupation 1941-1945). *Lietuvos istorijos metrastis* (Yearbook of Lithuanian History), 1978, 36-49.

Rusmandel, Vaino J. "The Continued Legal Existence of the Baltic States." *Baltic Review*, 12 (7 November 1957), 48-68.

Sabaliunas, Leonas. "Baltic Perspectives: The Disillusionment with the West and the Choices Ahead." *Lituanus*, 14, 2 (Summer 1968), 5-18.

Schechtmann, Joseph B. "The Option Clause in the Reich's Treaties on the Transfer of Population." *American Journal of International Law*, 38 (1944), 356-374.

Schlesinger, Arthur, Jr. "West European Scholars Absolve Yalta." *The Wall Street Journal*, 16 June 1987, p. 26.

Schmidt, Folke. "Nationality and Domicile in Swedish Private Law." *The International Law Quarterly*, 4 (1951), 39-52.

_____. "Construction of Statutes." *Scandinavian Studies in Law*, 1 (1957), 188-190.

Schnorf, Richard A. "The Baltic States in U.S.-Soviet Relations, 1939-1942." *Lituanus*, 12, 1 (Spring 1966), 33-53.

_____. "The Baltic States in U.S.-Soviet Relations: The Years of Doubt, 1943-

1946." *Lituanus*, 12, 4 (Winter 1966), 56-75.

_____. "The Baltic States in U.S.-Soviet Relations: From Truman to Johnson." *Lituanus*, 14, 3 (Fall 1968), 43-60.

Schodolski, Vincent J. "Baltics Lead Perestroika Push: 3 Republics May Provide Test for Gorbachev's Reforms." *Chicago Tribune*, 9 October 1988, sec. 1, p. 8.

_____. "Independent Lithuanian Group Urges Cut in Ties to Moscow." *Chicago Tribune*, 24 October 1988, sec. 1, p. 7.

Schultz, Lothar. "The Soviet Concept of the Occupation and Incorporation of the Baltic States." *Baltic Review*, 10 (29 March 1957), 3-18.

"Secret Yalta Displaced Persons Clauses." *Baltic Review*, 1, 4-5 (July-August 1946), 238-240.

Sherwood, John. "The Keeper of Lithuania's Fading Flame." *Chicago Tribune*, 13 July 1978, section 2, pp. 1, 4.

Shtromas, Alexander. "Political and Legal Aspects of the Soviet Occupation and Incorporation of the Baltic States." *Baltic Forum*, 1, 1 (Fall 1984), 24-38.

Shub, Anatole. "Tell Defector's Stirring Plea for Free Lithuania." *Chicago Sun-Times*, 7 August 1971, p. 1.

_____. "Report on the Trial Testimony of Simas Kudirka-Lithuanian Sailor." *Lituanus*, 18, 3 (Fall 1972), 7-12.

Sidzikauskas, Vaclovas. "On the Seizure and Forced Incorporation of the Baltic States by the USSR." *Baltic Review*, 4 (April 1955), 76-79.

_____. "The United Nations and the Baltic States." *Baltic Review*, 25 (October 1962), 5-11.

Slavenas, Julius P. "Nazi Ideology and Policy in the Baltic States." *Lituanus*, 11, 1 (Spring 1965), 34-47.

_____. "Klaipeda Territory." *Encyclopedia Lituanica*. Ed. Simas Suziedelis and Vincas Rastenis. South Boston: Lithuanian Encyclopedia Press, 1973, vol. 3, 134-137.

Smulkstys, Julius. "The Incorporation of the Baltic States by the Soviet Union." *Lituanus*, 14, 2 (Summer 1968), 19-44.

"The Soviet Baltic Quislings in Paris." *Baltic Review*, 1, 6 (November 1946), 319-320.

"Soviets Face Baltic Crisis: Politburo Members Sound alarm." *Chicago Sun-Times*, 16 November 1988, p. 7.

Spekke, Arnolds. "The Baltic Case in the Light of History." *Baltic Review*, 35 (August 1968), 27-38.

Stewart, J. F. "The Changed Baltic." *The Scottish Geographical Magazine*, 56, 3 (November 1940), 115-126, ill., map.

Surdokas, C. "Lietuvos diplomatine ir konsularine tarnyba" (Lithuania's diplomatic and consular corps). *Karys*, 8 (October 1987), 362-364; 9 (November 1987), 405-412, ill.

Taagepara, Rein. "De-Choicing of Elections: July 1940 in Estonia." *Journal of Baltic Studies*, 14, 3 (Fall 1983), 215-246.

Tiede, Tom. "Legation is last bit of Lithuania." *Huntington Park [CA] Daily Signal*, 2 April 1979, p. 1.

Trimakas, Antanas. "Satellite Status for the Baltic States-A Possible Opening for Freedom." *Baltic Review*, 7 (16 June 1956), 3-11.

_____. "The Soviet Disregard of the Right of Peoples to Self-Determination." *Baltic Review*, 16 (April 1959), 36-43.

Truska, L. "Visuomenes klasines sudeties pakitimas Lietuvoje socializmo statybos metais 1940-1941 m." (The change in the class structure of Lithuania while building socialism 1940-1941." *Lietuvos TSR Mokslu Akademijos darbai* (Proceedings of the Lithuanian SSR Academy of Sciences), Series A, 2 (19) (1965), 193-211, figures.

Vahter, Leonhard. "Molotov-Ribbentrop Pact of August 23, 1939." *Baltic Review*, 18 (November 1959), 58-64.

Vardys, V. Stanley. "The Baltic Peoples." *Problems of Communism*, 16, 5 (September-October 1967), 55-64.

Vilkatas, V. "Which Way Krushchev Aims at Indirect Recognition." *Baltic Review*, 21 (December 1960), 37-41.

Vitols, Hugo. "L'Annexion de la Lettonie par L'Union Sovietique et le Droit" (The annexation of Latvia by the Soviet Union and the law). *Baltic Review*, 1, 4-5 (July-August 1946), 193-203.

Vizulis, Jazeps. "Die Baltischen Lander-Opfer Sowjetischer Aggression" (The Baltic States-victims of Soviet aggression). *Acta Baltica*, 8 (1968), 74-105.

_____. "The Diplomacy of the Allied Powers toward the Baltic States (1942-1945)." *Baltic Review*, 35 (August 1968), 49-61.

Vuorjoki, Asko. "The Baltic Question in Today's World." *Baltic Review*, 38 (August 1971), 2-7.

Williams, G. Mennen. "Global Self-Determination and the Baltic States." *Baltic Review*, 31 (April 1966), 3-6.

Wright, Quincy. "The Legal Foundations of the Stimson Doctrine." *Pacific Affairs*, 8 (1935), 439-446.

Zygas, Juozas. "Lietuvos diplomatines tarnybos testinumas" (Continuity of Lithuania's diplomatic service). *Draugas*, 31 January 1987, pp. 3, 6.

Legal Cases

In re Adler's Estate, 197 Misc. 104, 93 NYS 2d 416 (Sur. Ct. Kings), appeal dismissed, 279 App. Div. 745, 109 NYS 2d 175 (1951), order vacated, 110 NYS 2d 283 (NYAD 1952); 122 *The New York Law Journal* 1777.

In re Alexandravicius, 83 NJ Super. 303-312, 199 A. 2d 662-666 (App. Div. 1964), cert. denied, 43 NJ 128, 202 A. 2d 702 (1964).

In re Estate of Bielinis, 55 Misc. 2d 191 NYS 2d 819 (Sur. Ct. Kings), affirmed 30 AD 2d 778; 292 NYS 2d 363 (1968).

In re Braunstein's Estate, 202 Misc. 244, 114 NYS 2d 280 (Sur. Ct. NY) (1952).

Buxhoeveden v. Estonian State Bank, et al., New York Supreme Court, Special Term, Queens County, 21 April 1943; 41 NYS 2d 752-757; *Ibid.*, Part I, 8 October 1948; 84 NYS 2d 2.

Compagnie Belgo-Lithuanienne d'Electricite v. Societe des Centrales Electriques Regionales. Decision of High Court of Belgium, 26 October 1946. *Journal du Droit International* (Journal of international law), 77 (1950), 865-887.

Daniunas v. Simutis, 481 F.Supp. 132 (SDNY 1978).

The Elise, C.Ex., Canada, 1948.

Estonian State Cargo and Passenger S.S. Line et al. v. United States, 116 F.Supp. 447 (Ct. of Cl., 1953).

The Florida, 133 F 2d. 719.

Gerbaud v. de (von) Meden, The Cour de Cassation, Chambre Civile, affirming on 10 January 1951 the judgement of the Court of Appeals in favor of the apellee. *Journal du Droit International* (Journal of international law), 78 (1951), 168-173.

Jordan v. The Austrian Republic and Taubner, Austrian Supreme Court, 15 October 1947. Annual Digest (1947), 41.

In re Kapocius, 36 Misc. 2d. 1087, 234 NYS 2d 346 (Sur. Kings 1962).

Kling and Others v. Lesser and Rotterdamsche Bank, Netherlands, 1955, *International Law Review*, 1955, 101.

The Kotkas, 35 F. Supp. 810 ff., District Court, EDNY, 22 November 1940; 37 F. Supp. 835 ff., do. 31 March 1941.

Laane and Baltser v. Estonian State Cargo and Passenger S.S. Liney, 1949 *Canada Law Reports* 539.

Republic of Latvia Case, West Germany, *International Law Review*, 1955, 230.

Latvian State Cargo and Passenger S.S. Line v. Clark, F. Supp. 453 (1948).

Latvian State Cargo and Passenger S.S. Line v. McGrath, 188 F. 2d 1000 (DC Circuit), 1951.

Latvian State Cargo and Passenger S.S. Line v. United States, 116 F. Supp. 717 (Ct. of Cl., 1953).

Laurine v. Laurine, Swedish Supreme Court (Hogstra Domstol), 25 February 1949, *Nytt Juridiskt Arkiv*, 1949, part 1, p. 82.

In re Linnas, A8 085 628, U.S. Immigration Court, New York City, 5 April 1985.

Lohk v. Lohk, Swedish Supreme Court (Hogstra Domstol), 12 December 1948, *Nytt Juridiskt Arkiv*, 1948, part 1, p. 805.

Matter of Luberg's Estate, 19 AD 2d 370; 243 NYS 2d 747 (1963).

McEvoy v. Owners of Otto, 4 July 1942, *The Irish Law Reports*, p. 148.

The Maret, 145 F. 2d 431, USCA, 3rd Circuit, 1944.

A/S Merilaid & Co., v. Chase National Bank of City of New York, 71 NYS 2d 377

(1947).

In re Mitzkel's Estate, 36 Misc. 2d 671; 233 NYS 2d 519 (Sur. Ct. Kings 1962).

In re Niggol's Estate, 115 NYS 2d 577 (1952).

North Sea Continental Shelf, West Germany v. Denmark; West Germany v. The Netherlands, 1969 International Court of Justice 3 (Judgment of 20 February 1969).

In the Estate of Pikelny, United Kingdom, *International Law Review*, 1955, 97.

Pulenciks v. Augustovskis, Divorce decision of the Tribunal Civil de Bruxelles (Civil Tribunal of Brussels), 5 April 1951, *Pasicrisie Belge*, 1952, III, 40-42.

The Regent, 35 F. Supp. 985 ff, District Court, EDNY, 22 November 1940.

Reports of Selected Cases Decided in the Courts of the State of New York. James M. Flavin, State Reporter. Volume 36, *Miscellaneous Reports* 2d Series. Albany: William Press, 1963.

R[ussian]. S[ocialist]. F[ederated]. Soviet Republic v. Cibrario, NYCA, 1923, 235 NY 255; 139 NE 259.

The Matter of Mike Shaskus, 131 *The New York Law Journal* 12 (1954), in the King's County Surrogate Court, New York.

The Signe, 37 F. Supp. 810, District Court, ED Louisiana, New Orleans Division, 4 March 1941; 39 F. Supp. 810, do. 22 July 1941; 133 F. 2d 719, Circuit Court of Appeals, Fifth Circuit, 20 February 1943.

A/S Tallinna Laeviihisus and Others v. Tallinn Shipping Company, Ltd., and Estonian State Steamship Line, 79 *Lloyds List Law Reports* 245 (1946); 80 *Ibid.* 99 (1947).

United States v. Rumsa, 212 F. 2d 927 (7th Circuit, 1954); cert. denied, 348 US 838.

The Matter of the Estate of Julius Yuska, 128 Misc. 2d 98; 488 NYS 2d 609 (Sur. Kings 1985).

Zarine v. Owners of the S.S. Ramava, Eire High Court, 29-30 April, 1, 10 May 1941; Eire Supreme Court, 3 July 1941. 1942 *The Irish Law Reports* 148; 36 *American Journal of International Law* 490.

Documents

Ad Hoc Committee Consisting of the World Councils of Byelorussians, Estonians, Latvians, Lithuanians, Turkestanians and Ukrainians. *A Memorandum Concerning the Decolonization of the Union of Soviet Socialist Republics Submitted to the Members of the 35th U.N. General Assembly.* New York: Ad Hoc Committee, 1980, 22 pp.

Allied Expeditionary Force. Supreme Headquarters. G-5 Division. Displaced Persons Branch. *Guide to the Care of Displaced Persons in Germany.* Revised May 1945.

Aiello, Stephen, White House Office of Public Affairs. "Draft Statement." *Draugas*,

28 October 1980, p. 1.

Arums Zinta. *Joint Baltic American National Committee (JBANC) 1986 Annual Report*. Rockville, MD: JBANC, 1987, 35 pp., ill., maps.

Assembly of Captive European Nations (ACEN). *First Session*, Plenary Meetings of September 20 and 21, 1954. New York: ACEN, 1954, 68 pp.

_____. *First Session*, September 20, 1954-February 11, 1955. Organization, Resolutions, Reports, Debate. New York: ACEN, 1955, 191 pp.

_____. *First Session (Second Part)*. February 12, 1955- September 20, 1955. Organization, Resolutions, Reports, Debate. New York: ACEN, 1955, 175 pp.

_____. *Third Session*. November 1956-September 1957. Organization, Resolutions, Reports. New York: ACEN, 1957, 126 pp.

_____. *A Few Facts on the New Colonialism*. New York: ACEN, 1960, 30 pp., figures, maps.

_____. *International Agreements and Pledges Concerning East-Central Europe*. New York: ACEN, 1960, 48 pp.

_____. *Facts on the Captive Countries*, 2d rev. ed. New York: ACEN, 1961, 22 pp.

Baltic Committee in Scandinavia (BCS). *The Baltic States 1940-1972: Documentary Background and Summary of Developments*. Stockholm: BCS, 1972, 121 pp., map.

_____. *Memorandum Regarding the European Security and Cooperation Conference and the Baltic States*. Stockholm: BCS, 1972, 4 pp.

Baltic Council of Australia (BCA). *Notes and Documents on Australian Recognition of the Incorporation of the Baltic States into the USSR*. n.p.: BCA, 1974, 18 pp.

Bilmanis, Alfred, ed. *Latvian-Russian Relations: Documents*. Washington, D.C.: Latvian Legation, 1944, 255 pp., map.

Brazil. Ministry of Foreign Affairs. *Lista do Corpo Consular Estrangeiro* (List of the foreign consular corps), 31 December 1955. Rio de Janeiro: Departamento de Imprensa Nacional, 1956, 71 pp.

Brownlie, Ian, ed. *Basic Documents in International Law*. London: Oxford University Press, 1967, 243 pp.

Canada. House of Commons. *House of Commons Debates*. Official Report, 17 May 1954, vol. 96, column 1767.

Canada. Ministry of Foreign Affairs. *Canadian Representatives Abroad and Representatives of Other Countries in Canada*. Published annually by the Canadian Ministry of Foreign Affairs.

Chinese Delegation [to the League of Nations]. Press Bureau. *Japanese Aggression and the League of Nations*, 1939. V. Geneva: PBCD, 1939, 82 pp.

Comite Supreme de Liberation de la Lithuanie (Supreme Committee for the Liberation of Lithuania). *Memorandum Relatif a la Restitution de l'Independance d L'Etat Lithuanien* (Memorandum relative to the restoration of the independence of the Lithuanian state). Fulda, West Germany: Lithuanian Executive Council, 87 pp., maps.

Conference of Free Byelorussians, Estonian World Council, Lithuanian World Community, World Congress of Free Ukrainians, World Federation of Free Latvians. *To the United Nations General Assembly: A Resolution with Appended Documents Concerning the Decolonization of the Union of Soviet Socialist Republics*. Toronto-New York: Joint Committee, Ucrainica Research Institute, 1978, 148 pp., ill., figures.

Council of Europe. *The Baltic States and the Soviet Union*. Reprinted from a Report of the Council of Europe, with a Preface and Supplementary Comments. Stockholm: Estonian Information Centre, Latvian National Foundation, Supreme Committee for the Liberation of Lithuania, 1962, 52 pp., figures, map.

Derwinski, Rep. Edward J. "Remarks in the House of Representatives on Proposed Consular Convention With the Soviet Union." *News Release*, 9 August 1965, 5 pp.

_____. "Derwinski-Paletskis [*sic*] Debate Again." *News Release*, 16 October 1970, 1 p.

_____. "Derwinski Introduces New Baltic States Resolution." *News Release*, 18 November 1977, 1 p.

Dobriansky, Lev E. *Captive Nations Week: Red Nightmare, Freedom's Hope*. Speeches of Hon. Daniel J. Flood of Pennsylvania and Hon. Edward J. Derwinski of Illinois, et al. in the House of Representatives and in the Senate of the United States. Washington, D.C.: National Captive Nations Committee, 1966, 310 pp.

Estonia. Consulate General. *Policy of the United States of America towards Estonia*. New York: Consulate General of Estonia, n.d., 12 pp.

Estonian National Council (ENC). *Estonian National Council 1947-1957*. Stockholm: ENC, 1957, 21 pp., ill.

Holy See and the Republic of Lithuania. *Konkordatas tarp Sventojo Sosto ir Lietuvos valdzios* (Concordat between the Holy See and the Government of Lithuania). Chicago: Draugas, 1928, 16 pp.

International Commission of Jurists (ICJ). *The International Commission of Jurists: Basic Facts*. Geneva: ICJ, 1962, 19 pp.

International Refugee Organization. *Tarptautines Tremtiniu Organizacijos Konstitucija* (International Refugee Organization constitution). Augsburg, West Germany: Ziburiai, 1947, 12 pp.

Italy. Foreign Ministry. *Ambasciate e legazioni estere in Italia* (Foreign embassies and legations in Italy). Published annually by the Italian Foreign Ministry.

Jacovskis, E., E. Rozauskas, and J. Ziugzda, eds. *Tarybu valdzios atkurimas Lietuvoje 1940-1941: Dokumentu rinkinys* (Reconstitution of Soviet rule in Lithuania 1940-1941: Documentary collection). Vilnius: Mintis, 1965, 347 pp., ill.

Jurgela, Constantine R. Letter to Robert A. Vitas, 22 May 1986.

Kaslas, Bronis J., ed. *The USSR-German Aggression against Lithuania*. New York: Robert Speller and Sons, 1973, 543 pp., ill., maps.

Kaslas, Bronis J. *La Lithuanie et la Seconde Guerre Mondiale: Recueil des Documents* (Lithuania and the Second World War: Documentary study). Paris: G.-P. Maisonneuve et Larose, 1981, 347 pp., map.

Kudirka, Simas. *In Defense of Human Rights*. Testimony of Simas Kudirka at the Bicentennial Convocation on Global Justice convened by the National Conference of Catholic Bishops Committee for the Bicentennial, 14 July 1976. Maspeth, NY: Lithuanian Roman Catholic Religious Aid, 1976, 24 pp.

Latvian Legation. *Latvia in 1939-1942: Background; Bolshevik and Nazi Occupation; Hopes for Future*. Washington, D.C.: Latvian Legation, 1942, 137 pp., figures, maps.

_____. *Latvia under German Occupation 1941-1943*. Washington, D.C.: Latvian Legation, 1943, 114 pp., figures, map.

_____. *Latvian-U.S.S.R. Relations: Memorandum*. Washington, D.C.: Latvian Legation, 1944, 16 pp.

Ligue des Droits des Peuples. *Les Etats Baltes* (The Baltic States). Conference at the Sorbonne, 31 May 1948. Toulouse: Impremerie Toulousaine R. Lion, 1948, 43 pp.

Lithuania. Chancellory of the Cabinet. *Vyriausybes zinios* (Government news). Kaunas: Ministru tarybos kanceliarija/Chancellory of the Cabinet, 1920-1940.

Lithuania: The Road to Independence 1917-1940. A Documentary Survey. Moscow: Novosti, 1987, ill., maps.

Lithuanian Consulate General, Chicago. Official documents and correspondence regarding the case of Simas Kudirka 1970-1975. Now housed at the Dauzvardis Consular Archive of the Lithuanian Research and Studies Center, Chicago.

Lithuanian Consulate General, Los Angeles. Letter of Consul General Julius J. Bielskis to Lithuanian Minister Juozas Kajeckas, 17 July 1971.

Lithuanian Legation. Letter of Minister Povilas Zadeikis to Acting Secretary of State Dean Acheson, No. 1237, 29 July 1946.

_____. *Some Aspects of the Soviet Russian Rule in Occupied Lithuania June 15, 1940-June 15, 1950: Ten Years of Lithuania's Sufferings under Foreign Tyranny*. Washington, D.C.: Legation, 1950, 45 pp.

_____. *Lithuania's Occupation by the Soviet Union*. Washington, D.C.: Lithuanian Legation, 1960, 28 pp.

Lithuanian Provisional Government. Chancellory of the Cabinet. *Laikinosios vyriausybes zinios* (Provisional Government news). Kaunas: Ministru tarybos kanceliarija/ Chancellory of the Cabinet, 1918-1920.

Lithuanian SSR Ministry of Justice. *Lietuvos TSR istatymu, Auksciausiosios Tarybos Prezidiumo isaku ir Vyriausybes nutarimu chronologinis rinkinys I: 1940-1947*

(Chronological collection of the laws of the Lithuanian SSR, decrees by the Lithuanian SSR Supreme Soviet, and decisions of the Lithuanian SSR government I: 1940-1947). Vilnius: State Political and Scientific Press, 1956, 320 pp., figures.

_____. Supreme Soviet. *Lietuvos TSR administracinis-teritorinis suskirstymas 1959 m. vasario 1 dienai* (Lithuanian SSR administrative-territorial divisions as of 1 February 1959). Vilnius: State Political and Scientific Press, 1959, 1034 pp., figures.

Merkys, Antanas, ed. *Lietuvos istatymai: Sistematizuotas istatymu, instrukciju ir isakymu rinkinys* (Statutes of Lithuania: Systematic collection of statutes, instructions and orders). Kaunas: A. Merkys and V. Petrulis, 1922, 1031 pp., figures.

_____, ed. *Lietuvos istatymai: Sistematizuotas istatymu, instrukciju ir isakymu rinkinys. Pirmas tesinys ligi 1924 m. liepos 1 d.* (Statutes of Lithuania: Systematic collection of statutes, instructions and orders. First supplement to 1 July 1924). Klaipeda: Rytas, 1925, 905 pp., figures.

Pennsylvania Commission on Displaced Persons (PCDP). *Third Annual Report 1951*. Harrisburg, PA: PCDP, 1952, 78 pp., ill., figures.

Percy, Senator Charles H. Statement on the planting of Baltic flags on the moon by the crew of Apollo 16. 21 March 1972.

Polish American Congress (PAC). *A Memorandum to the Senate of the United States on the Crimea Decisions Concerning Poland*. n.p.: PAC, 1945, 8 pp.

Prunskis, Juozas, ed. *Lithuania Must Be Free: Congressional Voices for Lithuania's Independence*. Chicago: Lithuanian American Council, 1981, 72 pp., ill.

Rei, August. *Nazi-Soviet Conspiracy and the Baltic States: Diplomatic Documents and Other Evidence*. London: Boreas, 1948, 61 pp.

Representatives of the Baltic Nations. *Appeal of the Representatives of the Baltic Nations to the General Assembly of the United Nations*. Jointly presented on November 24, 1947 by the Envoys of the Three Baltic States-Lithuania, Latvia and Estonia-in Washington to His Excellency Dr. Osvaldo Aranha, President of the General Assembly of the United Nations. Flushing Meadows, NY: n.p., 1947, 32 pp.

Rumsa, Antanas Juratis. *A Short Review of the Legal Status Determination Related to My Foreign Citizenship and the Military Service in the Armed Forces of the United States*. Chicago: Author, 1971, 49 pp.

Soviet Information Bureau. *The Soviet Union, Finland and the Baltic States*. n.p.: Soviet War News, 1941, 6 pp.

_____. *Falsificators of History (An Historical Note)*. Washington, D.C.: Embassy of the USSR, 1948, 61 pp.

Supreme Lithuanian Committee of Liberation. *Appeal to the United Nations on Genocide*. n.p.: Lithuanian Foreign Service, n.d., 80 pp.

_____. *Memorandum on the Restoration of Lithuania's Independence*. n.p.:

Lithuanian Executive Council, 1950, 93 pp., maps.

United Kingdom. *The Foreign Office List and Diplomatic and Consular Yearbook.* London: Foreign Office. Issued annually.

_____. *Parliamentary Debates (Hansard).* House of Commons. Official Report. London: H.M. Stationery Office, 21 December 1944, vol. 406, column 1953; 31 January 1945, vol. 406, column 1464; 23 May 1947, vol. 437, column 2785; 15 February 1954, vol. 523, column 1637; 22 January 1969, vol. 776, column 611.

United Nations. *UNO Yearbook 1946-47.* New York: U.N., 1947.

_____. *Vienna Convention on Consular Relations.* Doc. A/Conf. 25/12, 23 April 1963. New York: U.N., 1963.

United Nations. Department of Public Information. Press and Publications Division. "USSR Submits Draft Resolution on Repatriation of Refugees." Press Release GA/SHC/469, 5 October 1955, 4 pp.

United Nations. International Refugee Organization (IRO). *The Facts About Refugees.* Geneva: IRO, 1948, 24 pp., ill., figures.

_____. *Le Probleme des Refugies* (The problem of the refugees). Geneva: IRO, 1948, 24 pp., ill., figures.

_____. *Report to the General Council of the International Refugee Organization by the Executive Secretary of the Preparatory Commission.* 1 July 1947-30 June 1948. Geneva: IRO, 1948, figures.

_____. *The Forgotten Elite: The Story of Refugee Specialists.* Geneva: IRO, 1949, 12 pp., ill., figures.

_____. *Rapport du Directeur General au Conseil General de l'Organisation Internationale pour les Refugies* (Report to the director general of the general council of the International Refugee Organization). 1 July 1948-30 June 1949. Geneva: IRO, 1949, 95 pp., ill., figures.

United States. Armed Forces. *The USSR: Institutions and People.* A brief Handbook for the use of Officers of the Armed Forces of the United States. Washington, D.C.: U.S. Government Printing Office, 1945, 130 pp., ill., figures.

United States. Army Institute for Advanced Russian and East European Studies (USAIAREES). *50 Years of Soviet Power.* Soviet Affairs Symposium, 5-7 June 1967. Garmisch, West Germany: USAIAREES, 1967, 140 pp.

United States. Commission on Security and Cooperation in Europe (USCSCE). *Report to the Congress of the United States on Implementation of the Final Act of the Conference on Security and Cooperation in Europe: Findings and Recommendations Two Years after Helsinki.* Washington, D.C.: USCSCE, 1977, 254 pp., figures.

_____. *The Belgrade Followup Meeting to the Conference on Security and Cooperation in Europe: A Report and Appraisal.* Transmitted to the Committee on International Relations, U.S. House of Representatives.

Washington, D.C.: U.S. Government Printing Office, 1978, 105 pp.

————. *Implementation of the Final Act of the Conference on Security and Cooperation in Europe: Findings and Recommendations Five Years after Helsinki*. Report submitted to the Congress of the United States. Washington, D.C.: U.S. Government Printing Office, 1980, 341 pp.

————. *Implementation of the Final Act of the Conference on Security and Cooperation in Europe: Findings and Recommendations Seven Years after Helsinki*. Report submitted to the Congress of the United States. Washington, D.C.: U.S. Government Printing Office, 1982, 258 pp.

United States. Congress. *Congressional Record*. 29 March 1945, p. A 1707; 1 May 1948, p. 6795; 11 July 1974, pp. H 6443-H 6444; 2 December 1975, pp. H 11587-H 11594; 5 December 1975, pp. H 11587-H 11594; 10 October 1979, pp. E 4944-E 4945; 13 November 1979, pp. H 10583-H 10586, H 10603; 28 November 1979, p. S 17441; 4 February 1980, p. S 2257.

————. *Freedom for Lithuania: Lithuania's Independence Day in the Congress of the United States*. Excerpts from the Proceedings of the United States Senate and House of Representatives, February-June 1955. Washington, D.C.: U.S. Government Printing Office, 1955, 75 pp.

————. *Lithuania's Independence Day in Congress of the United States*. Excerpts from Proceedings of the Senate of the United States and House of Representatives. Washington: US Government Printing Office, 1953, 49 pp.

————. *Public Law 774*. 25 June 1948.

————. *Public Law 555*. 16 June 1950.

————. *Public Law 203*. 7 August 1953.

————. *Public Law 95-549*. 30 October 1978.

————. *Public Law 97-252*. 8 September 1982.

United States. Displaced Persons Commission. *Second Semiannual Report to the President and the Congress*. 1 August 1949. Washington, D.C.: U.S. Government Printing Office, 1949.

United States. Executive Office of the President. Letter of Henry A. Kissinger to Senator Hugh Scott, 28 October 1972.

United States. Office of the Federal Register. *Code of Federal Regulations*. Title 3-The President, 1938-1943 Compilation. Washington, D.C.: U.S. Government Printing Office, 1968, 1,442 pp., figures.

United States. General Accounting Office. *Helsinki Commission: The First 8 Years*. Report to the Chairman of the Commission on Security and Cooperation in Europe. GAO/NSIAD-85-57, 1 March 1985. Washington, D.C.: U.S. Government Printing Office, 1985, 33 pp.

————. *Asylum: Uniform Application of Standard Uncertain-Few Denied Applicants Deported*. GAO/GGD-87-33BR, 9 January 1987. Washington, D.C.: U.S. Government Printing Office, 43 pp., figures.

United States. High Commission for Germany. *Report to the U.S. High Commissioner for Germany on the International Refugee Organization.* U.S. Zone of Germany, 22 October 1951, 22 pp., annexes, figures.

United States. House of Representatives. House Resolution 346, 20 July 1953.

_____. *House Report 95-1452,* 1978.

_____. *House Concurrent Resolution 57,* 4 February 1981.

United States. House of Representatives. Committee on Foreign Affairs. Special Subcommittee. *Voluntary Foreign Aid: The Nature and Scope of Postwar Private American Assistance Abroad, with Special Reference to Europe.* 80th Congress, 2d Session. Washington, D.C.: U.S. Government Printing Office, 1948, 91 pp., figures.

_____. *Background Information of the Soviet Union in International Relations.* 81st Congress, 2d Session, 22 September 1950. Washington, D.C.: U.S. Government Printing Office, 1950, 54 pp., figures, maps.

United States. House of Representatives. Committee on Foreign Affairs. Subcommittee on Europe. *Captive European Nations.* 87th Congress, 2d Session. Washington, D.C.: U.S. Government Printing Office, 1962, 377 pp., figures.

_____. *Conditions in the Baltic States and in Other Countries of Eastern Europe.* 89th Congress, 1st Session. Washington, D.C.: U.S. Government Printing Office, 1965, 92 pp.

United States. House of Representatives. Committee on Foreign Affairs. Subcommittee on State Department Organization and Foreign Operations. *Attempted Defection by Lithuanian Seaman Simas Kudirka: Hearings.* Washington, D.C.: U.S. Government Printing Office, 1971, 247 pp., ill.

_____. *Attempted Defection by Lithuanian Seaman Simas Kudirka: Report.* Washington: US Government Printing Office, 1971, 11 pp.

United States. House of Representatives. Committee on the Judiciary. *Proceedings of the National Resettlement Conference for Displaced Persons.* 81st Congress, 1st Session. Washington, D.C.: U.S. Government Printing Office, 1949, 72 pp.

_____. *Displaced Persons Act...with Amendments of June 16, 1950...and Notes of Amendments.* Washington, D.C.: U.S. Government Printing Office, 1950, 18 pp.

United States. House of Representatives. Committee on International Relations. *Second Semiannual Report by the President to the Commission on Security and Cooperation in Europe.* 95th Congress, 1st Session. Washington, D.C.: U.S. Government Printing Office, 1977, 45 pp.

United States. House of Representatives. Committee on International Relations. Subcommittee on International Political and Military Affairs. *Conference on Security and Cooperation in Europe.* 94th Congress, 1st Session. Washington, D.C.: U.S. Government Printing Office, 1975, 52 pp.

_____. *Conference on Security and Cooperation in Europe II.* 94th Congress, 2d Session. Washington, D.C.: U.S. Government Printing Office, 1976, 191 pp., figures.

United States. House of Representatives. Select Committee on Communist Aggression. *Communist Takeover and Occupation of Latvia*. Special Report No. 12. 83d Congress, 2d Session. Washington, D.C.: U.S. Government Printing Office, 1954, 25 pp.

————. *Investigation of Communist Takeover and Occupation of the Non-Russian Nations of the U.S.S.R.: Eighth Interim Report of Hearings*. 83d Congress, 2d Session. Washington, D.C.: U.S. Government Printing Office, 1954, 370 pp.

————. *Second Interim Report of the Committee on Communist Aggression*. 83d Congress, 2d Session. Washington, D.C.: U.S. Government Printing Office, 1954, 25 pp.

————. Select Committee on Communist Aggression. *Communist Takeover and Occupation of Estonia*. Special Report No. 3. 83d Congress, 2d Session. Washington, D.C.: U.S. Government Printing Office, 1955, 34 pp.

————. *Communist Takeover and Occupation of Lithuania*. Special Report No. 14. 83d Congress, 2d Session. Washington, D.C.: U.S. Government Printing Office, 1955, 20 pp.

————. *Summary Report*. 83d Congress, 2d Session. Washington, D.C.: U.S. Government Printing Office, 1955, 44 pp., figures.

————. Subcommittee on Poland, Lithuania, and Slovakia. *Investigation of Communist Takeover and Occupation of Poland, Lithuania, and Slovakia: Sixth Interim Report of Hearings*. 83d Congress, 2d Session. Washington, D.C.: U.S. Government Printing Office, 1954, 214 pp., figures.

United States. House of Representatives. Select Committee to Investigate the Incorporation of the Baltic States into the U.S.S.R. *Baltic States Investigation I*. Washington, D.C.: U.S. Government Printing Office, 1953, 678 pp., ill.

————. *Third Interim Report of the Select Committee on Communist Aggression*. Washington, D.C.: U.S. Government Printing Office, 1954, 537 pp.

United States. Department of Justice. Order of the Attorney General, Transfer of Functions of the Special Litigation Unit within the Immigration and Naturalization Service of the Department of Justice to the Criminal Division of the Department of Justice. 851-79. 4 September 1979.

————. Department of Justice. Letter of Assistant Attorney General Steven Trott to Rep. Frank Annunzio, 7 November 1983.

United States. Legislative Reference Service. *Events Leading up to World War II 1931-1944*. Washington, D.C.: U.S. Government Printing Office, 1944, 421 pp.

————. *World Communist Movement: Selective Chronology 1818-1957. I: 1818-1945*. Washington, D.C.: U.S. Government Printing Office, 1960, 232 pp.

United States. Office of Military Government for Germany. Legal Division. *Gesetzliche Vorschriften der Amerikanischen Militarregierung in Deutschland* (Compilation of statutes of the American military government in Germany). Issue A, 1 June 1946-Issue H, 16 January 1948. Printed by Publishing

Operations Branch, Information Control Division, Office of Military Government for Bavaria.

United States Senate. Letter of Senator Charles H. Percy, 21 March 1972.

_____. *Senate Resolution 406.* 5 May 1976.

_____. *Senate Calendar. No. 520.* 13 December 1979.

_____. Committees on Armed Services and Foreign Relations. *Hearings on the Military Situation in the Far East.* 82d Congress, 1st Session. Washington, D.C.: U.S. Government Printing Office, 1951.

_____. Committee on Commerce. Subcommittee of the Subcommittee on Communications. *Freedom of Communications I: The Speeches, Remarks, Press Conferences, and Statements of Senator John F. Kennedy. 1 August-7 November 1960.* 87th Congress, 1st Session. Washington, D.C.: U.S. Government Printing Office, 1961.

United States. Senate. Committee on Foreign Relations. *Lithuania-Consular Convention.* 76th Congress, 3d Session, Executive Report No. 8, 22 May 1940. Washington, D.C.: U.S. Government Printing Office, 1940, 9 pp.

_____. *Consular Convention with the Soviet Union.* Hearings, 90th Congress, 1st Session, on Executive D, 88th Congress, 2d Session. Washington, D.C.: U.S. Government Printing Office, 1967, 374 pp., figures.

_____. *United States Recognition of Foreign Governments.* 91st Congress, 1st Session. Washington, D.C.: U.S. Government Printing Office, 1969.

_____. *Third Semiannual Report by the President to the Commission on Security and Cooperation in Europe.* Washington, D.C.: U.S. Government Printing Office, 1977, 34 pp.

_____. Committee on Foreign Relations. "Baltic Radio Service to Be Transferred to Radio Free Europe at Percy Request." *Media Notice,* 2 October 1984, 1 p.

_____. Subcommittee on the International Convention on the Prevention and Punishment of the Crime of Genocide. *The Genocide Convention.* 81st Congress, 2d Session. Washington, D.C.: U.S. Government Printing Office, 1950, figures, map.

United States Senate. Committee on the Judiciary. Subcommittee to Investigate Immigration and Naturalization. *Displaced Persons in Europe.* 80th Congress, 2d Session. Washington, D.C.: U.S. Government Printing Office, 1948, 84 pp., figures.

United States. Department of State. *The Belgrade Followup Meeting to the Conference on Security and Cooperation in Europe, 4 October 1977-9 March 1978.* Special Report No. 43. Washington, D.C.: U.S. Government Printing Office, 1978, 36 pp.

_____. "Case Studies in Soviet Colonialism." *Soviet Affairs Notes,* 249. 22 November 1960. n.p., 1960, 24 pp.

_____. Circular to State Governors. March 1948.

_____. *Department of State Bulletin*. 27 July 1940, p. 48; 1 August 1942, p. 660; 5 August 1945, pp. 153-161; 11 August 1975, pp. 204-206; 26 September 1977, pp. 404-410.

_____. *Digest of International Law*. Ed. Marjorie M. Whiteman. Washington, D.C.: U.S. Government Printing Office, 1964.

_____. *Diplomatic List*. Washington, D.C.: U.S. Government Printing Office. Published quarterly.

_____. *Documents on German Foreign Policy 1918-1945*. Series D (1937-1945), Volume X: The War Years. 23 June-31 August 1940. Washington, D.C.: U.S. Government Printing Office, 1957, 615 pp.

_____. "For the Press No. 67: Statement by Acting Secretary of State Walter Bedell Smith on the 36th Anniversary of the Declaration of Lithuanian Independence." 15 February 1954, 1 p.

_____. "For the Press No. 90: Statement by Secretary of State John Foster Dulles for Lithuanian and Estonian National Days." 16 February 1953, 1 p.

_____. *Foreign Consular Offices in the United States*. Washington, D.C.: U.S. Government Printing Office. Published quarterly.

_____. *Foreign Relations of the United States: Diplomatic Papers, 1940, Volume I, General*. Washington, D.C.: U.S. Government Printing Office, 1959, 832 pp.

_____. *Foreign Relations of the United States: Diplomatic Papers, 1940, Volume III*. Washington, D.C.: U.S. Government Printing Office, 1958.

_____. *Foreign Relations of the United States: Diplomatic Papers, 1941, Volume I*. Washington, D.C.: U.S. Government Printing Office, 1958.

_____. *Foreign Relations of the United States: Diplomatic Papers, 1942, Volume III*. Washington, D.C.: U.S. Government Printing Office, 1961.

_____. *Foreign Relations of the United States: Diplomatic Papers, the Conferences at Cairo and Teheran, 1943*. Washington, D.C.: U.S. Government Printing Office, 1961.

_____. *Foreign Relations of the United States: Diplomatic Papers, 1944, Volume IV, Europe*. Washington, D.C.: U.S. Government Printing Office, 1966.

_____. *Foreign Relations of the United States: Diplomatic Papers, the Conferences at Malta and Yalta, 1945*. Washington, D.C.: U.S. Government Printing Office, 1966.

_____. *Foreign Relations of the United States: Diplomatic Papers, the Conference at Berlin (The Potsdam Conference), 1945, Volumes I and II*. Washington, D.C.: U.S. Government Printing Office, 1960.

_____. *Fourth Semiannual Report by the President to the Commission on Security and Cooperation in Europe. 1 December 1977-1 June 1978*. Special Report No. 45. Washington, D.C.: U.S. Government Printing Office, 1978, 30 pp., figures.

_____. *Implementation of Helsinki Final Act*. Washington, D.C.: U.S. Government Printing Office. Published semi-annually.

_____. *In Quest of Peace and Security: Selected Documents on American Foreign*

Policy 1941-1951. Washington, D.C.: U.S. Government Printing Office, 1951, 120 pp.

_____. *The Kremlin Speaks: Excerpts from Statements Made by the Leaders of the Soviet Union*. Washington, D.C.: U.S. Government Printing Office, 1951, 37 pp.

_____. Letter of Assistant Secretary David M. Abshire to Rep. Frank Annunzio, 22 June 1972. Copies of all U.S. State Department letters are located in the Department's archives.

_____. Letter of Assistant Secretary J. Brian Atwood to Rep. Clement J. Zablocki, 8 February 1980.

_____. Letter of Assistant Secretary Carol C. Laise to Antanas Sukauskas, 14 March 1974.

_____. Letter of Assistant Secretary William B. Macomber, Jr., to Senator J. William Fulbright, 16 June 1969.

_____. Letter of Acting Assistant Secretary John Richardson, Jr., to Ilmar Pleer, 21 September 1973.

_____. Letter of Acting Assistant Secretary Alan D. Romberg to Jonas Urbonas, 18 January 1985.

_____. Letter of Secretary of State George P. Shultz to Minister Stasys A. Backis, 15 February 1983.

_____. Letter of Secretary of State Cyrus Vance to Minister Stasys A. Backis, 9 February 1978.

_____. "List of Foreign Service Posts." Revised July 1970, 2 pp.

_____. *Madrid CSCE Negotiations 1980-1981*. Washington, D.C.: U.S. Government Printing Office, 1982, 54 pp.

_____. *Nazi-Soviet Relations 1939-1941: Documents from the Archives of the German Foreign Office*. Ed. Raymond James Sontag and James Stuart Beddie. Washington, D.C.: U.S. Government Printing Office, 1948, 362 pp.

_____. *Soviet World Outlook: A Handbook of Communist Statements*. Washington, D.C: U.S. Government Printing Office, 1959, 247 pp.

_____. Statement by Robert L. Barry, Assistant Secretary of State for European Affairs, before the Subcommittee on International Organizations, House Foreign Affairs Committee. 26 June 1979.

_____. *Status of the World's Nations*. Geographical Bulletin No. 2. Washington, D.C.: U.S. Government Printing Office, 1965.

_____. *Treaties in Force*, 1 January 1966. Washington, D.C.: U.S. Government Printing Office, 1966.

_____. "United States Policy Toward the Baltic States." Public Information Series P-317-870, c. 1970, 1 p.

_____. "US Policy: The Baltic Republics." *Gist*, August 1984, 2 pp.

_____. U.S. Mission to the United Nations. "The United States Reaffirms Recognition of Independence of Estonia, Latvia and Lithuania." *Press Release*, 29 July 1983, 3 pp.

USSR. Supreme Soviet. *Constitution (Fundamental Law) of the Union of Soviet Socialist Republics*. Adopted at the Seventh (Special) Session of the Supreme Soviet of the USSR, Ninth Convocation, 7 October 1977. Moscow: Novosti, 1977, 127 pp.

Visinskis [Vishinsky], A. J., and A. A. Gromiko [Gromyko]. *Del pabegeliu ir perkeltuju asmenu: Kalbos Suvienytuju Naciju Generalineje Asamblejoje Niujorke 1946 m.* (On refugees and displaced persons: Addresses to the United Nations General Assembly in New York, 1946). Vilnius: State Political Press, 1947, 35 pp.

Von Lowzow. *Report on the Present Situation in the Baltic States*. n.p.: Council of Europe Consultative Assembly, 1963, 34 pp., figures.

We Demand Freedom for Estonia: Memoranda Presented to the Delegations at the Paris Conference, 1946. London: Boreas, 1947, 40 pp.

Ziugzda, J., ed. *Lietuvos TSR istorijos saltiniai IV: Lietuva burzuazijos valdymo metais (1919-1940)* (Sources of the history of the Lithuanian SSR IV: Lithuania during the years of bourgeoise rule (1919-1940)). Vilnius: State Political and Scientific Press, 1961, 863 pp.

Index

About the Author

Robert A. Vitas received his Ph.D. in political science at Loyola University of Chicago, and a diploma in history from the Lithuanian Institute of Education.

He has published in *Air University Review*, *Presidential Studies Quarterly*, *Proceedings of the Institute of Lithuanian Studies*, *The Russian Review*, and *Lituanus*. Dr. Vitas' books include *U.S. National Security Policy and Strategy: Documents and Policy Proposals*, co-edited with Sam C. Sarkesian, *U.S. National Security Strategy: New Challenges and Opportunities*, a report issued by the Inter-University Seminar on Armed Forces and Society to the Chief of Staff of the U.S. Army, and *Lithuanian Immigration History*, edited for the Lithuanian Institute of Education.

Dr. Vitas is currently at the Great Books Foundation in Chicago, while serving as Vice President of the Lithuanian Research and Studies Center, and Assistant to the Executive Director of the Inter-University Seminar on Armed Forces and Society at the University of Chicago.